Interwoven Lives:
Adolescent Mothers
and Their Children

Research Monographs in Adolescence

Nancy L. Galambos/Nancy A. Busch-Rossnagel, Editors

Interwoven Lives:
Adolescent Mothers
and Their Children

Thomas L. Whitman
John G. Borkowski
Deborah A. Keogh
University of Notre Dame

Keri Weed
University of South Carolina – Aiken

Foreword by Sharon Landesman Ramey

LAWRENCE ERLBAUM ASSOCIATES, PUBLISHERS
2001   Mahwah, New Jersey   London

Lawrence Erlbaum Associates, Inc., Publishers
10 Industrial Avenue
Mahwah, NJ 07430

Cover design by Kathryn Houghtaling Lacey

Library of Congress Cataloging-in-Publication Data

Interwoven Lives : adolescent mothers and their children /
Thomas L. Whitman ... [et al.]; foreword by Sharon
Landesman Ramey.
     p. cm.
Includes bibliographical references and index.
ISBN 0-8058-3127-4 (cloth : alk. paper)—ISBN 0-8058-3128-2
(pbk. : alk. paper)
1. Teenage mothers—United States—Longitudinal studies.
2. Children of teenage mothers—United States—Longitudinal studies. I. Whitman, Thomas L.

HQ759.4+
306.874'3—dc21   00-050286

Books published by Lawrence Erlbaum Associates are
printed on acid-free paper, and their bindings are chosen
for strength and durability.

Printed in the United States of America
10   9   8   7   6   5   4   3   2   1

For Kathy, Martha, Sam, and Mike

Table of Contents

sense of responsible science expanded to include thinking about the implications of these findings for designing and implementing more effective programs to prevent the negative toll that adolescent parenting takes on the majority and to consider policies that might better prepare our nation's youth to become competent parents at the right time and with the right supports in their lives. The awareness that this study truly represents an important and much more up-to-date story of what adolescent parenting is all about permeates these chapters, and culminates in thoughtful reflections on the implications of what this research team has learned. These insights and suggestions warrant serious attention and active discussion in policy circles, as well as among the many social service agencies, schools, health departments, and programs that work with young parents throughout our country.

And the story is not over yet. The participants are continuing to share their lives as the children progress through school and the families themselves change in terms of size and life circumstances. The multigenerational aspect of this study is a key theme. So is the contribution of multiple societal institutions and supports, with a crucial role attributed to schools. The failure of schools to detect early learning difficulties and social adjustment problems is striking, and further compounds the hardships that the majority of these children endure year after year. The multiple and accumulating negative consequences associated with teen unplanned parenthood on the lives of their young children are compelling. So too are the personal needs of the mothers as they continue their own development and seek to avoid or overcome depression, ignorance, and a sense of being trapped and unable to be effective change agents. That these children began their lives as healthy, inquisitive, and responsive babies should not be overlooked. With each few years that passed, their development has lagged—strikingly so by 3 years of age, with less than one third performing at age level, and even more profoundly by second grade. These outcomes in no way appear to be some inevitable result of "bad genes." Rather, they reflect the cumulative toll of failing to provide children with appropriate learning opportunities, stable home environments, extra supports for special needs, and high quality early care and education to foster normal growth and development.

For the reader of this new study, please do not skim over or skip the detailed presentation of the data analyses. The story of these lives does not reduce to a simple model, and what seems to matter for different outcomes and at different ages changes. This complexity and the interdependencies among the major constructs in the theory guiding this longitudinal study are worthy of continued reflection by any student of human development, as well as anyone who engages in designing and offering supports or policies to counteract the harmful effects of teen pregnancy—or any other set of life circumstances that takes young people out of the mainstream and limits their opportunities to develop into fully capable, contributing citizens with a strong sense of hope and fulfillment in their own lives.

I hope that *Interwoven Lives* will herald a new era in developmental science, continuing to expand the fine tradition of commitment to careful longitudinal study of both individuals and their life contexts in multiple sites, using multi-site data analyzed with sophisticated and appropriate quantitative strategies and complemented by real life stories that fill in the richness that important numerical data can never completely provide. Not only are the data interesting and important, so too are the multiple perspectives by this team of scientists and practitioners. A next stage to this research, which builds on a solid and current database, undoubtedly will provide the true test of the theory—by determining what interventions, for whom and at what stages in their lives, can help to improve the life trajectories for those at risk of non-optimal outcomes. In that process of translating basic social science findings into rigorously designed and tested prevention interventions, then we are likely to realize major advances that result in a more caring and a more competent world for all of us.

Preface

Although adolescent parenting is not a new phenomenon in the United States, the familial and cultural setting in which it is embedded has changed dramatically during the past several decades. In the first half of the 20th century, young single women who became pregnant often married or received physical supports from the fathers of their children. In other cases, families absorbed the newborn and its mother into their supportive network. Alternatively, it was common for unmarried mothers to place their children for adoption. In the 1960s, a new trend emerged in which teenage mothers increasingly rejected adoption as an option and raised their children as single parents, sometimes within the context of an extended family, but often on their own. Frequently, these mothers lived in poverty, surviving through welfare assistance and support from friends, partners, or family of origin.

With the emergence of this new trend in adolescent parenting, societal concerns were registered about its potentially adverse effects for both the child and the mother. Although considerable research on adolescent parenting has been conducted, it has tended to be narrow in the scope of the inquiry. Minimal attention has been given to investigating systematic changes in adolescent mothers and their children's psychological functioning over time. Moreover, little attempt has been made to understand individual differences in outcomes. For instance, why do some teen mothers and their children fare better than others?

In 1984, a longitudinal study was launched at the University of Notre Dame to evaluate the social and psychological consequences of teen parenting for both mothers and their children. In contrast to previous research, the mothers in this sample, although poor, were not enmeshed in "deep poverty." At the inception of the study the adolescent mothers were, for the most part, in school. Generally, their children had normal birth weights and gestational ages, were without congenital anomalies, and showed no evidence of cocaine addiction or fetal alcohol effects. Compared to studies of samples originating in large urban settings, our sample appeared more advantaged, and the infants healthier.

At the time of the writing of this book, data collection had been completed for a period extending from the last trimester of a mother's pregnancy until the time her first child was 5 years of age. Comprehensive information on the cognitive, socioemotional and behavioral functioning of both mothers and children was collected at five timepoints: prenatally and when the mothers' first born children were 6 months, 1 year, 3 years and 5 years of age. Similar data were being collected at 8 years; although incomplete, they are examined to give a glimpse of the children's academic functioning. Although the majority of the analyses presented in this book have not been reported elsewhere, we also summarize our previous published research where it is consistent with the purpose of this book.

The book is divided into three sections. In the first, background information about adolescent parenting and the Notre Dame Parenting Project is provided. In chapter 1, societal and scientific perspectives on adolescent parenting are described. In chapter 2, conceptualizations of adolescent development and adolescent parenting are introduced, along with a model formulated by us to explain parenting in adolescent mothers and development in their children. Chapter 3 describes the research participants, the measures employed to index the central constructs contained in our adolescent parenting model, and other measures used to evaluate maternal and child functioning over time.

Section two summarizes the basic results of the project. In chapter 4, the developmental status and adjustment of mothers in the Notre Dame Parenting Project are examined, including information regarding their prenatal psychological status and social resources; their parenting skills (including cognitive, affective and behavioral aspects); and their socioemotional adjustment. Relationships between the mothers' early development and their later adjustment are also generally described in this chapter. In chapter 5, the validity of our model of adolescent parenting is assessed, specifically, its ability to predict early parenting behavior, maternal risks for child abuse, and later maternal socioemotional adjustment.

Chapter 6 describes the development of the children of adolescent mothers in the Notre Dame Parenting Project from birth through 5 years of age. Data are presented regarding their physical, intellectual, linguistic, socioemotional, adaptive, and early academic functioning. Preliminary data are also presented on the children's academic achievement when they reached 8 years of age. Both concurrent relationships between child functioning in these various domains of development as well as predictive relationships between early and later child development are examined. Chapter 7 evaluates relationships between early maternal functioning and later child development, including the maternal antecedents of child development at 6 months, 3 years, and 5 years of age. Special attention is given to how maternal child abuse potential is related to later child functioning. Finally, this chapter examines relationships between attachment security and later development. In writing these chapters, we tried to present a comprehensive empirical picture of our project's findings while making the results as reader-friendly as possible.

In the last section, the data are analyzed qualitatively as well as quantitatively in order to understand why some mothers and children fared better than others, and hence might be called *resilient*. Implications of these data for framing social policy are also discussed. More specifically, chapter 8 evaluates factors that distinguish resilient mothers and children from those who were vulnerable. Chapter 9 presents the life stories from the mothers' perspectives; we show how their insights supplement the "objective" story derived from quantitative data. The use of case studies in both these chapters allows us to examine the validity and limitations of our model of adolescent parenting from a different vantage point. Finally, chapter 10 places the project's findings within the context of past theory, research and conventional wisdom about adolescent parenting. We develop recommendations about intervention programs and social policies to help adolescent parents and their children achieve developmental success and find happiness. A major theme emphasized throughout the book is that the lives and developmental trajectories of adolescent mothers and children are inextricably interwoven and closely linked to the social contexts in which they live.

ACKNOWLEDGMENTS

The Notre Dame Parenting Project and writing of this book has been generously funded by a series of grants from the Office of Adolescent Family Life (AR-000936) and the National Institute of Child Health and Development (HD-26456). Especially noteworthy is the history of support and assistance from the Mental Retardation and Developmental Disabilities Branch of NICHD. There are many people to thank for their assistance in the development and execution of the Notre Dame Parenting Project. Without their help this book could never have been written. First, and most important, are the parents and children for sharing their lives with us, and the children's teachers who gave, and continue to give, so much of their time and personal resources to make this project possible. Special thanks go to our valuable colleagues: Sebrina Tingley (our project manager who "stayed close" to the participants throughout the project) as well as a host of research assistants (Toni Bisconti, Jennifer Burke, Melissa Clearfield, Luis Cordon, Christine Davin, Claire Docherty, Tammy Dukewich, Donna Evangelisti, Dawn Gondoli, Joan Martin, Penny Miceli, Cindy Miller, Kristie Mitchell, Deirdre Mylod, Pam Nath, Deborah Newbill, Mary O'Callaghan, Marjorie Pinard, Lisa Rellinger, Kristie Sommer, Jane Stentz, Anna Valdez, Christine Willard, and Anne Wurtz Passino). Also special thanks to Joy, Constance, and Pat at the Mental Health Association in Aiken, South Carolina. Special appreciation is due to several important individuals, including Cindy Schellenbach who helped formulate our model of adolescent parenting, Scott Maxwell for his statistical assistance, Virginia Colin for her assistance in scoring the Strange Situation assessment, and Pauline Wright, Rhonda Singleton, and Jennifer Souders for their considerable help and patience in the preparation of this book.

Although this volume is an authored text, we gave special credit to several colleagues who, although not book authors, made important contributions to specific chapters. Their contribution is acknowledged by placing their name under the appropriate chapter heading. If this were an edited text their contribution in most cases would be significant enough to list them as second in the order of authorship for that chapter.

Finally, we would like to express our gratitude to our spouses and companions by dedicating this book to them. To Kathy Whitman, wife and best friend; Martha Borkowski, for 40 years of friendship, love, and support; Sam Saffren, for his humor, insights and support; and Mike Keogh, friend and confidante.

1

Adolescent Parenthood: A Changing Phenomenon

Teenage parenting continues to be a significant social problem despite dramatic declines in the rates of adolescent pregnancy and childbearing in the United States since the early 1990s. More than 750,000 teens become pregnant each year, with more than 50% resulting in live births. Of these births, approximately 90% of the mothers choose to assume the responsibilities of parenting themselves, rather than placing their children for adoption. Considerable research suggests that many teen mothers and/or their children are at risk for a variety of developmental problems (Furstenberg, Brooks-Gunn, & Morgan, 1987). This book describes the fate of a representative sample of teen mothers and their children—born in the late 1980s and early 1990s—across the first 8 years of their lives.

In this book, we search for factors in adolescent mothers and their environments that predict their own and their children's developmental outcomes. Additionally, we attempt to understand the mechanisms and pathways through which these factors exact their influence on development. We search for answers to questions such as the following: "Are the sources of influence on adolescent mothers the same as observed with adult parents or are new constructs and new variables required for a full developmental explanation?" "To what extent are teen mothers and their children at risk for developmental problems?" "In what ways do adolescent mothers influence their children's development, both positively and negatively?" "What factors produce successful outcomes for adolescent mothers?" "Are the lives of teenage mothers and their children intimately "interwoven" or, instead, do they assume divergent, noninteractive paths?" Answers to these questions will shed new light on the important phenomenon of teenage parenthood.

The existing literature suggests that the life trajectories of adolescent mothers are highly variable, with perhaps only 33% doing reasonably well as young adults (Furstenberg et al., 1987). It is likely that more than 50% of children with teen mothers will experience academic difficulties in their early school years; problems perhaps due to delays in intelligence, language, cognition, socioemotional adjustment, and social competence. More information is needed about the causal mechanisms that account for these delays in children's development as well as a more detailed understanding of the differences between resilient and vulnerable teenage mothers and children. It is important to understand the precise nature of problems associated with teenage parenting in order to form more effective social policies and to establish appropriate prevention and intervention programs. Greater knowledge about teen parenting will lead to programs that take into account the factors predictive of developmental delays and target those mothers and children most at risk.

Currently, federal and state agencies are responding to the country's educational crisis by toughening standards in order to increase the accountability of teachers, schools, and students. Although accountability is admirable and may produce positive results, this approach will likely fail if millions of children—many born each year to unmarried adolescents—enter kindergarten and the first grade with preexisting delays in school readiness, including cognitive and social self-regulation. More knowledge is required about the specific types of developmental delays, along with their causes, in the infants and children of adolescent mothers in order to prevent or remediate these problems as early as possible and to prepare future cohorts of at-risk children for academic and life course successes.

ADOLESCENT PARENTING: TRENDS AND PATTERNS

There are a variety of misconceptions about adolescent parenthood in the United States. Many are held by the public and some by professionals who deal with the problems associated with adolescent parenting:

- Teen pregnancy has increased dramatically since World War II and continues to increase.
- Adolescents have always been unmarried, single parents.
- Their partners are typically much older men.
- Most infants born to adolescents are unwanted and neglected.
- Repeat pregnancies are inevitable.
- An early, off-time pregnancy, by its very nature, will alter the life course.
- The phenomenon of teenage pregnancy in the year 2000 and beyond will be much like the teen pregnancy we observed in earlier decades, such as the 1960s or 1980s.

- Children who have teen mothers will likely benefit from existing federal or state assistance, such as minimal job training for mothers and compensatory programs, such as Head Start, for their children.

In the following sections, we discuss each of these beliefs as well as other related issues. We present recent data on trends in birth-rates to teenagers and relevant demographic information. Next, we discuss the development of adolescent mothers and their children. We also offer a provocative new perspective that has emerged from sociological and economic inquiry suggesting that adolescent parenthood may not be as important in determining maternal development as the factors that caused the pregnancy in the first place. Relatedly, we observe that the social contexts associated with teen parenting may have changed since the 1960s and 1970s, influenced by the insidious nature of poverty, drugs, and family instability; the result is a fundamental change in the phenomenon of adolescent parenthood. Finally, we begin to build a case for coordinated federal, state, and community-based assistance in order to prepare all at-risk infants and children for academic success through very early, comprehensive and intensive interventions during the first 5 years of life. Effective interventions for children and mothers are especially critical given the demise of the welfare system and the introduction of new work requirements that most single adolescent mothers, who live in poverty, are struggling to comply with as they raise their children.

Historical Trends in Teen Pregnancy and Early Childrearing

Changing Birth Rates. In 1997, births to teenagers continued a decline that began in the early 1990s. For every 1,000 girls 15 to 17 years old, 30 had babies in 1997; this number represents a 17% drop since 1991. The trend cuts across regional and racial boundaries; almost all sections of the country have experienced a drop. A 24% decline from the 1991 birth rate to African-American adolescents is especially noteworthy: In 1997, 70 per 1,000 African-American teens gave birth, versus 90 per 1,000 in 1991. The birth rate among Hispanic adolescents has shown less decline (only 6% from a 1992 high) than other ethnic groups (Elo, King, & Furstenberg, 1999).

Most of the decline for both White and Black adolescents occurred among the oldest cohort (those ages 18 and 19), which accounts for more than 60% of the births to teenagers. In contrast, the birth rate has not decreased for the youngest teens (ages 10 to 14). Although this group accounts for less than 3% of births to adolescents, they and their children appear to be at higher risk for delayed development (Elo et al., 1999).

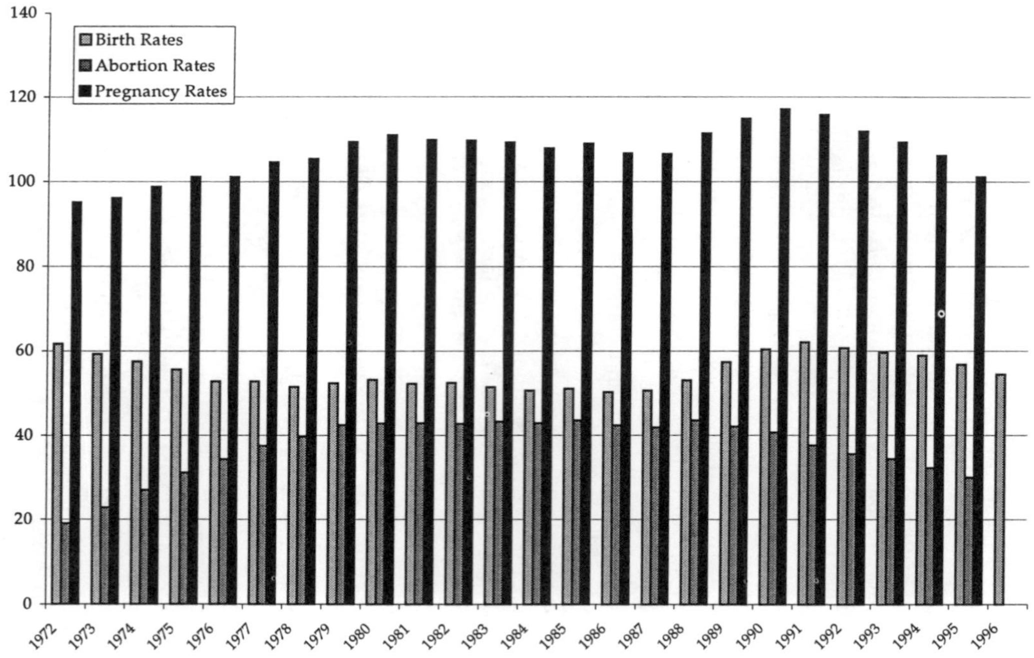

FIG. 1.1

Birth, pregnancy, and abortion rates per 1,000 women, ages 15 to 19, 1972-1996 (Alan Guttmacher Institute, 1999).

Not only are birth rates changing but so to are pregnancy and abortion rates. Figure 1.1 shows the birth, pregnancy, and abortion rates per 1,000 adolescents between ages 15 and 19 over a 25-year period. Several trends emerge from these data and other recently available information:

- From a high of nearly 62 per 1,000 teens in 1972, the birth rate declined to 50 per 1,000 in the mid-1980s and then rose again to the 1972 level, until the current declining trend began in 1992.
- The abortion rate increased dramatically from the early 1970s and remained consistent (around 43 per 1,000) throughout the 1980s. The abortion rate then declined more than 30% from a 1986 high of 43 per 1,000, to a current level of below 30 per 1,000 women.
- Not surprisingly, the decline in birth and abortion rates in the 1990s was accompanied by a decline in the rate of pregnancy, from 115 per 1,000 in 1988 to 101 per 1,000 in 1995.
- The declines in birth and pregnancy rates were accompanied by changes in sexual activity, with the percentage of teens under age 15 engaging in sex increasing and the proportion over age 15 decreasing.
- In 1996, Nevada, California, and Arizona had the highest pregnancy rates, with California and Texas having the highest absolute numbers of births to adolescents. The lowest rates were in the upper midwest (North Dakota and Minnesota, with Iowa also having a low pregnancy rate).
- Finally, it should be noted that the decline in births to adolescent mothers needs to be interpreted in the context of the overall decline in total births in the United States.

A variety of interest groups are quick to point out, and often claim credit for, the decline in birth rates among adolescents. Those advocating abstinence, more widespread and improved use of contraception, welfare reform, AIDS education, and right-to-life all claim at least some credit for recent population-based changes. The precise causes of the declining birth rate to adolescents, however, are unknown although our best guess is that the decreases are not the result of any single factor but rather the confluence of multiple factors. For instance, 66% of women now use condoms at first intercourse, up 18% from 1970; contraceptive use is also increasing among adolescents, in part due to the fear of AIDS and sexually transmitted diseases (National Survey of Family Growth, 1997). From another perspective, teenagers who feel connected to their families are less likely to begin sexual activity at an early age. "Perception of parental attitudes" about postponing sex and using birth control—but not "actual parental attitudes"—are associated with delayed sexual activity (Demographic and Behavioral Science Branch, 1999). Clearly, more demographic research is needed to identify the precise factors leading to the recent declines in pregnancy and birth rates, especially the role of novel prevention programs (cf. Allen, Philliber, Herrling, & Kuperminc, 1997).

Changes in Marital Status. Another demographic phenomenon affecting family structure, especially among teens, is the change in the number of out-of-wedlock births. In the early 1960s, it was relatively uncommon for adolescent girls to give birth outside of marriage (Elo et al., 1999). But by 1994 it was rare for younger White teens—between ages 10 and 17—to be married at childbirth: Only about 20% in this age range were married, in contrast to about 70% in 1960. Within this broad age group, the biggest change from 1960 to 1990 occurred for those between 15 and 17 years of age, a shift from 15% to 75% in out-of-wedlock births. Among all White teens, those ages 18 and 19 showed the least change in marriage rates (from about 5% unmarried to 55%), although even this shift was sizable.

Among African-American teens, the rise in out-of-wedlock births is even more dramatic. In this group, the change was nearly 60% across three decades. The sharp increase was experienced by all African-American adolescent mothers, even those in the 18 to 19 age group (Elo et al., 1999). By 1990, nearly 85% of African-American teen mothers were unmarried at the time of childbirth. These relatively recent changes in marital status—occurring over a brief span of 30 years—have major financial, emotional, and social implications for single mothers and their children. As McLanahan (1999) noted, the lack of an adequate and stable financial base—together with a fragile family structure—represent major obstacles for single mothers trying to become successful parents. The situation is even more problematic for unmarried teenage mothers.

Who Are the Fathers? Elo and colleagues (1999) presented fresh information about the fathers of infants born to teen mothers. Surprisingly, the mean difference in age between partners was only 3.3 years among 15- to 19-year-olds. Stated another way, approximately, 85% of infants born to adolescent mothers have fathers in their late teens or early 20s. These data run contrary to the widely held perception that older men (over age 25) are typically the fathers of babies born to adolescent girls.

There is an important exception: Younger girls are more likely to be sexually exploited by older males. In the under 15 age group, 45% reported that their partners were at least 4 years older. Particularly troubling is the fact that 16% of girls, whose age at first intercourse was under 15, reported that their first sexual contact was either rape or not voluntary, compared with approximately 7% for older teens (National Survey of Family Growth, 1997). As Elo et al. (1999) noted: "Even though birthrates and intercourse among young girls and adolescents are low, relative to older teens, young girls constitute the most vulnerable and exploitable group. Our results suggest that sexual exploitation of younger girls is likely to be more common than sexual exploitation of older girls" (p. 83).

The age of the father is an important factor for both mothers and their children for two additional reasons: family structure and financial support. Lindberg, Sonenstein, Ku, and Martinez (1997) found that among 15- to 17-year-olds, whose partners were 5 or more years older, the likelihood of living together increased, thus providing greater potential income as well as the presence of a male role model. Interestingly, adolescent mothers with older partners are more likely to already have had a child prior to forming these relationships as well as to have experienced more behavior problems when compared with adolescent mothers who have similar age partners. Both of these factors place a "new relationship" with an older man on shaky ground.

Intentionality and Wantedness. Recent data suggest that only 34% of teen births are planned (National Survey of Family Growth, 1997), compared with about 73% for women between ages 20 and 44. Unplanned pregnancies often occur because of the very nature of adolescence as a unique stage of development—including a sense of self-centeredness, feelings of invulnerability, and difficulties in foreseeing and understanding the long-term consequences of current actions. These characteristics of adolescence make it less likely for a sexually active teen to use contraception effectively and/or consistently (Demographic and Behavioral Science Branch, 1999).

Although most births to adolescents are unintended and mistimed, their infants are generally "wanted" rather than "unwanted," when carried to term. Adolescent and adult mothers are similar in their feelings about wantedness: Among births to adolescents, less than 11% of infants are unwanted in contrast to 9% for adult mothers. Unwanted babies are at high risk; infants classified as unwanted at birth often show delayed cognitive development during childhood and lower self-esteem as adults (Demographic and Behavioral Science Branch, 1999).

One final point regarding the feelings of adolescents toward their babies: Whereas adult mothers are reasonably "happy" (7.5 on a 10-point scale) with their pregnancies, teen mothers feel significantly less happy (5.6; Demographic and Behavioral Science Branch, 1999). This difference in happiness may play an important role in determining the quality of parenting that differentiates primiparous adult and teen mothers. It also suggests a certain caution in accepting the wantedness data reported by teen mothers at the time of birth. Adolescents may need to be interviewed in depth, on multiple occasions, to assess their sustained commitment to their infants and their parenting roles. It may be important to evaluate more carefully the "actual wantedness" of newborns with teen mothers if we are to reduce the frequency of child neglect and/or abuse.

Repeat Pregnancies. Many teen mothers have a second child within 2 years after their first child. For instance, East and Felice (1996) found that 35% of the 200 adolescent mothers in their sample had a repeat pregnancy within 18 months after the first birth. The second pregnancy was often associated with a failure to return to school and, hence, an inability to gain financial independence and security. It should be noted that women who have their first child before age 20 average close to three children whereas those who delay childbearing average around two (Furstenberg et al., 1987).

An often ignored factor that can lead to a repeat pregnancy is the sense of responsibility and independence developed by the teen mother while raising her first child. Apfel and Seitz (1999) recently reported that family support predicted subsequent childbearing: Either too much (e.g., the grandmother provided total replacement care) or too little (e.g., the adolescent received little or no help) were associated with a 42% rate of second pregnancies within 30 months, versus 24% among similar mothers who receive moderate support, supplementary care, and coaching from family members, especially the grandmother. A moderate amount of family support not only helps to prevent an immediate repeat pregnancy but also serves as an obstacle to teen mothers in "dropping out" of their parenting roles: Moderate support is associated with meaningful commitments to rearing their first-born children (cf. Apfel & Seitz, 1999).

DEVELOPMENTAL TRENDS FOR ADOLESCENT MOTHERS AND THEIR CHILDREN

Maternal Outcomes and Adolescent Childbearing

The reality of teen pregnancy—although less devastating than the listing of misconceptions might predict—still presents serious challenges for most adolescents mothers, their families, and society in general. A constellation of problems are associated with an off-timed pregnancy, often hindering an adolescent mother's progress into adulthood and, simultaneously, compromising her parenting skills (cf. Duncan & Brooks-Gunn, 1997; East & Felice, 1996; Horowitz, Klerman, Kuo, & Jekel, 1991):

• Absence of the biological father and/or unavailability of a reliable and stable male role model.
• Insufficient income, which prevents the newly created family from moving out of poverty and into the middle class.
• Lack of commitment to postponing additional children until personal and financial problems are resolved.
• High levels of stress.
• A lack of awareness about preparing children emotionally, socially, and cognitively for successful entry into school.
• The tendency to use physical punishment and/or to condone emotional neglect.
• A changing, and sometimes unreliable, social support system.

These problems often interact to compromise the formidable parenting tasks facing the typical teenage mother, placing both mother and child at risk for a variety of developmental delays. A number of longitudinally based studies have examined the maternal outcomes following a birth during the teenage years, revealing much about the nature of the lives of adolescent mothers.

Important Longitudinal Projects. Furstenberg and colleagues (1987) conducted an influential longitudinal study examining the fate of adolescent mothers and their children from early childhood through early adolescence. Primiparous mothers were recruited in Baltimore in the mid- to late-1960s, a period of optimism for many in poverty, in part because of the promises of the Great Society. The adolescent mothers who enrolled in this "Baltimore Project" experienced a variety of outcomes 17 years following their transition to parenthood. Although the project did not focus intensively on process variables—such as maternal depression, self-esteem, and stress—it did measure important maternal outcomes, such as income level, welfare status, and number of subsequent children.

More successful mothers were economically secure, or had modest incomes, compared with the "working poor" or welfare recipients; they also tended to limit further childbearing. The strongest predictor of welfare status at the adult follow-up was the education level of the grandparents, independent of the teen mother's own educational status.

Furstenberg and colleagues (1987) surmised that grandparents with more education had greater economic and social resources to assist their teenage daughter in becoming an independent adult and a more effective parent. Not surprisingly, the strongest predictor of fertility was the length of time before the second child was born: The success of some teens in delaying the second pregnancy and in limiting their total number of pregnancies was attributed, in part, to participation in school and community intervention programs, suggesting that these types of assistance may have compensated for limited family supports and personal resources.

A second major longitudinal project was initiated in New Haven at about the same time as the Baltimore Project. Follow-up data, collected nearly 20 years later, supported the general findings of the Baltimore project: 66% of teen mothers had completed high school; the majority had recently been on welfare; most had more than one but less than four children (Horowitz et al., 1991). It should be emphasized that it is difficult to tell whether these outcomes are due to an off-timed birth and/or to the factors that helped to produce the pregnancy in the first place. More will be said on this issue in a later section of this chapter.

East and Felice (1996) recently conducted another important longitudinal project investigating the development of adolescent mothers and their children across the first 3 years of life. The project was unique in its frequency of assessments of parenting quality (every 6 months), use of medical care, measurement of repeat pregnancies, and the roles of fathers and grandmothers in parenting. The following factors emerged as predictors or correlates of maternal and parenting outcomes:

1. Older adolescents who had frequent prenatal medical visits and abstained from alcohol and other drugs showed more positive mother–child outcomes.
2. Delayed pregnancies (especially for at least 6 months after the first birth) were associated with less alcohol and drug use during the second pregnancy and, not surprisingly, resulted in better child outcomes.
3. Positive parenting and high confidence were associated with good social development in children, and low natural stress was associated with fewer displays of aggression in children.
4. Hispanic mothers and children were more at risk for developmental problems if they reported less mature parenting values (e.g., unrealistic expectations, less empathy, and greater use of punishment), less confidence in their parenting skills, and lower levels of child acceptance.

5. Adolescents who had more favorable parenting attitudes and skills generally lived apart from their mothers, but still received high amounts of child care and support.

6. Although 60% of the fathers were involved with their children at 3 years, only about 30% provided substantial financial supports. No clear associations were uncovered regarding father involvement and child outcomes. Although fathers rarely provided hands-on-care, it is possible that more "involved fathers" provided at least a minimal protective mechanism, especially in the domain of social development.

In short, favorable outcomes were more common in older teens who sought pre- and postnatal care, who expressed positive parenting values early during the first year of their child's life, who were supported by their families and partners but who lived apart from their mothers, and who managed to delay a second pregnancy until adulthood (East & Felice, 1996).

Major Outcomes for Adolescent Mothers. Although the long-term outcomes for teenage mothers are highly variable, there are a number of studies that point to potential developmental problems surfacing during adulthood (cf. Furstenberg et al., 1987; Horwitz et al., 1991; Hotz, McElroy, & Sanders, 1997):

• About 30% of adolescent mothers fail to complete high school, whereas many others do not graduate on time but eventually complete their education as adults.

• Among graduates and GED recipients, many adolescent mothers do not have sufficient functional reading and math skills or the necessary work and motivational habits to compete successfully in the job market.

• About 25% of teenage mothers do not become economically self-sufficient and many of these then move on and off of public assistance as adults.

• Approximately 55% of all mothers on welfare at any given time were teenagers when their first child was born.

• Although a majority of adolescent mothers have a second child within 3 to 4 years, only around 15% to 20% have four or more children prior to age 30.

• Teen mothers are likely to spend twice as much time unmarried prior to age 30 compared to those who delay childbearing.

The Transition to Parenthood

The Importance of Preparing for Parenting. Adolescent mothers—as do all mothers—need to be prepared for the challenging parenting tasks that lie ahead, if they are to assume full responsibility for optimizing their children's development. The term, *cognitive readiness to parent*, captures this kind of preparation (Sommer et al., 1993). An additional problem for many adolescents is that they do not become "prepared through experience," and fail to develop effective parenting skills even after having additional children.

The concept of *cognitive readiness* involves three interrelated components: (a) knowledge about how children develop, (b) mature attitudes about the parenting role, and (c) understanding appropriate parenting practices. The development of each component may be restricted because of the nature of adolescence as a unique stage of development. For instance, the ability to learn about developmental milestones, such as the timing of sitting up or talking, may be hindered by the adolescent's egocentrism or inexperience with children. Attitudes toward parenting may be influenced by role reversal, that is in the belief that the child is responsible for the parent's well-being rather than vice versa. Furthermore, an understanding of appropriate parenting practices—such as the advantage of an authoritative versus authoritarian style—may be limited by an inability to gain empathic awareness of children's needs, as well as by an overly simplistic endorsement of the role of physical punishment in promoting infant and child development. Research on the components of cognitive readiness has found that adolescent mothers have imprecise knowledge concerning child development and often report negative attitudes about parenting (Jarrett, 1982; Roosa & Vaughn, 1984; Sommer et al., 1993). They sometimes have children for their own sake, are conflicted when children fail to meet their "mythical expectations," and are harsh or punitive in their response when faced with perceived or real inappropriate behaviors. We cover the concept of *cognitive readiness* in greater depth in the next chapter.

Personal Factors That Effect Maternal Development and Parenting. In general, adolescent mothers have more adjustment problems—such as depression and aggression—than first-time adult mothers. In understanding teenage parenting, it is important to take into account preexisting personality factors, such as maternal adjustment and stability, in order to predict whether teen mothers can adequately assume their new and demanding parenting roles.

In a longitudinal study, Leadbeater and Linares (1992) focused on depression and its impact on the adjustment of African-American and Puerto Rican poor, inner-city, adolescent mothers. Concurrent and reciprocal relationships among depression, stressful life events, and social supports were investigated. Whereas nondepressed adolescent mothers were more likely 3 years after the birth of their children to return to school and exhibit more positive interactions with their infants, mothers who were chronically depressed were more likely to live alone and to have experienced less residential stability. Trends were found relating chronic depression to low graduation rates, further childbearing, and welfare status. It was concluded that the ability to cope with stressful life events was impaired by depression and that chronic depression may be related to rejection of parenting roles. In turn, negative perceptions about the future and social isolation likely created even greater stress and less effective parenting practices (Leadbeater & Linares, 1992), with abuse and/or neglect as possible consequences. Hence, the transition to parenthood for many teen mothers is made more difficult by inadequate preparation, both cognitively and emotionally.

DOES ADOLESCENT PARENTHOOD CHANGE A MOTHER'S LIFE COURSE?

There is an ongoing debate about whether or not teen pregnancy and parenthood adversely affect the development of mothers, as we have implied in an earlier section. Recently, respected scholars have suggested that it is the factors that lead the teenager into pregnancy in the first place—such as academic failure, personal instability, poor role models, a history of abuse, or negative visions about "future selves"—that actually produce the economic and personal hardships that adolescent mothers frequently encounter in their adult years. In this scenario, most teenage mothers would be in exactly the same situation in their transition to adulthood even if they did not became pregnant as adolescents (Furstenberg, 1998; Hotz et al., 1997). Thus, it is unclear whether an early, off-timed pregnancy is an important causal event in altering the life course of adolescent mothers, or whether pre-existing factors serve as the real causal agents.

In an interesting analysis using data from the National Longitudinal Study of Youth, Hotz et al. (1997) compared developmental outcomes of adolescent girls who became mothers to a comparison sample of girls who became pregnant but experienced unintentional miscarriages, thus delaying their transition to motherhood for several years. This methodology provided a "quasi-random" comparison group for the adolescent mothers, presumably controlling for factors predisposing the teen to an early pregnancy. Hotz and colleagues concluded that adolescent child-bearing had little effect on maternal self-sufficiency. In fact, adolescent mothers actually worked more hours, and had higher earnings at age 34, than the comparison group. Although adolescent mothers were initially less likely to have graduated from high school, when the percentage acquiring GEDs were also considered, the difference later disappeared. However, adolescent mothers spent more time as single mothers and had 12% more children. After considering public expenditures for 17- to 34-year-old women who gave birth prior to age 18, as well as average earnings for the adolescent mothers and comparison mothers, Holz came to the surprising conclusion that programmatic efforts to delay childbearing, without addressing other background factors associated with early childbearing, actually incur additional public costs with questionable long-term benefits.

Hotz et al.'s (1997) conclusions are consistent with those of Harris (1997), who found that women who participated in the Baltimore Longitudinal Project, although spending more time on welfare, actually had greater total earnings than comparison women who delayed childbearing. The explanation for the somewhat better outcomes of the adolescent mothers is unclear. It is possible, however, that their pregnancies and transitions to motherhood provided these adolescents access to services for which they might not have otherwise been eligible.

Alternatively, the reality of motherhood might have provided them the incentive needed in order to make major changes in their lives. In any case, more data are required to fully assess the impact of early parenthood, per se, on life course development. Particularly needed are assessments of psychological states—such as depression and self-esteem—that might be influenced by an off-timed pregnancy. Here we take a more in-depth look at maternal development among teenage mothers.

The Changing Context of Adolescent Parenthood

Although the average age of mothers at first birth has increased for all socioeconomic groups during the past decade, delayed childbearing has been most dramatic among well-educated adult women. The primary reason here is economic: The cost of leaving the workforce and the potential loss in advancement seem to be critical motivating factors for well-educated adult women delaying childbirth, until their mid- to late-30s. Lower educated women—who are more likely to become teenage mothers—appear less motivated by economic considerations in making decisions regarding the timing of childbearing. Whatever their reasons, differences in patterns of childbearing likely result in an amplification of income disparities among first-time adult and adolescent mothers which, in turn, magnify the effects that socioeconomic factors have on subsequent child development (McLanahan & Sandefur, 1994).

Because of this differential trend in childbearing, the economic and social contexts for parenting infants and young children among highly educated adults versus poorly educated adolescents are as different as they have been in this century. Although the percentage of adults in poverty, especially the elderly, has declined precipitously since 1960, the percentage of children in poverty remains remarkably high (around 20%), especially given the prosperity of the United States (Duncan & Brooks-Gunn, 1997). To emphasize the scope of childhood poverty, consider the following data from the early 1980s: In a 6-year period, about 75% of White children were never poor, in contrast to 33% of Black children (Duncan, Brooks-Gunn, & Klebanov, 1994). What this means is that although approximately 20% of children are in poverty at any one time, many more have recently been, or will soon be, living in poverty. In other words, the percentage of children who are in, have been in, or will soon be in poverty is likely greater than 30% nationwide, and even greater for African-American and Hispanic children.

Recent social changes (e.g., increases in single-parent families) and economic changes (e.g., welfare reform) have likely influenced also altered the extent and type of poverty across America, increasing the real as well as psychological distances between the "haves" and the "have nots." As a consequence of such changes, the next generation of children born in poverty to adolescent mothers is likely at even greater risk than children in prior generations as they progress through often inadequate educational systems. The chances of succeeding in school for those enmeshed in poverty are extremely low, given their lack of school readiness and system wide failures to deal with learning problems early and effectively. Already, there are growing complaints from kindergarten teachers around the United States about declines in student motivation, short attention spans, and diminished self-regulatory skills.

These signs of change in the phenomenon of adolescent parenthood were anticipated by Baumeister (1988) in his discussion of the "new morbidity." The concept of *new morbidity* identifies complex, multivariate linkages between poverty and a host of related developmental delays. It emphasizes the predisposing, catalytic, proximal, and outcome factors associated with poverty, including drugs, alcohol, unplanned and unprepared for pregnancies, low birth weight, environmental risks, accidents, and violence. Added to these risks factors are changing and unstable family structures, inadequate community-based social programs, new and untested welfare systems, weak educational systems and a ceiling on job advancement for the unskilled. Although these problems are not new in society, they have multiplied in recent years and are more likely to occur in combination with one another. It is in this sense that the phenomenon of adolescent parenting has changed during the past several decades making it more complex and challenging than in prior generations.

Children's Development: The Heart of the Problem

Although the precise contributing role of teenage pregnancy and parenthood to the life course development of children is difficult to determine because of the unusually large number of causal and correlated factors, it is clear that children born to teenage mothers do not prosper as well as their mothers or children born to adult parents (East & Felice, 1996; Furstenberg et al., 1987): It is not uncommon to find that more than 50% of children with teen mothers experience academic and/or personal problems during their elementary and middle school years.

Intellectual Declines. Children with adolescent mothers are at risk for a host of developmental problems related to cognition and intelligence. These problems often have their inception in pregnancies that result in lower birth weight, prematurity, and greater neonatal mortality. Data from the Perinatal Longitudinal Project of Broman, Nichols, Shaughnessy, and Kennedy (1987)—which analyzed the outcomes of more than 38,000 high-risk births—also showed a higher percentage of mild retardation in the offspring of teen mothers versus adult mothers, from similar socioeconomic status (SES) and educational backgrounds. The actual percentage of mild retardation—due to nonorganic causes— may be up to three times higher among children of teen mothers.

Relatedly, data from the Baltimore longitudinal project of Furstenberg et al. (1987) and the New Haven project of Seitz and Apfel (1993) showed profound developmental delays: More than one half of the children with teen mothers had major behavioral and school-related problems, and many showed intellectual deficits as well. These longitudinal projects suggested that the social and psychological consequences of early pregnancy and teenage parenting are considerable, both for the children themselves as well as for the society that hopes to guide and mold their future development.

Although the long-term "fate" of many children with teen mothers is not promising, dramatic improvements in intelligence and cognitive skills have been described in several comprehensive intervention projects with children in poverty, many of whom had adolescent mothers. Both the North Carolina Abecedarian and the Milwaukee projects found that intellectual development declined precipitously over time for the children with low IQ mothers (Garber, 1988; Ramey & Ramey, 1990). For instance, the average intelligence level of children in the control group in the Milwaukee Project declined up to 20 points by age 10, if early intervention was not provided. Similarly, children with low IQ mothers in the Abecedarian Project showed an even more dramatic decline in IQ, up to 25 points, by age 10. In both intervention projects, children in the treatment and control conditions were similar on early measures of development, with most infants functioning within the normal range of intelligence during the first 6 months of life. In the Abecedarian Project, children in the control condition were 3.5 times as likely to have cognitive-educational deficits as children in the intervention condition (Ramey & Campbell, 1987). These findings support the general conclusion that intelligence and academic readiness generally decline for children in poverty across the first 5 years of life if they do not receive early, intensive, and consistent educationally based interventions.

Emotional Well-Being. Just as depression seriously impacts the life course development of adolescent mothers, maternal depression and anxiety appears to influence the socioemotional development of children. Spieker, Larsen, Lewis, Killer and Gilchrist (1999) recently studied the developmental trajectories of disruptive behavior problems between the ages of 3 and 6 for children of adolescent mothers. More than twice as many children as expected based on normative data exceeded the borderline-clinical cutoff, with boys showing higher levels of disruptive behaviors at age 6 than girls. In addition, negative maternal control—yelling, threatening and spanking—was related to the levels of disruptive behaviors and mediated the effects of maternal depression and anxiety. At the end of the preschool period, many mother–child dyads with high negative control were likely involved in "coercive power struggles" with their children. These interpersonal struggles exacerbated other problems such as poor educational preparation, thus hindering subsequent cognitive-social development and limiting the chances for life successes, for both the mother and her child.

THE INSIDIOUS NATURE OF POVERTY: A NEED FOR NEW PROGRAMS

Researchers are beginning to understand more fully how poverty in infancy is associated with long-term academic and personal problems

(Duncan & Brooks-Gunn, 1997). If poverty, and its correlates, are not fully addressed, most children with unmarried teen mothers will experience delays in their development. It is also becoming clearer that enhancing income, through good jobs and better tax-related incentives together with comprehensive interventions for both mothers and children, have the potential to increase cognitive skills and school readiness for children born into poverty (Smith, Brooks-Gunn, & Klebanov, 1997) and to improve their mothers' life trajectories.

Anticipating changes in federal programs, the Department of Health and Human Services launched the Teenage Parent Demonstration project in 1986 to assess the short- and long-term effectiveness of programs designed to improve the economic self-sufficiency of more than 5,000 adolescent parents on welfare. Agencies in Illinois and New Jersey that served teenage mothers, developed prevention programs and kept them in operation until the early 1990s. The programs required participation in education, job training, or employment-related activities, offering individual case management, child-care, and transportation. Participants were assigned randomly to an enhanced services condition (the intervention) or to a regular service condition (the control). Most of the mothers had educational deficits at intake and lacked basic skills (e.g., more than 50% read below the eighth-grade level).

There were several positive, short-term outcomes associated with participation in the Teenage Parent Demonstration Project (Zaslow, Tout, Smith, & Moore, 1998):

1. All sites demonstrated that they could operate mandatory work-oriented programs for teenage mothers, with good participation rates.
2. During the 2 years following intake, increased rates of school attendance and employment were found in the intervention condition versus the control, but no personal-social changes were noted (e.g., marriage, child support, and repeated pregnancies rates were not different).

With respect to enhanced self-sufficiency over the long-term, results were even less promising: Seven years after intake, 90% of the participants remained in poverty in both conditions. Ninety percent of the mothers were unmarried and those who were employed often remained in or near the poverty level. In addition, the program had no apparent effect on parenting practices. Thus, the short-term gains did not alter life course trajectories for mothers, or for their children who generally were unprepared for kindergarten and the start of elementary school.

Although the pace of welfare reform has accelerated since the Teenage Parent Demonstration Project, most states have failed to introduce comprehensive programs to assist first-time teenage mothers and their children. In addition to focusing on educational and job training needs—the specific goals of the Teenage Parent Demonstration Project—programs are needed that address maternal maladjustment (e.g., depression and self-esteem); low self-efficacy (e.g., pessimism about obtaining a better future); and inadequate social supports. Equally important for teen mothers, and especially for their children, is the acquisition of parenting skills. Mothers need to become competent in carrying out their new adult roles as responsible parents, and children need the "early start" provided by loving, responsible, and sensitive parents. In addition, most infants will require high-quality day care or preschool if young mothers are to assume jobs outside the home as mandated by new welfare laws. The availability and quality of that day care needs to be assured: If children receive 4 years of consistent, high quality care prior to the commencement of formal schooling, they will be in a much better position to succeed academically and to lead productive, happy lives as adolescents and adults (Ramey & Ramey, 1990).

It is possible that the poverty of today is more devastating, in terms of children's development, than in prior decades. This may, at first glance, seem contradictory given the recent expansion of Head Start, which now serves a greater proportion of 4-year-olds than ever before. However, as the effects of poor prenatal maternal medical care; unstable family lives and inadequate parenting; the ready availability of drugs and alcohol; the presence of violence in our neighborhoods; and low-level jobs have a cumulative adverse effect on child development (cf. Duncan & Brooks-Gunn, 1997), this increased availability of Head Start programs may be too little and too late. As an alternative, the emergence of the Early Start program holds promise of solving the problems associated with the traditional form of Head Start. The difficulty is that Early Start is not widely available for most needy, eligible children.

MODELS OF RESILIENCY

Although many adolescent mothers experience developmental problems as a result of their off-timed pregnancies and most of their children encounter academic delays, other teen mothers and their children prove to be resilient—overcoming obstacles and achieving success in the home, school, and workplace. If problems traditionally associated with adolescent parenting are to be averted, it is as important to identify the protective mechanism of resilient teen mothers as it is to find causal factors that lead to developmental problems in vulnerable mothers. Three related models—*compensatory*, *protective*, and *challenge* or *inoculation*, first described by Garmezy, Masten, and Tellegen (1984) and later elaborated by Zimmerman and Arunkumar (1994)—provide different ways of thinking about resiliency among adolescent mothers and children.

In the compensatory model, exposure to specific stressors or risks is neutralized by compensatory factors which exert a direct effect on the targeted outcomes and, generally, do not interact with risk factors. Garmezy et al. (1984) found SES to be an important compensatory factor, with children from higher socioeconomic backgrounds demonstrating less disruptive behavior, regardless of their levels of stress. Education is another example of a strong compensatory factor for adolescent mothers. Regardless of the amount of stress experienced, the degree of social support, or even the extent of cognitive preparation, young mothers with more education tend to adjust better to the challenges of early parenthood. The co-existence of compensatory processes and fewer risk factors promotes resilience.

A protective factors model provides a second way of conceptualizing resiliency. In this model, one or more factors interact with the risk factors to reduce the probability of a negative outcome. Protective factors function as moderating variables. That is, the effects of protective factors are greater within the context of a specific risk than they would be if that risk was not present (Werner & Smith, 1992). Results from Project Competence (Garmezy et al., 1984) highlight the protective effects of intelligence under conditions of high life stress: When confronted with greater life stresses, children with higher intelligence maintained adequate achievement scores, whereas the school achievement of children with lower intelligence declined; intelligence served as a protective factor against high stress. Similarly, cognitive readiness for parenting may serve as a protective factor for adolescent mothers: Cognitively prepared mothers will probably be more effective in parenting children with difficult temperament, whereas this protective factor may make less difference with children who have easy temperaments.

The third model discussed by Garmezy et al. (1984) and by Zimmerman and Arunkumar (1994) is the challenge model. Rutter (1985) described this model as providing a steeling or inoculation effect. For example, limited social support from parents—a potentially undesirable situation for many adult parents—can actually enhance adaptation among adolescent mothers: Young mothers who are unable to turn to their own mothers for total material support and child care are forced to accept their own role as mother, accelerating their transition from adolescence to adulthood. An early acceptance of the maternal role "steels or inoculates" teens from further stressors in their environments and equips them for other developmental challenges associated with adulthood. These three models are not mutually exclusive. Resilient adolescent mothers and their children may be influenced by compensatory factors that serve to neutralize some of the stressors or risks associated with early childbearing. Protective factors may moderate the influence of other risk factors associated with an off-time transition. Finally, compensatory and protective factors may co-occur with inoculation variables. All three models suggest the existence of factors that shield adolescent mothers from high risks and provide them a means of successfully coping with the stressors associated with early parenthood. Although resiliency involves a process for successfully coping with and adapting to stressors, it is often inferred from successful outcomes. However, Luthar and Zigler (1991) warned that resilience does not imply invulnerability, and that many resilient individuals may show evidence of scars, suggesting that successful adaptation or seeming resilience may mask underlying problems. It is not surprising that Luthar and Zigler (1991) encouraged researchers to attend to possible underlying signs of internalizing disorders in children of adolescent mothers who appear otherwise resilient. Clearly, more information is needed about the protective mechanisms used by adolescent mothers and their children who are resilient.

CONCLUSION

Although researchers and family practitioners now understand more about the phenomenon of adolescent parenting, it remains a serious issue—for those immediately involved as well as for society at large—for three major reasons:

1. Although the birth rate to teens has declined in recent years, the absolute number of adolescent births in the United States is sizable, more than 400,000 per year.
2. The impact of parenthood on a mother's transition to adulthood may be more deleterious today than ever before; this is due to the insidious nature of poverty, increases in substance abuse, breakdown of traditional supports, elimination of many components of federal and state assistance, and the ever increasing level of violence in our society.
3. Increases in aggression and depression among today's adolescents, the unavailability of effective preschool services in the first 3 years of life, and declines in the quality of parenting are likely to further ex-

acerbate the developmental problems of children raised by teenage mothers.

The adolescent parenting project described in this book is aimed at understanding more about the processes that adversely influence, or facilitate, development in adolescent mothers and their first-born offspring. The goal here is to describe, in considerable detail, the interwoven lives of adolescent mothers and their children through the first 8 years.

2

Theoretical Perspectives on Adolescent Parenting

with Elizabeth Rellinger

Since the 1970s, there has been an emergence of exciting new perspectives on the importance of parenting for successful child development (e.g., Baumrind, 1971; Belsky, 1984; Gottman, 1997). These new theories provide information about the role of parenting beliefs and practices; about the historical, cultural, and personal factors that give rise to specific parenting practices; and about the characteristics of successful parents as they raise and mentor their children. Although different in their emphases, they share a common focus on active, responsive parenting, thus countering the cultural trend toward laissez faire, permissive parenting that emerged following World War II. Despite an impressive amount of research on parenting since 1970, relatively little is known about how the parenting styles, beliefs, and practices of adolescent parents differ from those of adult parents and how these factors influence child development.

It is possible, of course, that all that is claimed about adult parenting will hold, with only slight modification or a minor change in emphasis, for adolescent parents. However, given the cognitive and emotional immaturity of most adolescents, it is possible that what is true for adults holds only in part, or not at all, for adolescents. New theories, or major theoretical modifications in existing theories, may be necessary for a full accounting of adolescent parenting and its impact on child development.

In this chapter, we review selective research on adult parenting with an eye toward assessing its "fit" with adolescent parenting. Next, we examine the unique aspects of adolescence, as a critical stage of human development, with a view toward understanding how challenges associated with the developmental tasks of the period complicate the acquisition and use of parenting skills, especially under stress and in the context of poverty. Finally, we develop the argument—based on our analysis of the adult parenting literature and the uniqueness of adolescence as a de-

23

velopmental stage—that existing perspectives on parenting require a reconsideration or reemphasis in order to fully understand the emergence of parenting practices in adolescent mothers and their translation into the lives of children. The aim is to show that factors explaining variability in adult parenting practices may not fully account for variability among adolescent parents.

A PERSPECTIVE ON ADULT PARENTING AND ITS APPLICABILITY TO ADOLESCENTS

Perhaps the most comprehensive view of the causes and consequences of parenting is presented by Belsky's (1984) multidimensional model. As can be seen in Fig. 2.1, Belsky emphasized three main sources of influence on parenting: psychological resources of parents, including their developmental histories and adjustment strategies; contextual–environmental sources of support; and child characteristics. These factors work together, sometimes in reciprocal fashion, to influence child development. Although the Belsky model has failed to generate a substantial body of research supporting its dynamic character (such as the bidirectionality between personality and social support and their links to parenting), each construct in the model has been individually validated, to varying degrees, in the empirical literature. What is most valuable about the Belsky model, however, is its conceptual framework, which is especially useful in understanding the interacting, multiple causes of successful and unsuccessful parenting, and their evolution over time.

The centerpiece of Belsky's model lies in its emphasis on parents' personality traits, reflected in their personal histories and current adjustments to life's stressors, as a major determinant of parenting behavior. Operating as a second essential component, often in concert with personality, is the quality of the social support network, which not only acts directly on parenting but also can interact with personality. For instance, the inconsistent or insensitive parenting practices of a depressed mother may be much less harmful to her child if the grandmother, siblings, and/or spouse are available to provide understanding, support, and assistance to the mother. Other important social factors, especially for adults, are work and marriage; a stable job and a secure marriage contribute to both adjustment and happiness, which in turn enlarge the parents' pool of personal resources as well as contribute to the development of positive parenting practices (see Fig. 2.1). Finally, the child's own characteristics—such as an easy temperament, hyperactivity, aggression, or depression—can influence the type and quality of parenting, especially if the child has behavioral problems that are not addressed and remediated, decreasing parental responsivity and sensitivity over time.

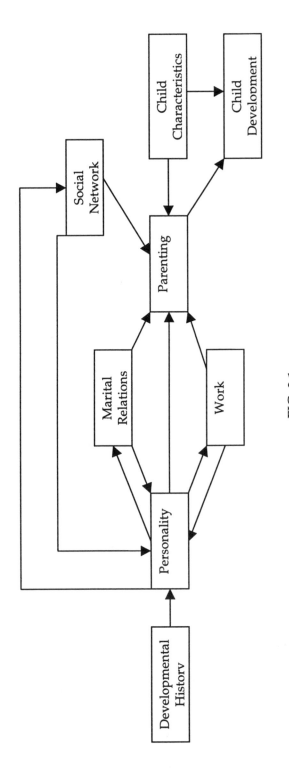

FIG. 2.1
Belsky's (1984) model of parenting.

25

Although the same components in Belsky's (1984) model appear to be important for adolescent as well as adult parents, there is also evidence that the extent of their influence may differ (Nath, Borkowski, Whitman, & Schellenbach, 1991). In contrast to adult mothers, adolescent mothers often need and receive more support from their own parents and their extended family, especially during pregnancy and early parenthood. During the first few years of parenting, the presence of supportive friends typically becomes an important factor—more so than for adult parents. Moreover, the social supports provided through marriage, or a stable relationship, as well as through work seem more important in understanding variability among adults than among adolescents who are just developing the maturity necessary to sustain serious relationships. These latter factors, although vital in maintaining high-quality parenting, occur infrequently and sporadically in the lives of adolescent mothers. That is, the vast majority of adolescents are unmarried (Furstenberg & Crawford, 1978), sometimes have unstable relationships with their partners (Unger & Wandersman, 1985), and frequently are unemployed or underemployed (Jorgensen, King, & Torry, 1980; Moore, Hofferth, Wetheimer, Waite, & Caldwell, 1981). Hence, these factors are less useful in explaining variability in adolescent parenting.

In addition to differences in the pattern of relationships among core constructs and the lack of variation in jobs and relationships, the personal resources of adolescents for coping with the stresses associated with parenting are often less developed and sometimes qualitatively different from those of adult mothers. Compared to adult mothers, adolescent mothers are more likely to be in poorer health, behaviorally maladjusted, less educated, lower in intellectual ability, and less equipped for the challenges of parenting (Patten, 1981; Vukelich & Kliman, 1985). Hence, many teens are less prepared for and less "ready" to parent—both cognitively and emotionally—than adult parents. These "readiness" factors have potential significance for problematic parenting practices and subsequent delayed development in children. A new construct, cognitive readiness to parent, is featured in the model of adolescent parenting we develop in the final section of this chapter.

Although Belsky (1984) emphasized that there is a bidirectional influence between child characteristics and parenting, child characteristics may have, for several reasons, an even more critical impact on adolescent parenting. First, children of adolescent mothers are more likely to develop problematic behaviors such as inattention, hyperactivity, and aggression. Second, adolescent mothers may be more quickly overwhelmed as they attempt to cope with a challenging child. Adolescents sometimes tend either to retreat from or deny their children's problems, or punish excessively, rather than facing constructively difficulties head on, with the support and positive assistance of family, agencies, clinics, or schools. In short, differences in patterns of social relationships, in the early emergence of unanticipated childhood problems, and in the relevance of key potential exploratory constructs, such as work and marriage, between adult and adolescent parents suggest that a revised model is necessary to account for individual differences in teen parenting and its impact on child development. The next section develops more fully the rationale for a unique model of adolescent parenting.

ADOLESCENT DEVELOPMENT AND PARENTING

Although there are multiple frameworks for understanding adolescent development, an exhaustive review of this literature is beyond the scope of this chapter. Nonetheless, a brief overview of two of the most relevant theories of adolescent development, and their implications for adolescent parenting, are summarized. First, a Piagetian view of social and cognitive development is discussed. Next, Erikson's theory of adolescent identity development is summarized. The aim is to show how "the uniqueness of adolescence" as a stage of development complicates the emergence of effective parenting practices. After the presentation of these two theories, the stage is set for building a framework for a developmentally oriented model of adolescent parenting.

A Piagetian View of Adolescent Cognitive Development

According to Piaget (1972), children and adults differ in their ability to deal with abstractions. In his view, the shift from concrete operational thought to formal operational thought brings about the ability to deal with the world in a more complex, systematic, and logical fashion. Although Piaget (1952) initially believed that formal operational thought becomes consolidated between the ages of 11 and 15, he later revised this age range to somewhere between the ages of 15 and 20 (Piaget, 1972). Because researchers have indicated that many college students do not think in formal operational ways (Elkind, 1961; Lapsley, 1990; Tomlinson-Keasey, 1972), it seems safe to assume that most teens are, at best, operating in an emergent subperiod of formal operational thought. This may be especially the case for teen parents who frequently have difficulty performing well in school.

Early emergent formal operational thought, which falls short of "adult thinking," is characterized by the development of hypothetical reasoning that is not constrained by reality, resulting in perceptions of the world that are both too subjective and too idealistic (Broughton,

1983). Thus, the adolescent period is marked by paradoxical contrasts: dramatic changes that indicate growth in cognitive processes but somewhat distorted ways of thinking about, and operating within, the social world. Two of these paradoxes are idealistic thinking and adolescent egocentrism.

Within the Piagetian view, idealistic thinking emerges as adolescents begin to compare the real to the possible, thus discovering the shortcomings and inconsistencies that surround them (Piaget, 1926, 1950). As they find their environments lacking in comparison "to the imagined," adolescents can become both cynical about the world and overly optimistic about their own ability to make changes. The consequences may lead to a tendency to find fault with authority figures and accepted modes of behavior, as well as to faulty judgments. These faulty judgments are often due to failures to anticipate the possible consequences of their own behaviors, and a tendency to oversimplify explanations (Klaczynski, 1997).

The form of egocentrism that emerges during adolescence also develops from this newfound ability to engage in higher order thinking. During the stage of emergent formal thought the adolescent is able to realize that others have thoughts, but is unable to differentiate between the focus of his or her own thoughts and the focus of other's thoughts (Elkind, 1967). Because adolescents are so often concerned with the "physiological metamorphoses" they are undergoing, they are convinced that others are as preoccupied with their appearance and behavior as they are (Elkind, 1967). This belief leads to a phenomenon referred to as the "imaginary audience" in which the adolescent sees him or herself as being the center of attention in almost all social situations. Furthermore, the imaginary audience assumption leads adolescents to believe that their private thoughts and concerns are known—and are of importance— to those around them.

Because adolescents believe that they are of central importance to so many people, they may come to regard themselves and their feelings as somewhat unique. According to Elkind (1967), this leads to the "personal fable," which explains a number of frequently noted adolescent thought patterns. These personal fables, or untrue stories that adolescents tells themselves, include feelings of uniqueness as well as feelings of immortality. Feelings of uniqueness lead adolescents to believe that whatever emotion is experienced—be it loneliness, passion, despair, or confusion— has never before been experienced as strongly or as exquisitely. Because the person experiencing the personal fable believes him or herself to be absolutely unique, he or she can also believe that he or she is exempt from the rules by which others must live; in essence, he or she feels immortal. In explaining the impact of such thinking, Elkind (1967) stated that, "many young girls become pregnant because, in part at least, their personal fable convinces them that pregnancy will happen to others but never to them and so they need not take precautions" (p. 1032). From a Piagetian perspective of development, adolescent girls can be viewed as at risk for pregnancy for a number of other reasons:

1. They make faulty judgments based on an oversimplified and overly idealistic view of the world.
2. They believe that they are of primary importance to others, and that their romances are truly unique and meaningful.
3. They engage in risk-taking behaviors because they do not believe that they are subject to the same biological laws as others.

This perspective is partially supported by a study of Arnett (1992) in which egocentrism was related to "reckless sexual behavior" among high school students. It may also explain why so many educational programs to prevent adolescent pregnancy have produced inconsistent and inconclusive results (Levinson, 1995): If adolescents are immersed in strong personal fables, it is unlikely that programs to prevent pregnancy will have much impact because they will see this information as being applicable to others, but not themselves. Additionally, as explained by Cobb (1988), many adolescents may be facing sexual decisions while still approaching daily problems in a concrete fashion, limiting their thinking to what is immediate and apparent. Thus, the immediate desire of pleasing a male may be seen as more pressing than concerns about pregnancy and disease, which often times seem distant and dim possibilities.

Of course, all teenage pregnancies are not unplanned. However, researchers working in clinical settings have provided evidence that among adolescents who intentionally become pregnant, immature and egocentric reasons often lie behind this choice. For instance, Black and DeBlassie (1985) reported several cases in which 14- and 15-year-old girls attributed their pregnancy to a desire to rebel against their domineering parents. Battle (1995) reported on young women who cited reasons for becoming pregnant, such as "wanting to keep a boyfriend" and "wanting to rectify one's sense of isolation." Whether planned or unplanned, it is likely that many adolescents become pregnant due, at least in part, to thought processes that are distorted by egocentrism and an inconsistent ability to engage in systematic, long-term decision making.

Once an adolescent becomes pregnant, it is possible that her egocentrism may determine the choices she makes about the pregnancy. This hypothesis has not been tested directly, but in one study, adolescents who chose adoption over keeping the baby, cited concerns for the baby's welfare as their primary consideration, whereas adolescents who chose to keep their babies cited concerns for their own welfare. Specifically, this second group endorsed the statement that "adoption was too emotionally upsetting to consider" (Resnick, Blum, Bose, Smith, & Toogood, 1990). Once young women elect to raise their children, many express not only egocentrism, but also idealistic visions of motherhood and overly optimistic consequences of their pregnancies. This idealism was clearly expressed by young women interviewed by Battle (1995) who reported narratives that "revealed an idyllic fantasy to mend a broken world through a desired pregnancy" (p. 25). It is also interesting to note these women later reported feelings of resentment toward the infants who, rather than satisfying the mothers' unrealistic hopes, had needs of their own. Furthermore, these young women admitted that they continued to engage in various risk-taking behaviors, sometimes exposing their children to dangerous situations. It seems clear that adolescent egocentrism is likely linked to role reversal and immature attitudes about why a woman chooses to become a parent.

A cognitively immature and idealistic view of the world was also shown by pregnant teens and adolescent mothers in a study by Medora, Goldstein, and von der Hellen (1994). In this study, 255 pregnant teens, 121 adolescent mothers, and 273 nonpregnant and nonparenting adolescents were compared in terms of their levels of romanticism about pregnancy, motherhood, and romantic relationships. Although it is not surprising that pregnant adolescents tended to hold an idealized view of relationships, it was surprising that the adolescent mothers had not lost this romanticized view. This finding, however, makes sense in that romantic individuals were described in this study as also being more illogical and irrational, and as holding unrealistic and simplistic expectations about relationships. In other words, a high sense of romanticism is typical of the idealistic adolescent—whether a parent or pregnant—who is engaging in the personal fable. These data also lend credence to the idea that the experience of motherhood is insufficient to change an adolescent's cognitive structure or to bring on the consolidation of formal operational thought. Moreover, because many adolescent mothers are already showing cognitive delays (Coll, Hoffman, & Oh, 1987; Sommer et al., 1993), they may be less able to profit from their unique life experiences (Whitman, Borkowski, Schellenbach, & Nath, 1987).

The picture that emerges from taking a Piagetian view of adolescent motherhood is that of a parent entering a complex and demanding new world with inadequate problem-solving skills, an idealized view of that world, and unrealistic expectations about what to expect from her child. To the extent that adolescent mothers are experiencing "personal fables," they are less likely to believe that their children can come to harm and more likely to believe that their children will turn out fine despite the environmental or emotional deprivations they sometimes experience. More generally, Piaget's perspective on development reinforces the need for a model of parenting sensitive to the actual cognitive beliefs and attitudes of adolescents.

An Eriksonian View of Adolescent Identity Development

According to Erikson (1960), the rapid body growth and sexual maturity that comes with puberty forces adolescents to grapple with conflicts about personal identity. It is not until the individual has done "the work of this stage," and begins to feel secure in his or her identity, that Erikson believes true intimacy and commitments to others can be established.

Intimacy and commitment are the hallmarks of successful parenting. Before an adolescent girl can take on adult roles, such as parenting, she must grapple with the tasks of adolescence that include obtaining an education, developing an identity, and moving away from home (Erikson, 1963). As Spieker and Bensley (1994) pointed out, the adolescent mother is often caught between competing roles: The fulfillment of typical adolescent developmental tasks can mean a neglect of maternal duties and a lack of attention in preparing for the adult tasks of forming intimate relationships and rearing the next generation. Spieker and Bensley compared adolescent mothers who lived with their mothers to those who moved away from their mothers' homes and found that those who continued to live with their mothers were more likely to continue in their adolescent roles. Although this had some positive implications for the adolescents—most notably that these adolescents were more likely to remain in school—they also experienced a high level of conflict and experienced role confusion regarding their relationships with their children. Moving away from home can serve as a rite of passage for adolescent mothers and may have positive consequences for both the teen and her child. Indeed, Spieker and Bensley (1994) found that the mothers who live with neither grandmother nor a partner were rated as being more skilled when they interacted with their infants. What is not clear is whether there are negative long-term consequences for mothers who move abruptly from the role of young adolescents to the role of "adult" parent.

The question about the long-term consequences of taking on the maternal role during adolescence is critical if Erikson's (1968) warning about a "double-edged danger" at this stage is taken seriously. By selecting an identity too quickly, the adolescent may become identity foreclosed, but by avoiding making decisions the adolescent may continue in a state of identity confusion. Because adolescents who are foreclosed enter into the parenting role without having an opportunity to adequately experiment with other roles, they may be less likely to feel truly comfortable in the parenting role and may be more likely to interact with their children in a rigid and stereotyped manner. Because little work has been done on the identity status of young mothers, research on the characteristics of foreclosed individuals is reviewed.

Orlofsky, Marcia, and Lesser (1973) found that the intimate relationships of foreclosed individuals tend to be stereotyped and marked by a lack of self-disclosure and sharing. Relatedly, Lutes (1981) studied couples who had entered into marriage at early ages and found that individuals in these marriages tended to be foreclosed. Young married people displayed a significant amount of impulsivity, were more concerned with social desirability, and had weaker abstract problem-solving skills. In an impressive longitudinal study of female identity status, Josselson (1989) described foreclosed women as being unable to tolerate ambiguity, being self-centered and unreflective, and as showing few signs of personal development. It seems likely that foreclosed adolescents would parent in a way that is rigid, cold, and focused on adhering to social standards. In essence, this parenting profile mirrors that of the authoritarian parent. This position is supported by Marcia's (1966) study in which foreclosed individuals received significantly higher scores of the F Scale (which measures authoritarian submission and conventionality) than individuals in the other identity status groups.

Although Erikson feels that some amount of confusion during adolescence is normative, he also believes that adolescents should enter into a psychological moratorium during which they experiment with alternative roles and new personal options. Otherwise, sustained identity confusion can lead to a state of identity diffusion that is marked by excessive self-centeredness and emotional immaturity (Marcia, 1966). For instance, an adolescent girl who is raising a child while being parented by her own mother, may end up drifting among various immature roles (girlfriend, part-time GED student, gang member, or Burger King chef), often with few commitments and little introspection, rather than more systematically experimenting with new "possible selves." According to Waterman (1985), identity diffusion can occur as the adolescent relinquishes efforts to choose an identity because no attractive options appear open. This can easily happen to teen mothers residing with their parents; that is, the teen feels a sense of forced dependency on the parents, a dependence that directly contrasts with the adolescent's need for independence (Spieker & Bensley, 1994).

When intimacy patterns are analyzed, diffused adolescents are often described as *isolates*, who experience casual relationships that lack depth and commitment (Orlofsky et al., 1973). This lack of deep friendship is attributed to the tendency to be self-centered, self-doubting, and distrustful of others. In Josselson's (1989) study, isolated women developed few coping skills and tended to use fantasy as a means of escaping personal challenges. The diffused approach to life decisions was described as haphazard; hence, these young women reacted to life events like "leaves blown by the wind." Much like foreclosed adolescents, diffused teens show limited problem solving skills and are likely to underachieve in math, a subject that requires systematic thinking (Streitmatter, 1989).

The portrait that emerges of the diffused adolescent as a mother is a person who believes that the child should try to meet her needs, has few concrete plans for her own or for her child's future, and who learns little from her interpersonal experiences. This profile is quite similar to that which emerges from the profile of the egocentric adolescent because both egocentrism and diffusion are typical of young or immature adolescents.

The contention here is that the adolescent's personal search for an identity leaves her with little time or interest for deep reflection on new parenting responsibilities (Sommer et al., 1993). Whether the adolescent deals with her identity crisis by becoming foreclosed or by remaining diffused, she most likely will experience some or all of the following developmental problems: (a) trouble accurately interpreting and learning from her life experiences, (b) a view of herself and her child that is both egocentric and rigid, (c) poor social problem-solving skills, and (d) stress associated with her relationship with her mother. All of these factors make it likely that adolescents who are faced with the dual tasks of identity development and parenting will be less prepared, and more stressed, in responding to their children's needs.

A DEVELOPMENTAL MODEL OF ADOLESCENT PARENTING

The review of Piaget and Erikson's theories highlights several important characteristics of adolescents that likely affect their abilities to enter into demanding maternal roles. The goal of the rest of this chapter is to integrate theories of adult parenting with theories of adolescence as a developmental stage into an age-appropriate model of adolescent parenting. It is our belief that this model will help explain the tendency of adolescent mothers to be less responsive and sensitive to their children (Osofsky & Osofsky, 1970; Roosa, Fitzgerald, & Carson, 1982), more authoritarian (Sommer et al., 1993), less able to foster emotional self-regulation skills, and less prepared to confront early appearing developmental delays in their children.

In developing our model of adolescent parenting, we focus on the impact of five important characteristics in the mother, her child, and their environment on parenting competence:

1. The adolescent's lower level of cognitive readiness for parenting.
2. Limited intellectual resources.
3. Restricted social support system.
4. Psychological adjustment problems and emotional immaturity.
5. Raising a challenging child.

Although each of these factors is discussed in the next section, we emphasize the concepts of cognitive readiness and learning ability for parenting because these constructs are not contained in Belsky's (1984) parenting model.

The Importance of Cognitive Readiness for Adolescent Parenting

Whitman et al. (1987) proposed a comprehensive model of adolescent parenting that focuses on the impact of cognitive readiness on parenting and child development. Cognitive readiness, as described by Sommer and colleagues (1993), involves three interrelated components: knowledge about how children develop, attitudes about the parenting role, and understanding of appropriate parenting practices. It seems likely that the development of each component might be inhibited because of the nature of adolescence as a unique stage of development. For instance, the ability to learn about developmental milestones, such as the timing of walking and talking, may be hampered by the adolescent's identity diffusion, egocentrism, or inexperience. Maternal attitudes toward parenting may be marked by tendencies toward authoritarianism and role reversal, as reflected in the belief that the child is responsible for the parent's well-being rather than vice versa. Furthermore, an understanding of appropriate parenting practices may be limited by an inability to decenter and gain empathic awareness of their children's needs, as well as by a simplistic endorsement of the value of physical punishment.

Indeed, descriptive research on cognitive readiness has shown that adolescent mothers often have imprecise knowledge concerning child development and espouse negative attitudes about parenting (Jarrett, 1982; Roosa & Vaughn, 1984). They sometimes have children for egocentric reasons, are conflicted when children fail to meet their "mythical expectations," and are harsh in their response when faced with perceived or real inappropriate child behaviors. Recent research has emphasized the importance of cognitive factors—such as parenting attitudes, values, and knowledge—as the earliest socioenvironmental risk factors influencing infants and children (C. Miller, Heysek, Whitman, & Borkowski, 1996; Sigel, McGillicuddy-DeLisi, & Goodnow, 1992).

Examining the relationship of cognitive readiness to parenting outcomes, Sommer and colleagues (1993) found that adolescent mothers were less cognitively prepared for parenting prior to the birth of their children when compared with adult mothers. Furthermore, less prepared adolescent mothers experienced greater parenting stress and were less responsive to their children. In contrast, research has indicated that mothers with accurate expectations regarding children's development are more likely to facilitate their own children's acquisition of developmental milestones, such as early verbal and sensorimotor skills (S. Miller, Manhal, & Mee, 1991; Stoiber & Houghton, 1993). For example, Stoiber and Houghton found that adolescent mothers who reported more positive, realistic, and mature parental expectations about child development had infants who displayed more adaptive and effective sensorimotor skills and coping behaviors. Finally, O'Callaghan, Borkowski, Whitman, Maxwell, and Keogh (1999) found that cognitive readiness mediated relationships between several other important maternal characteristics— such as IQ and personal adjustment—and adolescent parenting. That is, rather than effecting parenting directly, IQ and personality influenced cognitive readiness, which, in turn, was directly related to parenting.

To the extent that adolescent mothers possess less accurate and inadequate knowledge about child development and parenting practices, they may be predisposed once they become parents to "miss" the connection between their children's behavior and their parenting practices (Sommer et al., 1993). Mothers may view the source of a child's behavior problem as residing solely in the child. These maternal perceptions, which can develop during the first months of parenting, can affect the quality of parent–child interactions and subsequently hinder child development, both in emotional and cognitive realms (C. Miller et al., 1996). Mothers who perceive their parenting roles as more difficult tend to experience feelings of helplessness and inadequacy about their abilities to parent effectively (Bugental, Blue, & Cruzcosa, 1989), and parents who perceive their parenting role as stressful are less effective in their parenting practices (Bell, 1976; Crnic, Greenberg, Ragozin, Robinson, & Basham, 1983; Crnic, Greenberg, & Slough, 1986). In turn, higher levels of reported parenting stress have been associated with a lack of maternal responsiveness to infant cues, lower levels of positive maternal affect, as well as insecure child attachment and child noncompliance (Crnic et al., 1986; Dix, 1991). Finally, inaccurate and negative maternal perceptions regarding children's behaviors have been associated with lower maternal responsiveness, greater interference, and increased irritability in the child (Crockenberg & Smith, 1982; Nover, Shore, Timberlake, & Greenspan, 1984).

The Importance of Learning Ability for Adolescent Parenting

Among adolescents who become pregnant, those who elect to raise their children tend to have more limited academic success than those who choose adoption (Grow, 1979) or abortion (B. Miller & Moore, 1990). When compared to older mothers, adolescent mothers tend to be less educated (Belmont, Cohen, Dryfoos, Stein, & Zayac, 1981; National Survey of Family Growth Cycle III, 1982) and score lower on tests of intellectual ability (Coll et al., 1987; Sommer et al., 1993). Additionally, Rauch-Elnekave (1994) suggested that many adolescents who become pregnant have undetected learning problems, problems that make it difficult for them to succeed in school as well as at work. It is not surprising to find that adolescents who have a second child within a few years of the first often have lower intellectual ability (Shearer, 1999). Impaired learning skills and academic failures may predispose the adolescent toward becoming pregnant as well as may inhibit her cognitive preparation for the task of parenting (Sommer et al., 1993).

These latter problems, in conjunction with the low intellectual abilities of some adolescent mothers, can affect their children's future cognitive attainment through direct, genetic transmission of mental retardation; inappropriate maternal teaching styles and a lack of knowledge about how to "scaffold" children's cognitive growth; and genetic and environmental factors that interact to determine a mother's parenting skills (Plomin, Loehlin, & DeFries, 1985). Thus, the development of cognition and intelligence in the children of teenage mothers may be affected directly via genetic factors and indirectly through inadequate parental cognitive and emotional readiness, which sometimes combine to produce unstable and nonstimulating childrearing environments.

Adolescent Socioemotional Adjustment

Teen mothers are often not emotionally ready to cope with the stressors associated with parenthood. In part, this lack of readiness is due to the fact that they often have reduced cognitive resources and are forced to cope with tasks associated with adolescent development, including a search for self-identity, self-esteem, and peer acceptance, while simultaneously attempting to resolve the challenging tasks associated with parenthood. Thus, it is not surprising that depression, frustration, and aggression occur with higher frequency among pregnant adolescents than pregnant adults (Passino et al., 1993).

Adolescents often bring excess emotional baggage with them as they adapt to their new roles as mothers. Research suggests that as they deal with conflicts with their own children, unresolved issues from their own childhood take on added significance and are not easily dropped. For example, pregnant teens often have experienced a higher rate of sexual abuse as children and young adults, a deeply rooted problem that can lead to punitive parenting practices with their own children (Dukewich, Borkowski, & Whitman, 1996). Other studies suggest that adolescent mothers may carry over hostility to their sons transferred from fathers who have abandoned their responsibilities. Even without added emotional baggage, an adolescent forced to parent a young child faces a demanding task, requiring patience, frustration tolerance, and emotional control—challenges that many adolescent mothers find difficult as they search for their own self-identity. Not surprisingly, a variety of studies suggest that pregnant adolescents have poorly integrated personalities and low self-esteem (cf. Passino et al., 1993). Although Belsky (1984) appeared justified in focusing on personal adjustment as a major construct in forming his model of adult parenting; it could prove to be an even more critical construct in explaining adolescent parenting.

Particularly critical for the adjustment of children is their mothers' emotional maturity and understanding of their roles in fostering emotional growth. Emotional maturity is necessary for handling parenting stress and for developing satisfactory interpersonal relationships. According to Gottman (1997), a mother's ability to understand the factors that produce emotional stability in her child is likely related to her own emotional awareness. Gottman identified the critical roles played by emotional awareness, emotional validation, and emotional coaching on the part of mature parents as they nurture their children's development and foster interpersonal relationships. Gottman's model represents a major advance in the understanding of the interface between the emotional, cognitive, and social domains of development; children who experience early emotional coaching tend to have more success academically, socially, and physically. Although "emotional sensitivity" is not all that common among adult parents, especially fathers, it is likely an even rarer commodity among adolescents.

At the heart of the Gottman model is the concept of meta-emotions (Gottman, Katz, & Hooven, 1997). The model, summarized in Fig. 2.2, suggests the critical paths through which meta-emotions, such as understanding the importance of a child's specific emotional experiences, influence parenting practices and eventually child development through the emergence of emotional self-regulation as reflected in the ability to self-sooth and manage anger. The opportunity "to coach" children's emotions is a critical "parenting moment" and an often neglected or misunderstood parenting task.

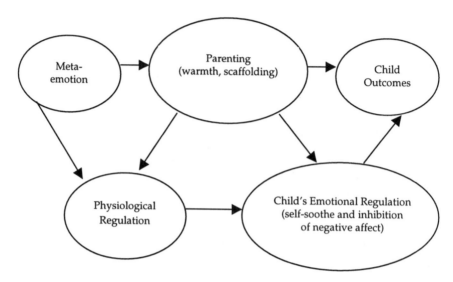

FIG. 2.2

Adapted from Gottman et al.'s (1997b) model of meta-emotional development.

The importance of children's emotional regulation shows up most clearly during the preschool years and later becomes a factor not only in emotional development but also in social, intellectual, and physical development as well. The problem for many adolescent parents is that their own emotional lives are often in disarray or undergoing rapid changes; hence, few are prepared to validate and coach the emergence of emotions, such as anger and sadness, in their children. It is likely that this component of successful adult parents is missing from the parenting repertoire of most adolescent parents.

The Role of Social Supports in Adolescent Parenting

From the perspective of attachment theory, adolescence is a time during which the primary social bonds formed in childhood are changed as the adolescent begins to seek a new partner who will, in time, replace the parent as the primary attachment figure (Colin, 1996). For teenage mothers, this may be a particularly daunting task because the person who they may have viewed as a new attachment figure, the child's father, may be unable or unwilling to fulfill this role: Seventy-two percent of adolescent mothers are unmarried (Alan Guttmacher Institute, 1994), and few unwed mothers live with their children's fathers (Navarro, 1996).

There is another shift in social support systems that is typically perceived as occurring during adolescence: Peer support sometimes supplants the role of parental support. Despite the widespread appeal of this notion, there is considerable evidence that parents continue to play primary roles in providing social supports to adolescents. For instance, parental counsel is often sought in important situations involving long-term decision making, such as exploring the implications of pregnancy (Rosenberg, 1965). Satisfaction with help from parents is more related to adolescent's psychological health than is satisfaction with help from peers (Burke & Weir, 1979); and the quality of attachment to parents is a more powerful predictor of well-being than is the quality of attachment to peers (Greenberg, Siegel, & Leitch, 1983).

Given the inaccessibility of many partners of adolescent mothers and the heavy reliance of most adolescents on their parents, it is not surprising that adolescent mothers frequently receive primary support from their families of origin, especially their mothers, rather than their partners (Lamb, 1988). Among teenage mothers, higher levels of familial social support are frequently associated with positive outcomes. For example, social support from family members is correlated with more sensitive parenting, greater responsivity, and affection toward their children (Colletta, 1981; Crockenberg, 1981). However, there is some reason to believe that too much involvement by the grandmother may be linked to confusion about authority and may lead to delays in the adolescent mother's assumption of parenting responsibilities and roles, perhaps resulting in negative consequences for children (Apfel & Seitz, 1999). In summary, although the mother of the adolescent is an important source of social support, the nature of this relationship is quite complex and still not fully understood.

Infant and Child Characteristics

Infant characteristics can interact with and influence the quality of parenting. For instance, difficult infant temperament, when combined with insensitive parenting, can have adverse affects on child development. Infants with difficult temperament likely increase the stress levels of immature mothers, which in turn can result in parental inattention, punishment, or neglect. Adolescents who are struggling to learn how to be sensitive and responsive mothers are asked simultaneously to deal with, and regulate, children's temperamental states.

An even greater problem arises for both adult and adolescent parents when they are called on to raise special needs children. Developmental delays occur more frequently in the children of adolescent than adult parents and the adolescent parent's preparation for dealing with special parenting challenges is likely less adequate (Whitman et al., 1987). The developmental course of childhood problems—such attention deficit disorder with hyperactivity (ADHD) and learning disabilities (LD)—are greatly influenced by parental behavior and planning. Both problems are representative of the types of challenges that adolescent mothers must face on a daily basis.

The rise of diagnosed cases of ADHD and LD in the United States cuts across economic, racial, and age boundaries. Children who show problems in attention, impulsivity, and self-regulation can succeed in school provided that parents find appropriate classroom therapies (including carefully prescribed and monitored medication in the case of ADHD). Often, they need to carry out well-chosen behavior modification plans that coordinate activities in the home with the school, using a program of rewards and restrictions. Barkley (1997) identified the specific components of attentional processing and executive functioning that can be modified through the judicious use of behavior modification programs when applied systematically in the clinic, home, and school. It is clear, however, that the typical, middle-class adult couple finds such educational tasks challenging, requiring considerable diligence and persistence throughout their son or daughter's childhood and adolescence. For a young mother, the problems are formidable.

Several problems confront the adolescent mother who is parenting a child with LD and/or ADHD:

1. She has difficulty locating an affordable and competent physician and behavioral therapist who have the requisite treatment skills.
2. She experiences obstacles setting up a behavioral system in the home, because of the irregular and often chaotic schedule in her life.
3. She finds it difficult negotiating with the school system, specifically in securing appropriate classroom instruction and consistent teacher cooperation.
4. Her own life stresses, including those associated with poverty, make implementation of these programs problematic, especially when many years of treatment are required.

Thus, the parenting of a child with ADHD and/or LD is more complicated and difficult for adolescent than for adult mothers. Because hyperactivity and the breakdown of regulation are often a precursor of later developing, more serious emotional problems, such as conduct disorders, the tasks of parenting can become overwhelming for the single, poorly educated mother as the child ages.

Adolescent and Adult Parenting

Although we have reviewed a number of studies showing differences in parenting practices and styles among adults and adolescents, we conclude this section with an explicit discussion on this construct because it is central to the model of adolescent parenting we develop in the next section. It is argued that consistent displays of parental warmth, responsivity, and sensitivity are vital for a child's emotional and cognitive development. We focus here on parenting styles and the potential ways in which these styles may distinguish adult and adolescent parenting practices. Baumrind (1971, 1980) cogently observed that parents tend to employ different parenting styles, that these styles occur with a reasonable degree of stability, and that they produce differential outcomes in children and adolescents. According to Baumrind, there are three main styles of parenting: authoritative, authoritarian, and permissive. These parenting styles, reflecting differential attitudes, beliefs, parenting behaviors, are relatively independent of context. They have powerful effects on children's behavior, especially when a particular style is practiced in the extreme.

Authoritative parents are demanding but responsive. They set limits and expect adherence to rules but are flexible in their dealings with children, especially in providing warmth and clear explanations for advocated goals, values, and standards. Children raised by authoritative parents tend to be energetic and friendly and exhibit good cognitive and emotional self-control. They tend to cope well, to be intellectually curious, and to show good achievement in school. In sharp contrast, authoritarian parents are harsh disciplinarians, often imposing unbending rules and strict limits. Most importantly, they are punitive when their children stray from the established rules. An authoritarian style is likely due to an oversubscription to the belief "spare the rod, spoil the child" as well as to underdeveloped skills in responding to children's emotional needs (Sommer et al., 1993). Their children are often characterized as unhappy, unfriendly, and having a diminished ability to self-regulate. Finally, permissive parents allow children considerable freedom and, although warm, they make few demands on their children. As a result, children with permissive parents tend to show impulsivity and aggression during the early school years, and often have underdeveloped or underregulated cognitive and social skills. It is likely that these problems evolve because of the children's failure to develop self-control in both domains.

Although these styles of parenting occur to varying degrees among adult parents, and differ according to class, culture, context, and behavioral domain (Smetana, 1994), it is likely that there is less variability in styles among teenage parents and that authoritarianism or permissiveness are their predominant styles (Sommer et al., 1993). Because of the likelihood of high rates of authoritarian and/or permissive parenting among adolescent mothers and because of the negative child outcomes associated with these styles, models of adolescent parenting need to be particularly sensitive to the possibility that early punitive parenting practices may be associated with later physical and emotional abuse as well as with child neglect.

A MODEL OF ADOLESCENT PARENTING

Although the perspectives on parenting reviewed in this chapter—especially those of Belsky (1984)—are extremely valuable in understanding adult parenting, they may be insufficient for several reasons in accounting for variability among adolescent parents. These reasons include the following: teen parents rarely have meaningful jobs or are in stable relationships (cf. Belsky, 1984); they tend to be authoritarian parents (cf. Baumrind, 1980); they are often unprepared by age and experience to foster emotional development (cf. Gottman, 1997); and adolescent mothers often encounter seemingly insurmountable problems in raising special needs children (cf. Greene, 1998). In short, most existing views on adult parenting fall short of adequately explaining adolescent parenting and the developmental challenges their children inevitably face.

Our proposed model of adolescent parenting contains five constructs that we believe are needed to understand the causes and consequences of teenage parenting and successful childrearing. In addition to the maternal adjustment, child characteristics, and social support constructs contained in Belsky's (1984) model of parenting, the interplay of two unique maternal constructs—cognitive readiness and learning ability—is highlighted in our model. Moreover, different roles are assigned to the adolescent's social support system.

The model in Fig. 2.3 depicts hypothesized relationships among maternal constructs, social support, and child characteristics, as well as illustrates how these constructs might conjointly affect parenting and subsequent child development. It is our view that a more complete understanding of adolescent parenting and child development will flow from an analysis of the interactions among these factors.

Although the model sketched in Fig. 2.3 postulates numerous direct and indirect influences on the parenting behavior of adolescents during the first 6 months of life, the most important relationships can be summarized as follows: To parent effectively, an adolescent mother must be cognitively and emotionally prepared. Her cognitive readiness is related to her socioemotional adjustment, learning ability, and social supports.

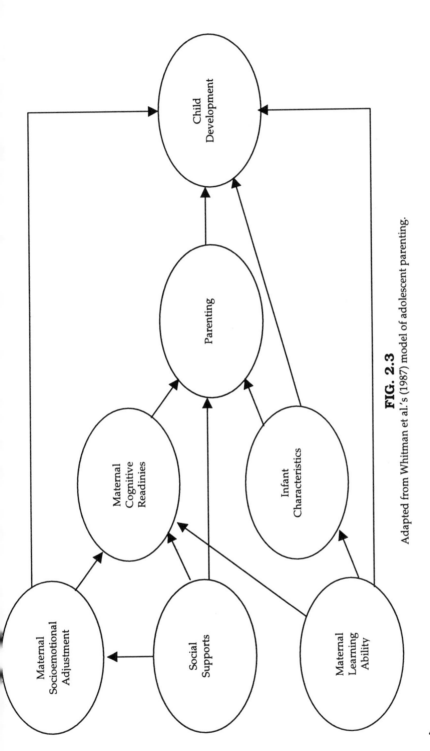

FIG. 2.3

Adapted from Whitman et al.'s (1987) model of adolescent parenting.

Social support, along with cognitive readiness, directly influence parenting. In addition, a mother's ability to deal emotionally with the stresses associated with parenting depends on whether her child displays challenging characteristics (e.g., hyperactivity) that can complicate the parenting task. By the end of the first year of life, the quality of infant cognitive (e.g., attentional flexibility) and emotional development (e.g., attachment) are likely related to the interaction of the factors represented in Fig. 2.3, with cognitive readiness to parent serving an important mediational role in explaining variability in the quality of adolescent parenting, which in turn influences child development. Rather than focusing on the overall impact of age and SES, the model suggests more specific constructs to explain individual variations in the parenting practices of adolescent mothers and subsequent consequences for their children's development.

In the next chapter, the constructs in our model of adolescent parenting are operationally defined along with other research methodologies that have been employed in the Notre Dame Parenting Project. In the following set of chapters, we describe the development of mothers and their children in the project and then search for the predictive and explanatory roles of the various constructs in our model. A major aim is to discover how the variables in the model combine to produce resilient and vulnerable mothers and children. These data should help us pinpoint constructs that can serve as targets for early interventions in order to forestall developmental delays that often characterize the life course of children with adolescent mothers. We recognize, however, that other variables—such as the availability of high quality preschools, safe neighborhoods, and constructive peers—combine with the core constructs in our model to determine developmental outcomes, especially during the elementary school years.

3

The Notre Dame Parenting Project: Design and Methodology

The Notre Dame Parenting Project has gathered data on adolescent mothers and their children from pregnancy through the first 8 years of life. The main goal has been to understand the unique and common factors that influence the children's intellectual skills, socioemotional development, and academic achievement through analysis of maternal and child factors operating during pregnancy and later as children proceed through their preschool and early school years. In addition, the project examined the mothers' life course and how the early personal characteristics of these mothers influenced their own later development.

The first phase of the project was guided by a model of child development that features social and psychological variables that predispose children of adolescent mothers to various developmental risks (Whitman et al., 1987). An initial goal was to identify personal and social factors that differentiated early childbearers from adult and nonpregnant adolescent comparison groups and to use prenatal maternal variables (intellectual, socioemotional, cognitive readiness to parent, and social support) to predict early childrearing practices and other parenting factors among the adolescent mothers as well as child development. The mothers participated in prenatal assessments and subsequently both mothers and children were assessed on multiple occasions.

The second phase, built on this database, charted the developmental trajectories of teen mothers and their children at ages 3 and 5. Maternal constructs included intelligence, social support, parenting, and socioemotional adjustment. Children's development was measured through standardized assessment of intellectual development, early academic skills, adaptive skills, and socioemotional functioning. The project also assessed the emergence of developmental delays and evaluated the antecedents and correlates of these problems. Finally, we were particularly

45

interested in finding resilient mothers and children and determining how they could be identified early in life.

The third phase of the project followed the mothers and their children through age 8, an age at which problems such as mild mental retardation, achievement-related difficulties, and conduct disorders are manifested. We present data based on the assessment of children's intellectual ability, academic achievement, and adaptive development as well as teacher-reported information gathered when the children were in Grade 2.

The project differs from other longitudinal projects with adolescent mothers in that the participants were generally healthy and had no known drug or alcohol problems during pregnancy. They participated in assessments on repeated occasions during a period of rapid change for both the children and the mothers as they moved from adolescence to adulthood. The focus was broader than most studies of adolescent parents in that multiple domains of development, with multiple measures of each were evaluated for both mothers and children.

PROJECT PARTICIPANTS

The first participants in the Notre Dame Parenting Project entered in 1984, with recruitment of new participants continuing through 1991. Two samples of primiparous adolescent mothers were included, with a total of 281 participants. The first sample, 233 adolescents in South Bend, Indiana, was recruited primarily from a school-age mothers program (62.4%), run by the school corporation. Other recruitment sites included family practice clinics associated with local hospitals and social services sites such as Women, Infants, Children (WIC). The second sample consisted of 48 adolescent mothers seeking prenatal care at a local health department or delivering at a small rural hospital in Aiken, South Carolina. At both sites, the sample was recruited from those seeking educational, medical, or social services; hence, we may have missed the most at-risk teen mothers in both locations (i.e., those who dropped out of school or failed to seek prenatal care).

Maternal Characteristics and Childbirth Information

Adolescent mothers, at the time of childbirth, ranged in age from 13.9 to 19.6 years, with an average age of 17.13 ($SD = 1.28$). Approximately 20% were 15 or younger, 23.7% were 16, 26.3% were 17, 25.2% were 18, and 4.9% had just turned 19 years of age when their children were born (see Fig. 3.1). Ethnic backgrounds included 62.5% African American, 33.2% Euro-American, and 4.3% Hispanic-American (see Fig. 3.2). The relative sizes of the ethnic subsamples limit analysis examining ethnic/racial differences, particularly with regard to evaluating our model of adolescent parenting.

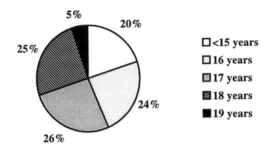

FIG. 3.1

Age composition of the sample.

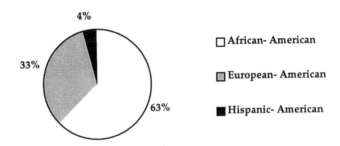

FIG. 3.2

Racial composition of the sample.

At the time of the prenatal interview, 72.5% of the adolescents were living with their biological mothers. Of these, 25% had their biological father also present in the home and 17% had a stepfather present. The majority lived in single-parent households headed by their mothers. Some participants (8.4%) resided with surrogate parents, such as extended family members or foster parents. Approximately 9% were married at the time of childbirth and many of these couples resided with their parents (or in-laws). Another 7% of the participants lived with their boyfriends, generally along with other family members.

Three years after the first child was born, 33.9% of the participants continued to reside with their mothers. In most cases other extended family members were also in the home, such as the siblings, nieces, and nephews. A slightly larger percentage (37.4%) resided on their own with their child or children. About 30% resided with their spouses or boyfriends, although a small percentage of these couples also resided with parents or extended family. There were a few mothers residing with relatives but not mother or boyfriend.

For the South Bend sample, neighborhood information was obtained through census reports. Data on rate of female head of household, male joblessness, high school drop out, poverty, and government assistance was summarized to form a Block Distress Index for each South Bend neighborhood. In South Bend, the average Block Distress Index was 58.61 ($SD = 41.74$) for 1990, ranging from 4.72 to 225.78. Higher numbers indicate more distress in a neighborhood. The neighborhoods where participants resided during their pregnancies had an average block distress score of 79.7 ($SD = 35.4$), significantly worse than the South Bend average. The participants moved frequently, often moving to similar or worse neighborhoods. For instance, 3 years later the average Block Distress Index was 94.8 ($SD = 34.8$) and 5 years later the average was 94.5 ($SD = 34.65$).

Socioeconomic status was determined at the initial interview based on the adolescent's report of education and employment status of the adults with whom they resided since the teens were not supporting themselves. Using the Hollingshead (1965) Two-Factor Index of Social Position, derived from a weighted composition of education and occupation, the average SES score was 56.25 ($SD = 12.89$), ranging from 15 to 77. Possible scores on this measure range from 11 to 77, with higher numbers indicating lower status. The adolescents generally came from lower SES homes. Utilizing the Hollingshead five-level classification system, approximately 75% of the households fell into the lower two levels of SES.

At the time of the initial interview, approximately 74% of the young women were attending high school, typically a school-age mothers' program run by the local school corporation. Years of education for the en-tire sample ranged from sixth grade to post-high school, averaging of 10.5 years (SD = 1.29). The mothers had an average estimated IQ of 87.06 (SD = 12.46), based on the Vocabulary and Block Design subtests of the Wechsler Intelligence Scale for Children–Revised (WISC–R) or Wechsler Adult Intelligence Scale–Revised (WAIS–R). In terms of employment, 27% of the sample was working, all on a part-time basis. Approximately 70% indicated involvement with at least one social service agency, typi-cally for financial and/or food assistance.

Comparison Samples

Data from two other samples were gathered in South Bend for compari-son purposes. Forty-two adult, primiparous, pregnant women were re-cruited from prenatal classes at area hospitals, and 60 nonpregnant ado-lescents were recruited from area schools. Most of the later sample were students attending summer school, some due to educational need, others due to a desire for educational advancement.

In the adult sample, participants ranged in age from 22 years to 33, with an average age of 25.17 (SD = 2.6) at childbirth. They were inter-viewed during the last trimester of pregnancy and again at 6 months postpartum. The ethnic composition of the adult sample was 76.2% Euro-American, 21.4% African-American, and 2.4% Hispanic American women. Average SES, measured by the Hollingshead Two-Factor Index, was 45.93 (SD = 14.59). The number of years of education averaged 13.29 (SD = 1.76) and the sample had an estimated IQ of approximately 91 (SD = 12.7). Thus, this sample was more educated and of slightly higher SES, had a somewhat higher IQ, and was comprised of a larger percentage of Euro-American participants.

The nonpregnant teens also participated in the initial interview and evaluations as well as a follow-up testing after approximately 6 months. This group was comprised of 50% African American, 38.3% Euro-American, 6.7% Hispanic American, and 3.3% Asian. Their average age was 15.9 (SD = 1.2) years, ranging from 13.8 to 19 years. All but one was attending high school and their education level averaged 10.24 (SD = 1.22). The average estimated IQ was approximately 93 (SD = 9.6). The average socioeconomic backgrounds of these adolescents was 43.6 (SD = 16.54). Thus the nonpregnant sample more closely resembled the preg-nant adolescents in terms of years of education but they tended to be younger, more intelligent, and from better economic backgrounds.

Child Information

All of the adolescent mothers received medical care during their pregnancy, generally on a regular basis, starting at an average of 11 weeks into the pregnancy. Their infants' weights ranged from 1,670 to 5,018 grams (3.68 to 11.06 pounds); average weight was 3204.7 grams (7.07 pounds). A relatively small percentage of infants (9%) had birth weights below 2,500 grams (5.51 pounds). Gestational age ranged from 32 to 44 weeks, with a mean of 39.56 (SD = 1.8). Apgar scores averaged 7.7 at 1 minute and 8.9 at 5 minutes. The babies of adolescent mothers did not significantly differ in weight, length, Apgar scores, or gestational age from the children of the adult sample. The gender distribution was 52.6% female and 47.4% male. It should also be noted that four babies died (one mother miscarried, one baby was stillborn, and two babies died within the first 2 months). At 6 months of age, the children were administered the Bayley Scales of Infant Development. Mental development generally fell within normal ranges with an average mental development index of 101.7 (SD = 17.65).

Father Information

At the initial prenatal interview, 73.9% of the young women indicated they were "in contact" with their partner, 7% indicated they "lived with partner" and 9% indicated they were "married." Approximately 10% reported they no longer had any contact with the father of their unborn child. More than half of the adolescents indicated that their relationship with the father had been longer than 1 year in duration. The average age of the fathers at the time of birth was just over 19 years of age (19.33) with 42.86% being 20 years or older. The fathers' average age was 2 years greater than the mothers. Further information about the fathers of the children was obtained during a phone interview when the children were 6 years of age. Eighteen percent of the children had daily or almost daily contact with their fathers. Another 34% of the fathers had maintained some contact with their child. Of the fathers, 35% had no contact at all with their children for various or unspecified reasons. Another 7% had no contact with their children due to being incarcerated and 5% of the fathers were deceased (cause of death was generally either gunshot wounds or motor vehicle accident). Given the fact that little information was gathered about the fathers, their role with regard to adolescent parenting and child development can only be examined in a limited fashion.

Comparison of the Two Adolescent Mother Samples

Teen mothers from Indiana and South Carolina were not significantly different in age at childbirth or years of education. Mothers in the South Carolina sample came from slightly but not significantly higher socioeconomic backgrounds, 53.43 (vs. 56.86 for the South Bend sample). Although there was no sample difference prenatally on the Vocabulary subtest of the WAIS–R, the Indiana sample scored higher on the Block Design task. Although Parenting Attitude and Parenting Style measures did not distinguish the groups, the South Carolina sample scored higher prenatally on Knowledge of Child Development. Finally, the South Carolina sample reported fewer behavior problems on the Youth Self-Report than did the participants from Indiana.

With respect to the children, there were no differences at birth. There were significant differences at 6 months on the Bayley Scales of Infant Development, with the children in Indiana scoring significantly higher than the South Carolina sample. Later analyses at 3 and 5 years revealed that children in the Indiana sample scored slightly, albeit significantly, higher on measures of cognitive ability at 3 years compared to the children in the South Carolina sample; however, differences on these measures were not significant at 5 years. The only difference found at 5 years was on the measure of adaptive skills; Indiana children scored higher in adaptive skills.

Attrition Information

Of the 233 South Bend mothers, 117 mother–child dyads participated in 3-year and 110 in 5-year assessments. Of the 48 South Carolina dyads, 27 took part in 3-year evaluations and 26 participated at 5 years.

The high mobility of these adolescent mothers contributed to the attrition rate. In the first 6 months following the birth of their children, 27% of the mothers moved within or outside the city. Between 6 months and the 3-year assessment, 64% of the sample moved, and over the next 2 years, 65% had moved. Many mothers moved out of town (often out of state) or could not be located as other family contacts had also moved. Sometimes letters and phone calls went unanswered but there was no firm evidence that the mother had moved.

Of those permanently lost, 26% (61) of the original sample from South Bend did not return after the initial interview; four babies died and two young mothers chose to give their children up for adoption. Another 19 participants were lost after the 6-month assessment. All but four of those seen at 1 year were contacted for a phone interview at 18 months.

Another 19 mother–child dyads were lost at the 3-year assessment and 7 more were lost at the 5-year assessment.

No significant differences in demographic information such as age, SES, and education emerged when comparing participants who remained in the project with those participants who left the project at any of the possible attrition exit points. However, a significant difference emerged relative to the ethnic composition of the sample. At 5 years, 53.8% of the African-American mothers continued to participate whereas 35.2% of the Euro-American participants remained. Eight of the 12 (67%) Hispanic-American mothers also remained in the project at 5 years. Therefore, at 5 years, the sample was 24% Euro-American, 70% African American, and 6% Hispanic American.

Comparisons of mothers who left the project with those who remained indicated no significant differences in major prenatal domains (described in the next section) with the exception of socioemotional status. The mothers who participated in the 3-year assessments indicated slightly fewer behavior problems prenatally than those who did not participate at 3 years. However, this difference was not found at 5 years.

DESIGN AND GENERAL METHODOLOGY

The adolescent mothers participated in an initial interview during their last trimester of pregnancy. Birth information was obtained from hospital records with mothers' consent. Mothers and children were evaluated when children were 6 months, 1 year, 3 years, 5 years, and 8 years of age. Each session with the mothers typically lasted between 1 and 3 hours; children's assessments usually lasted from 1 to 2 hours. The prenatal interview usually required two sessions.

Mothers were provided transportation to the interview site and a monetary reimbursement for their time. At 8 years, children also received a gift. Phone interviews were completed at 18 months and again at approximately 6.5 years to gain further information as well as to maintain contact with participants. Birthday cards as well as seasonal cards were also sent as a means of maintaining contact.

During the assessments, a wide range of information was obtained for each of the constructs included in our model of adolescent parenting: intelligence, cognitive readiness to parent, social support, socioemotional adjustment, and parenting. Children were assessed across intelligence, socioemotional, adaptive behavior, and achievement domains. Life history information was also gathered to determine current information regarding education, employment, relationship status, financial situation, additional children/pregnancies, and child-care arrangements. Whereas prenatally SES was based on the adolescents parents' education and employment, at all the other time points, the adolescent mothers' educational level and occupation were used to compute the two-factor score.

Typically, multiple measures were utilized to assess each construct and most measures were repeated across assessment times in order to evaluate developmental trajectories. At times, measures were changed due to their developmental sensitivities; for example, age-appropriate child intelligence assessments were administered (Bayley at 6 months and Stanford–Binet Intelligence Scale at 3 and 5 years). Table 3.1 lists the assessments utilized to measure the maternal constructs at each time point and Table 3.2 provides a listing of assessments used to index child constructs. In the next section each of these measures is described in detail.

TABLE 3.1
Maternal Assessments: Prenatal to 5 Years

Constructs	Prenatal	6 Months	1 Year	3 & 5 Years
Intelligence	WISC/ WAIS-R (short form)			WAIS-R
Cognitive Readiness	Knowledge Style Attitude	Knowledge Style Attitude		
Social Support	Support Interview	Support Interview	Support Interview	Support Interview
				Personal Network
Socioemotional	YSR Life stress		SEI IPPA	SEI BDI STAI Life stress
Parenting		MIS PSI	MIS CAPI MCRS	MIS CAPI

Note. WISC-R = Wechsler Intelligence Scale for Children–Revised; WAIS-R = Wechsler Adult Intelligence Scale–Revised; YSR = Youth Self Report; SEI = Self-Esteem Inventory; IPPA = Inventory of Parent and Peer Attachment; BDI = Beck Depression Inventory; STAI = State-Trait Anxiety Inventory; MIS = Maternal Interaction Scale; PSI = Parenting Stress Index; CAPI = Child Abuse Potential Inventory; MCRS = Mother-Child Relationship Scale

CONSTRUCTS AND MEASURES

In the following sections, the assessments used to measure each construct are described. For instruments that are widely known, relatively little information on psychometric properties is given; for assessments developed for this project or less commonly known, a fuller description is provided. Also, information regarding how each measure is indexed for statistical analyses is also given (e.g., standard scores vs. raw scores, subscale scores vs. total scores, etc.).

Maternal Measures

Intelligence. Intelligence was measured by a short form of the Wechsler scales, yielding an estimated total IQ. At the initial interview either the WISC–R or the WAIS–R Vocabulary and Block Design tests were administered depending on the age of the adolescent (Wechsler, 1974, 1981). At all subsequent administrations (3 and 5 years), the WAIS–R was employed. These subscales were chosen in part because the composite of the Block Design and Vocabulary tests correlate .94 with the Full Scale Score (Sattler, 1990). For data analysis purposes, either the estimated IQ or the separate Vocabulary and Block Design scaled scores (M = 10, SD = 3) were used.

Cognitive Readiness for Parenting. Cognitive Readiness for Parenting was measured through three questionnaires: Knowledge of Child Development, Parenting Style Questionnaire, and Parenting Attitudes Questionnaire.

Knowledge of Child Development assessed the teen's awareness of child developmental stages and of developmental milestones. The 39-item measure was a compilation of 20 items, scored agree–disagree, measuring expectations regarding child development and 19 multiple choice questions about developmental milestones. Examples of expectation items include "a 2-year-old child can be expected to toilet train his or herself with little help from parents" and "a parent can expect a young child (age 3 or 4) to know enough to behave in a supermarket so that the parent won't look foolish in front of others". An example of a multiple-choice question is "Most babies begin sitting up with some support at 3 months, 6 months, 9 months, or 12 months." Two texts in child development and introductory psychology served as informational sources for developing questions about child development (Bourne & Ekstrand, 1973; Yussen & Santrock, 1984). In addition, items were drawn from the inappropriate expectation scale of the Adult–Adolescent Parenting Inventory (AAPI; Bavolek, 1984). The internal consistency coefficient of the measure of Knowledge of Child Development was .70.

The Parenting Style Questionnaire evaluated parenting philosophy and style. It examined the mother's knowledge about skills and behaviors useful in child management and parenting as opposed to attitudes and knowledge about child development. Specifically, two subscales of this questionnaire, Empathetic Awareness and Physical Punishment, assessed empathy for the child's needs and child management approach. Both scales were derived from the AAPI. An additional 10 items were developed to measure authoritarianism and abuse/neglect. Each of the items was rated on Likert-type scale, ranging from 1 (*strongly agree*) to 5 (*strongly disagree*). Statements included "Children will quit crying faster if ignored," "Children will learn good behavior through physical punishment," "I believe too much attention and tenderness can harm or weaken a child," and "There is nothing wrong with punishing a 9-month-old child for crying too much." Internal consistency coefficients for empathetic awareness and physical punishment subscales have been shown to be .75 and .81, whereas test–retest reliability was assessed at .89 and .69 (Bavolek, 1984). For our sample, the Parenting Style Questionnaire had an internal consistency coefficient of .89.

The Parenting Attitude Questionnaire was developed to measure an individual's general attitudes and values about children. The questionnaire measures beliefs about role reversal (mother's expectations about the child's role in fulfilling her emotional needs) drawn from the AAPI and child-centeredness (the mother's orientation toward becoming a mother and putting the child's needs above her own). Statements were again rated on a 5-point scale. Items included "Young children should try to make their mom feel better when she is feeling sad or depressed" and "Being a parent is an important job but it sometimes gets in the way of things you want to do." The total scale has an internal consistency coefficient of .74.

When Knowledge of Child Development, Parenting Style, and Parenting Attitude are used in subsequent data analyses, a total score for each measure is used. Whenever an overall measure of cognitive readiness is utilized the totals for each measure are standardized and then summed in order to weigh each measure equally.

Social Support. Social support information was gathered throughout the study. Information about the mothers' social network, a list of important people in their lives including family; friends; boyfriends, partner, or spouse; social agency personnel and people at school or work was obtained. The mothers were asked to rate, on a 5-point scale, closeness, emotional support, and instrumental support expected or received from parents, relatives, friends, partner or boyfriend, and social agency personnel. Prenatally, they were asked about their "expected" levels of support; postnatally, they were asked if they were receiving too much, too little, or just the right amount of assistance. In data analyses, either a composite of overall support (a sum of all the ratings) is used or when a particular type or source of support appears important, a composite score for that source is utilized.

Socioemotional. Socioemotional functioning of the mothers was evaluated in a variety of ways. Initially, a broad measure, the Youth Self-Report (YSR; Achenbach, 1991c), was utilized to assess a range of behaviors and social competence; at 1-year, self-esteem and relationships with the teen's mother were examined; and, at 3 and 5 years, measures of depression, self-esteem, and anxiety were utilized. Life stress was also assessed prenatally as well as at 3 and 5 years.

The YSR was administered prenatally (Achenbach, 1991c). Alhough data collection began prior to 1991, assessments were scored using the 1991 norms. The YSR yielded a measure of social competence (involvement in extracurricular activities, peer relationships, and school success) as well as ratings of behavioral problems including withdrawal, somatic complaints, anxiety/depression, social problems, attention problems, delinquency, and aggressive behavior. Scores reflecting internalizing problems (withdrawal, somatic complaints, and anxiety/depression), externalizing problems (delinquent and aggressive behavior) and total problems were also obtained. Standardized T scores were utilized in the analyses. Higher scores indicate more behavioral difficulties, with a T $\geq$ 60 indicating a score within the clinical range. Achenbach (1991c) reported a Cronbach's alpha internal consistency index of .48 for social competence and .95 for total problems for girls. The 7-day test–retest reliability was .82 for social competence and .83 for total problems, for 15- to 18-year-old adolescent girls.

At 1, 3, and 5 years, the adult form of the Self-Esteem Inventory (SEI) was administered (Coopersmith, 1981). The short, 25-item SEI has been frequently used to measure self-esteem. The mothers indicated "like me" or "unlike me" following each statement. Statements included "I often wish I were someone else" and "I give in very easily." A sum of items indicating high self-esteem was utilized in the analyses. Multiplying the score by four gives the scores comparable to the longer version of the SEI. High scores correspond to high self-esteem. The SEI has a Cronbach alpha coefficient of .75 (Coopersmith, 1981).

The Beck Depression Inventory (BDI) is a 21-item self-report measure for evaluating the degree of depression (Beck, 1967, 1987). The BDI assesses motivational, cognitive, affective, and behavioral components of depression. The respondent selected one of four statements that best fit how they felt during the past week. For example, "I don't feel disappointed in myself," "I am disappointed in myself," "I am disgusted with myself," and "I hate myself." Total scores can be converted to four clinical ratings ranging from no or minimal signs of depression to extremely severely depressed. Total raw scores (range 0–84 possible) were utilized in data analyses. The scale has a split-half reliability of .86.

State-Trait Anxiety Inventory (STAI; Spielberger, 1983) is a self-report measure consisting of 40 brief items, 20 to assess how the individual feels right now (state anxiety) and 20 items to assess how the individual generally feels (trait anxiety). Each item is rated on a 4-point scale. For data analysis, state and trait were examined separately or summed for a total anxiety score. Alpha reliability coefficients for normative samples ranged from .83 to .92 for state scores and .86 to .92 for trait scores.

To measure life stress, a subtest of the Parenting Stress Index (PSI; Abidin, 1983) was administered at the prenatal interview and readministered at 3 years and 5 years. This instrument consists of a list of 18 possible events in an individual's life that cause stress, such as death of a relative, moving, and changing jobs. The events are weighted; some, such as marriage, are considered more stressful than others, such as changing schools. Scores of 17 and above (representing the 90th percentile) are considered high and suggest stressful situational circumstances that are often beyond an individual's control (Abidin, 1983).

A final measure of socioemotional status evaluated the mother's relationship with her mother. Parent attachment scores have previously been found to relate to a number of personality variables such as affect status, self-esteem, and life satisfaction. At 1-year, mothers were asked to complete a measure of their attachment to their mothers, the mother section of the Inventory of Parent and Peer Attachment (IPPA; Armsden & Greenberg, 1987). The 25 items were each rated on a scale ranging from 1 (*never true*) to 5 (*almost* or *always true*). Three scores were derived from this measure: trust in mother, communication, and alienation from mother. Internal reliability for mother attachment (a composite of the three scales) was found to be .87.

Parenting. Measures of parenting behavior, affect, and cognition were administered. Parenting affect was measured by assessing stress encountered in the parenting role as well as the potential for child abuse and neglect. Parenting cognition was evaluated through the readministration of the cognitive readiness measures 6 months after the birth of the child and a measure of mother–child relationship completed at 1 year.

Parenting behavior was measured through observational ratings of mother–child interactions.

Measures of *parenting affect* included a measure of stress at 6 months only, and abuse potential measured at 1, 3, and 5 years. Stress was measured by the PSI (Abidin, 1983). The PSI is a 101-item inventory that measures the stress experienced by a mother as a function of her newly acquired parenting role. Subscores are available for stress associated with specific child characteristics separate from stress associated solely with the parenting role. Reliability coefficients for the child domain and the parent domain have been reported as .89 and .93. Cronbach's alpha for the total score has been demonstrated at .98 with test–retest coefficient of .96 (Abidin, 1983).

Abuse potential was measured using an abbreviated form of the Child Abuse Potential Inventory (CAPI; Milner, 1986). The shortened CAPI contained 25 items selected primarily from the unhappiness and rigidity scales. These two scales have been found to distinguish abusive from nonabusive individuals (Milner, 1986). The mothers indicated their agreement or disagreement with statements such as "Everything in a home should always be in its place" and "I have several close friends in my neighborhood." Total raw scores are utilized in subsequent analyses.

Parenting cognition was assessed through the readministration of the three cognitive readiness measures 6 months after the birth of the child and the administration, at 1 year, of the Mother–Child Relationship Scale (MCRS; Roth, 1980). This scale provides an estimate of the mother's relationship to her child, specifically her acceptance, overprotection, overindulgence, and rejection of the child. Split-half reliabilities of .57 for acceptance, .53 for overprotective, .41 for overindulgent, and .47 for rejection have been reported (Roth, 1980). The developer of the scale felt that because of the low number of items these coefficients represent a lower bound estimate.

Parenting behavior was assessed in toy-play situations. At 6 months, each mother was asked to play with her child for 15 minutes, 5 minutes with each of three simple toys. Each mother was also given a card listing activities that she could have her child do with the toy, such as reach for, hold, shake, twirl moveable parts, or squeeze. At 1 year, the interactions were less formal in that mother and child sat on the floor with several toys and were asked to play for 5 minutes. At 3 and 5 years, the mother–child dyads sat at a table and were given three toys to play with: a jigsaw puzzle, a nesting toy, and a shape puzzle/sorter. The tasks were intended to challenge the child in order to examine the extent and type of assistance offered by mother.

These interactions were videotaped and rated using the Maternal Interaction Scale (MIS), a behavioral measure of parenting developed for this project to assess maternal sensitivity and child responsiveness. Maternal behaviors rated included interaction, flexibility, control, attention, verbalness, rate of stimulation, direction, appropriate motivation, positiveness, affectional match, and general quality of mothering. The three child behaviors evaluated were activity level, mood, and responsiveness. All behaviors were rated on a 6-point scale with the best score being 6. The ratings for the maternal items were summed to derive a total score of parenting. Internal consistency of the 11 items ranged from .93 to .94 for the four assessment periods. Interrater reliability was .81 at 6 months, .66 at 1 year, .73 at 3 years, and .90 at 5 years.

Construct validity for the MIS was assessed at 6-months, by examining correlations between the MIS and self-report measures of parenting attitudes, style, and knowledge and parenting stress (PSI). Specifically, the MIS total score correlated significantly ($r = .37$), with the cognitive readiness measures of parenting (i.e., attitudes, style, and knowledge). The correlation with parenting stress was lower, $r = -.21$, but still significant ($p < .01$). At 1-year, validity was assessed through correlations of MIS with the four subscales of the Roth Mother–Child Relationship Questionnaire and with the short-form of the CAPI. The MIS correlated with the Acceptance and Over Protection subscales of the Roth and the CAPI ($r = .33$, $p < .001$; $r = -.19$, $p < .05$; and $r = -.33$, $p < .001$, respectively). Only the short form of the CAPI was available at 3 and 5 years. Maternal interactive behavior at 3 years was significantly related to the CAPI at 3 years ($r = -.27$, $p < .001$) whereas the correlation of MIS and CAPI at 5 years was not significant.

Child Measures

Child information was gathered from birth, with information initially obtained from hospital records, through 8 years of age. Children began active involvement in the project at 6 months of age. Constructs measured included intellectual development, socioemotional well-being, adaptive behavior, and achievement (see Table 3.2).

Intelligence. Intelligence was assessed through a series of age-appropriate instruments. All of the measures have a mean of 100 and standard deviation of 15 or 16. At 6 months and 1 year, the Bayley Scales of Infant Development (Bayley, 1969) were administered. Both the Mental Development Index, including items measuring sustained attention, purposeful manipulation of objects, imitation, comprehension, expressive language, and problem solving, and Psychomotor Development Index, measuring gross and fine motor abilities, were utilized. The Stanford–Binet Intelligence Scale, Form L–M (SBIS) was administered at 3 and 5

TABLE 3.2

Child Assessments: 6 Months to 8 Years

Constructs	6 Months	1 Year	3 & 5 Years	8 Years
Intelligence	Bayley	Bayley	SBIS DVMI PPVT-R	WISC-III (short form) PPVT-R
Socioemotional	CITQ	Attachment	BSQ CBCL Attachment	CBCL TRF
Adaptive			VABS	VABS
Achievement			PIAT	PIAT-R

Note. SBIS = Stanford-Binet Intelligence Scale (Form L-M); WISC-III = Wechsler Intelligence Scale for Children–Third Edition; DVMI = Developmental test of Visual-Motor Integration; CITQ = Carey Infant Temperament Questionnaire; BSQ = Behavioral Style Questionnaire; CBCL = Child Behavior Checklist; TRF = Teacher Report Form; VABS = Vineland Adaptive Behavior Scale; PIAT = Peabody Individual Achievement Test; PPVT-R = Peabody Picture Vocabulary Test–Revised

years of age (Terman & Merrill, 1972). Form L–M was utilized as it was felt to be more discriminating at the early ages than the newer fourth edition. A shortened form of the Wechsler Intelligence Scale for Children–Third Edition (WISC–III) was employed when the children were assessed at 8 years of age (Wechsler, 1991). Four subtests were administered including Picture Completion, Information, Block Design, and Vocabulary. According to Sattler (1992), this shortened form has a high reliability of .94.

Two other measures, highly correlated with intelligence tests, were also employed, measuring language and visual motor development. Children's language development, assessed at 3, 5, and 8 years, was measured by the Peabody Picture Vocabulary Test–Revised (PPVT–R; Dunn & Dunn, 1981), a one-word receptive vocabulary test. The test involves the presentation of four pictures with a request for the child to point to the one named. The test is standardized with a mean of 100 and standard deviation of 15. Split-half reliability coefficients range from .67 to .88 (median = .80). Correlations between the PPVT–R and intelligence tests range between .38 and .72. The lowest correlations are with nonverbal tests (Dunn & Dunn, 1981).

At 5 years, visual-motor integration was evaluated through the Developmental Test of Visual-Motor Integration (DVMI; Beery, 1989). This test involves the presentation of simple line drawings to be copied. The DVMI is felt to be relatively culture-free and has been found to correlate with intelligence tests and measures of academic achievement, particularly reading, which require the integration of sensory inputs and motor action. Internal consistency reliability for 5-year-olds is .87.

Socioemotional. Socioemotional measures included assessment of child temperament beginning at 6 months; with a measure of behavioral problems added at 3 years and 5 years. In addition, the security of attachment was assessed at 1 and 5 years. Finally at 8 years, children's adjustment was assessed through teacher-report measures.

Temperament was initially assessed through maternal ratings on the Carey Infant Temperament Questionnaire (CITQ; Carey & McDevitt, 1978) at 6 months, and later with the Behavioral Style Questionnaire (BSQ; McDevitt & Carey, 1978) at 3 and 5 years. The nine categories that comprise the temperament ratings on both instruments include activity, rhythmicity of biological functions, initial approach–withdrawal, adaptability, intensity, mood, persistence, distractibility, and sensory threshold. A composite of the means of the five subscales used to derive the clinical ratings (rhythmicity, approach, adaptability, intensity and mood) was utilized to provide a continuous variable of easy–difficult temperament. Possible scores range from 5 to 30, with higher scores indicating more difficult temperament. Internal consistency reliability for the CITQ is .57, and for the BSQ, .70.

Security of attachment was evaluated through the Strange Situation paradigm (Ainsworth & Wittig, 1969) when children were 12 months old. Attachment was scored as secure (B), insecure-avoidant (A), insecure-resistant (C) (Ainsworth, Blehar, Waters, & Walls, 1978), or insecure-disorganized/disoriented (D) (Main & Solomon, 1986, 1990). Scoring was completed by Virginia Colin who was trained by Mary Ainsworth. Security of attachment at was also examined 5 years of age using the Strange Situation. Colin, trained by Bob Marvin, scored attachment using the Preschool Attachment Assessment System (Cassidy & Marvin, 1992). Each dyad was classified as secure (B), avoidant (A), resistant (C), insecure-other (I-O), or disorganized (D). The I-O category refers to an attachment pattern that does not fit avoidant or resistant categories but is not a pattern generally observed in disorganized attachment. However, for analytic purposes the I-Os are grouped with the disorganized category. Colin did establish interrater reliability of .87 with other trained raters.

The Child Behavior Checklist (CBCL) was employed to assess socio-emotional adjustment when the children were 3 and 5 years of age (Achenbach, 1991a). The mothers rated each of approximately 100 items on the checklist in terms of *never, sometimes,* or *always occurring.* The derived problem subscales include withdrawn, somatic complaints, anxious/depressed, social problems, thought problems, delinquent behavior, aggressive behavior, and other problems. Subscales can be grouped to obtain scores in internalizing behavior (withdrawn, somatic complaints, and anxious/depressed), externalizing behaviors (delinquent behavior and aggressive behavior), and total problems. *T* scores, available by age and gender, were utilized for data analysis. *T* scores of 60 or greater indicate behavior problems in the clinical range. Internal consistency, Cronbach's alpha, is .89 for internalizing, .93 for eternalizing, and .96 for total problems.

At 8 years of age, socioemotional information was obtained from the teachers who completed a scale comparable to the CBCL, the Teacher Report Form (TRF; Achenbach, 1991b). The TRF is very similar to the CBCL, using the same scales and *T* scores, and with adequate reliability as well.

Adaptive Behavior. Adaptive skills were assessed, at 3, 5, and 8 years, through the Vineland Adaptive Behavior Scale (VABS; Sparrow, Balla, & Cicchetti, 1984). The four domains evaluated are Communication (receptive, expressive, and written), Daily Living (personal, domestic, and community), Socialization (interpersonal relationships, play and leisure time, and coping skills), and Motor (gross and fine). Maladaptive behaviors (such as impulsiveness, temper tantrums, defiance, and lies/steals) were also measured beginning at age 5. This instrument was completed through an interview with the mother. Scores are standardized to a mean of 100 and a standard deviation of 15. Split-half reliabilities are reported to be .89 for Communication, .90 for Daily Living Skills, .86 for Socialization, .83 for Motor, and .86 for Maladaptive Behavior.

Achievement. To measure reading and math achievement the Peabody Individual Achievement Test (PIAT; Dunn & Markwardt, 1970) and PIAT–Revised (Markwardt, 1989) were administered at ages 5 and 8, respectively. The PIAT and PIAT–R involve a format similar to the PPVT–R in that the children responded to questions by pointing or indicating which of four options is correct, except when asked to read words. The PIAT reading recognition and mathematics tests were administered to the 5-year-olds. The PIAT–R reading recognition and comprehension were administered along with the mathematics test at age 8. Scores are standardized with a mean of 100 and standard deviation of 15.

Test–retest reliability coefficients of .52 for the mathematics subtest and .81 for the reading test have been reported for kindergarten children. Split-half reliabilities for PIAT–R range from .93 to .98 (median = .96) in reading recognition, .90 to .94 (median = .92) in reading comprehension, and .90 to .96 (median = .94) in mathematics.

DATA MANAGEMENT AND ANALYTIC PLAN

As indicated, information was gathered from participants across a period extending from the last trimester of pregnancy until children reached 8 years of age. Due to attrition, the number of participants varied across each time period. In addition, some participants chose not to, or failed to, respond to individual items or measures. The general procedure for dealing with missing data was either to exclude the nonparticipant from the analysis or to utilize mean substitution. For example, when one or two items were omitted on a questionnaire, the mean of other items on that scale was substituted for the omitted response so that a total score could be derived.

The next four chapters present analyses of mother and child data sets. In chapters 4 and 6, a variety of descriptive strategies were employed to examine mother and child development. Means and standard deviations for measures of the major outcomes are presented. Wherever possible, normative information is provided to illustrate how mothers and children were performing relative to normed or average expectations. For certain prenatal and 6-month measures, contrasts between teen and adult mothers and nonpregnant teens were made. Moreover, mean comparisons were conducted for measures administered at multiple time points. Correlations between measures of constructs were typically conducted at each time point, and across time, for measures that were repeated in order to assess the stability of functioning.

Analyses examining the early predictors of maternal behavior and adjustment are presented in chapter 5. Specifically, we explored the maternal predictors of parenting skills, potential for child abuse, and socioemotional adaptation. In chapter 7, the relationship of maternal measures and child development are examined, in particular, the early maternal predictors of later child intelligence, adaptive behavior, preacademic skills, and socioemotional development. For both chapters, simple correlational and multiple regression procedures were utilized.

In chapter 8, we identify distinctive pathways leading to resiliency for mothers and their children through discriminatory analyses. Relatedly, chapter 9 uses an interview format to explore in a qualitative fashion the life stories of four mothers and their children. The qualitative descriptions provided by the mothers are compared with quantitative data for each dyad.

In the final chapter, we integrate this information and discuss its implications for designing interventions. After discussing the extent to which adolescent mothers and their children experience adverse developmental outcomes, we identify how early factors that place them at risk can be utilized in structuring programs to prevent later developmental problems. Finally, we examine the results of the Notre Dame Parenting Project in the context of other research projects and make more general social policy recommendations.

4

Development of
Adolescent Mothers

with Mary O'Callaghan

As the incidence of teenage pregnancy rose in the 1960s and 1970s, research began to focus on the effects that teen mothers have on the development of their infants. Based on this research, children with adolescent mothers were often perceived as at risk because of their mothers' limited ability to cope cognitively and emotionally with the simultaneous challenges of adolescence and parenting (Whitman et al., 1987). In contrast, the developmental consequences that adolescent mothers experience as a result of their off-time transition to parenthood has been less well investigated, with several exceptions, including the landmark longitudinally based study of Furstenberg et al. (1987), East and Felice's (1996) San Diego project, and several reanalyses of the National Longitudinal Study of Youth (NLSY; e.g., Moore, Sugland, Blumentahl, Glei, & Snyder, 1995).

In contrast to the prevailing stereotype suggesting the inevitability of developmental problems in adolescent mothers, Furstenberg et al. (1987) found that teenage mothers actually differed considerably in their life course development.

> One of the most impressive findings was the diversity of responses to a common event. Despite the fact that virtually all the participants in the study were low-income black females in their midteens who were premaritally pregnant for the first time, the outcome at the five-year-follow-up was enormously varied. Whether it was the decision to wed, marital stability, subsequent childbearing, work and welfare experiences, or methods of childrearing, the young mothers were extremely dissimilar. (pp. 218–219)

Similar diversity existed among these mothers 17 years after the birth of their first child; however, when compared to women of SES and race who delayed childbearing, the teenage mothers in the Baltimore Study had fewer years of education, greater marital instability, and less career and economic success (Furstenberg et al., 1987). Contrary to popular stereotypes, the early childbearers did not have significantly more children nor did the majority rely on public assistance. The strongest predictor of welfare status at the follow-up was the education level of the parents of adolescent mothers, independent of their own educational status. Furstenberg et al. (1987) surmised that parents with lower education had fewer economic or social resources to assist their daughters. The authors also suggested that teens who were able to limit their future pregnancies did so because of participation in school and community intervention programs, with community supports often compensating for weak family supports. Furstenberg et al. (1987) also speculated that young mothers who delayed further childbearing were more motivated to continue their education and to support themselves. Motivational and cognitive resources, however, were not directly assessed in the Baltimore study.

Thus, although "common wisdom" argues that the birth of a child represents a major obstacle in the satisfactory transition of an adolescent into adulthood, this wisdom has been questioned. Furstenberg (1998) asserted that the direct effects of early childbearing on health, social, and economic outcomes are only modest to moderate. Hotz et al. (1997) argued that the adverse economic consequences accompanying teen parenting are due more to preexisting circumstances—which also likely contributed to the off-timed pregnancy—than to the birth of the child per se. From this perspective, early poverty, educational failure, and a history of abuse are the likely determinants of problematic adult development, rather than teen pregnancy and parenting per se.

An alternative perspective—one that was developed in chapter 2—stresses the importance of accelerated role transition caused by early pregnancy and its negative impact on adult development. The birth of a first child poses numerous challenges for even well-prepared parents. For many new parents, the joys of an infant are tempered by the stress resulting from the demands that the child places on the their time and energy. It is not surprising that marital satisfaction typically declines. Parents feel overwhelmed to the extent they are unprepared for the new challenges presented by their infant. For the teen mother, pregnancy, parenting, and intense interpersonal relationships must all be handled during a brief, but critical, period of development—adolescence—a period that has its own unique crises. Adolescent mothers are faced with many new developmental challenges, including identity development, the establishment of intimate relationships, and the consolidation of abstract thinking. Coping with these challenges during the transition to parenthood may be particularly stressful because the coping skills of adolescent parents are generally immature and still in the process of development (Passino et al., 1993).

In discussing the dynamics of accelerated role transitions, such as adolescent parenting, and their relation to personal adjustment, Elder and Rockwell (1976) suggested that increased stress is likely when such transitions are asynchronous with the typical sequence of life events. According to Elder and Rockwell, factors instrumental in determining the level of stress experienced by any individual depend on the importance of the role transition involved and the discrepancy between the actual timing of the role transition and socially acceptable norms. Those roles that are considered more socially important, and transitions that are more temporally discrepant from the norm, are most stressful. Russell (1980) pointed out that because culture places a high value on parenthood, premature transitions to parenting should be very stressful for young mothers. Because the normative age for becoming a parent has been increasing, early parenting runs against the cultural grain, representing a more atypical and perhaps more difficult transition than in previous decades. To the extent adolescents are unprepared cognitively and emotionally for the responsibilities and demands of an early transition to motherhood, this transition likely becomes even more difficult.

From this perspective, the demands and potential stress associated with adolescence and with parenting are hypothesized to produce adverse long-term effects on the lives of adolescent mothers. Their education may be curtailed, career opportunities restricted, and the likelihood of becoming dependent on public assistance increased. They may have additional children in quick succession. Moreover, because teen mothers often have out of wedlock births, as well as marriages ending in divorce, their social support resources may be insufficient during a period when their need for help and assistance is increasing. At a more personal level, they may be less sensitive and responsive parents. Particularly worrisome are the data that associate adolescent parenting with increased risk for child abuse and neglect (Wolfe, 1985). Although little is known about the socioemotional costs of early parenthood for the mother herself, young mothers appear to struggle more than adult mothers with low self-esteem, anxiety, and depression (Barth, 1983; de Anda, Darroch, Davidson, Gilly, & Morejon, 1990), setting the stage for potential child abuse, neglect or both.

Cognitive development may also be placed in jeopardy as a result of teen parenting. Typically, adolescence is a period of growth in abstract reasoning, perspective taking, hypothesis testing, and logical reasoning.

Cross-cultural research has supported the importance of formal schooling in the development of these skills. To the extent that parenting inter-
feres with school completion or induces high levels of stress, the acquisition of these cognitive skills may be compromised. Some adolescent
mothers may experience a decline in their cognitive skills following the
birth of a child as a function of dropping out of school prematurely and
living in stressful environments. As a consequence of these cognitive
limitations, young mothers may be less equipped to cope with the challenges of early parenting and less likely to finish school with a set of
work-related competencies.

Although these socioemotional and cognitive problems appear
common, adolescent mothers vary considerably in the extent to which
they are at risk for and experience adverse developmental outcomes. The
results of the Furstenberg et al. (1987) study suggests that many young
mothers fare reasonably well. In this chapter, we further explore the
story of adolescent maternal development. In the Notre Dame Parenting
Project, the teen mothers' cognitive, emotional, and social resources were
evaluated as they proceeded into and through their parenting career. In
contrast to previous research, the focus has been on understanding the
extent of their personal resources and how these resources, or lack
thereof, influence their later cognitive and socioemotional adjustment. In
the present chapter, the developmental status and adaptation of mothers
in the Notre Dame Parenting Project are described at five time points:
prenatally (during the last trimester of pregnancy) and subsequently
when their first children were 6 months, 1 year, 3 years, and 5 years of
age. At each of these time points, two or more of the following maternal
domains were evaluated: socioemotional adjustment, intellectual functioning, cognitive readiness (parental knowledge, style, and attitudes),
social supports, parenting affect, and behavior, and other demographic
information (e.g., marital, educational, and vocational status). Finally,
relationships between different domains of maternal functioning and the
stability of maternal development are described. The extent to which
adolescent mother's cognitive and socioemotional resources influence
their later development is discussed in chapter 5. We begin by examining
the prenatal characteristics of adolescent mothers in the sample.

ADOLESCENT MOTHERS: THEIR PRENATAL STATUS

Information was gathered regarding the psychological and social resources of adolescent mothers during the last trimester of their pregnancy. More specifically, their level of intellectual functioning, cognitive
readiness for parenting, socioemotional adjustment, and social supports

were evaluated (see chap. 3 for a full description of the measures). The developmental status of the adolescent mothers is interpreted through comparison, wherever possible, to standardized norms. When such norms are not available, comparisons are made to samples of nonpregnant adolescents and adult mothers. The prenatal data are interesting from several perspectives. They provide a more precise description of the maternal sample as well as an evaluation of their early resources and preparation for parenting before they began their challenging journey into parenthood. The data also provide a vehicle for gaining insights into the early markers of the teen mothers' later achievements and developmental problems.

Intelligence

Intelligence was measured prenatally by the Vocabulary and Block Design subscales of the WAIS–R or WISC–R, depending on the age of the mother. Both the Vocabulary and Block Design scales are normed with a mean of 10 and a standard deviation of 3; scores between 7 and 13 are considered average. The pregnant teens had a mean prenatal Block Design scaled score of 8.58 (SD = 3.02), which fell in the low end of the average range. Their mean prenatal Vocabulary scaled score, 6.82 (SD = 2.07), fell below the average range. Block Design scores were significantly higher than Vocabulary scores, $t(270)$ = -10.56, p < .01, suggesting that the teens in the sample possessed better perceptual than verbal skills.

Estimated full-scale standard scores were calculated from subscale scores. Both the WAIS–R and WISC–R are normed with means of 100 and standard deviations of 15. The average estimated full-scale IQ for the pregnant teen sample was 87.06 (SD = 12.46). The distribution of prenatal full-scale intelligence scores, according to traditional IQ classification, is shown in Table 4.1. As seen, the majority of adolescents (68.7%) tested in the normal and low average ranges at this time point. However, slightly more than 25% of the sample was estimated to be functioning in the borderline or mentally retarded range of intellectual functioning. Fewer adolescents fell into the high average category (5.2% of the sample), and only one teen was classified as having superior intelligence. Compared to the theoretical normal curve, the IQ scores of our adolescent group were markedly skewed toward the low end of the continuum.

Cognitive Readiness for Parenting

The average scores on the Parenting Attitudes Questionnaire (which is comprised of subscales evaluating role reversal and child-centeredness),

TABLE 4.1
Distribution of Prenatal Maternal IQ Scores

IQ Classification	IQ Range	Frequency	Actual Percent	Expected Percent[a]
Very superior	130–169	0	0	2.6
Superior	120–129	1	.2	6.9
High average	110–119	14	5.2	16.6
Normal	90–109	82	30.3	49.1
Low average	80–89	104	38.4	16.1
Borderline	70–79	46	17.0	6.4
Mentally retarded	30–69	24	8.9	2.3

[a]According to a theoretical normal curve.

the Parenting Style Questionnaire (which includes subscales measuring responsiveness/empathy, punishment, abuse/neglect, and authoritarianism), and the Knowledge of Child Development Scale (which consists of subscales assessing child development and expectations) are presented in Table 4.2. Although national norms are not available for interpreting scores on these cognitive readiness measures, the scores of the pregnant teens were compared to those of the pregnant adult and nonpregnant teen samples. In general, these analyses suggested that the pregnant adolescent mothers were more cognitively prepared for parenting than their nonpregnant teen counterparts but less prepared than the pregnant adult sample.

More specifically, independent sample t tests were conducted to compare adolescent and adult mothers on the three Cognitive Readiness scales, as well as their respective individual subscales, and overall Cognitive Readiness. As can be seen in Table 4.2, there were differences in Parenting Attitudes, Parenting Style, Parenting Knowledge, and total Cognitive Readiness (a composite z score formed by summing the individual z scores from the three scales). Adult mothers scored consistently higher than adolescent mothers on these measures, indicating a greater prenatal cognitive readiness to parent in this group.

It is interesting to note, however, that these overall differences between adult and teen mothers were not reflected in all of the individual subscales. In the analyses of subscale differences in Parenting Attitudes, adults were less likely than teen mothers to believe that their children

TABLE 4.2
Comparison of Adult and Adolescent Mother's
Prenatal Cognitive Readiness to Parent

Measure	Adolescent Mean	(SD)	Adult Mean	(SD)	t
Parenting Attitudes	59.63	(7.05)	64.78	(6.86)	
	4.32**				
		(n = 270)		(n = 40)	
Role reversal	22.99	(5.40)	27.95	(5.57)	5.40**
Child-centeredness	36.64	(4.40)	36.83	(4.66)	.25
Parenting Style	97.04	(13.36)	102.16	(11.76)	2.30**
		(n = 271)		(n = 40)	
Respons./empathy	28.81	(5.23)	31.25	(4.51)	2.80**
Punishment	33.09	(5.95)	34.19	(5.65)	1.10
Abuse/neglect	20.77	(2.56)	21.40	(1.95)	1.48
Authoritarianism	14.32	(2.42)	15.32	(2.41)	2.44*
Knowledge	23.22	(4.52)	26.58	(5.16)	4.29**
		(n = 267)		(n = 40)	
Information	10.33	(2.60)	12.13	(2.48)	4.10**
Expectancy	12.88	(3.06)	14.45	(3.73)	2.93**
Cognitive Readiness	.05	(2.20)	1.7	(2.25)	4.66**
Total (z score)		(n = 264)		(n = 40)	

*$p < .05$. ** $p < .01$.

should be expected to fulfill their (i.e., the mothers) needs (role reversal), but the groups did not differ in child-centeredness. In the area of Parenting Style, adults characterized themselves as more responsive and empathetic, and less authoritarian with their children than teen mothers. However, there were no differences between the two groups on subscales measuring their orientation toward punishment and abuse and neglect. Finally, t tests of the Knowledge subscales suggested that adult mothers were both better informed about child development and had more realistic expectations for their children's behavior.

The cognitive readiness scores of the pregnant and nonpregnant teen samples were also compared. These analyses indicated significant differences in prenatal parenting attitudes, and overall cognitive readiness for parenting, with pregnant teens showing more positive attitudes and more preparedness in general for the parenting role. Similar results were found when the nonpregnant teen and adult samples were compared. Adults had more positive attitudes, better knowledge of child development, more appropriate parenting styles, and overall demonstrated more cognitive preparedness for parenting. In conjunction with the pregnant teen versus adult comparisons reported in Table 4.2, these results also suggested that adolescents, whether pregnant or not, are not as cognitively ready for parenting as pregnant adults.

Socioemotional Adjustment

A behavioral measure of socioemotional well-being, the YSR was administered prenatally to evaluate behavioral problems and social competence. Behavioral scores were derived for internalizing (withdrawal, somatic complaints, anxiety/depression), thought, social, attention, and externalizing (delinquent and aggressive behavior) problems as well as for total problems. Table 4.3 shows the percent of the pregnant teen sample falling in the normal ($T < 60$), borderline clinical ($T = 60$–63) and clinical ($T > 63$) ranges for internalizing, externalizing, and total problems. As this table indicates, 24%, 23.3% and 26.7% of the sample fell in the borderline clinical plus clinical ranges for internalizing behaviors, externalizing behaviors, and total problems. Compared to other female adolescents, the sample of pregnant adolescents reported more behavior problems than a nonclinical group, but fewer problems than a clinical group referred for mental health services (Achenbach, 1991c). Compared to the adult sample, adolescent mothers had significantly higher internalizing [$t(307) = 3.23, p < .01$], externalizing [$t(308) = 3.16, p < .01$], and total problem [$t(307) = 3.31, p < .01$] scores.

Table 4.4 presents the cross-tabulation of scores by clinical category for the internalizing and externalizing scales. As seen, approximately 13% of the teen sample fell at or above a T score of 60 on both scales and thus were categorized as borderline clinical or clinical. Ten percent of the sample had scores above 60 on the externalizing but not internalizing scales, and another 10.7% had scores above 60 on the internalizing, but not the externalizing scale. Thus, 34% of the adolescent mothers had problems of either one or both types. The remaining adolescent mothers scored within normal limits on both scales.

TABLE 4.3
Distribution of Prenatal Youth Self-Report Scores

Range	Internalizing		Externalizing		Total	
	N	Percent	N	Percent	N	Percent
Normal	205	75.9	208	76.8	198	73.3
Borderline	29	10.7	25	9.3	41	15.2
Clinical	36	13.3	38	14.0	31	11.5

TABLE 4.4
Cross-Tabulation of Youth Self-Report Scores by Clinical Category

| | Externalizing Scale | |
| | T Score 60 or Above | T Score Below 60 |
Internalizing Scale	(Borderline or Clinical)	(Normal)
T-Score 60 or Above	13.3%	10.7%
(Borderline or clinical)	(n = 36)	(n = 20)
T-Score Below 60	10%	65.9%
(Normal)	(n = 27)	(n = 178)

In addition to their behavioral difficulties, the pregnant adolescent group was evaluated as less competent socially than the nonpregnant adolescent sample on the YSR [$t(339) = 6.06$, $p < .01$]. The Social Competence scale measures involvement in social activities with family and friends. The mean raw score for the pregnant adolescent group on the Social Competence scale of the YSR was 12.62 in contrast to an adolescent norm group average of 14.6. Higher scores indicate a greater competence, and a score below 12 is considered in the clinical range. In our sample, 18.3% of the adolescent mothers scored in the borderline clinical and 24.1% scored in the clinical range. Thus, only 57.6% of the adolescents scored within the normal range of social competence.

Social Support

Measures of social support were derived from questions asked during a structured prenatal interview. It assessed perceptions of closeness and emotional support from mothers, siblings, friends, partners, and extended families, as well as anticipated postnatal financial support and child care from these same sources. Three composite social support variables were created: expected support from mothers and siblings (range 6 to 30); expected support from primary partners as well as from friends (range 8 to 40); and expected support from extended family members (range 4 to 20). For all three composites, higher scores indicate a greater degree of social support. Descriptive analyses yielded a mean of 23.20 ($SD = 3.88$) for mother/sibling support, 25.87 ($SD = 5.33$) for friend/partner support, and 12.04 ($SD = 3.87$) for support from extended family.

The sample of pregnant adults served as a comparison group to evaluate the pregnant teens' social support scores since preexistent norms were not available. Results of independent sample *t* tests indicated that pregnant teens perceived themselves as receiving more support from family members than pregnant adults, while adults reported more support from friends and partners. Specifically, teens scored higher on the index of support from mothers and siblings [$t(309) = 2.75, p < .01$], as well as on the measures of support from extended family members [$t(311) = 2.15, p < .05$]. Adults reported more support from friends and spouses or boyfriends [$t(309) = -2.51, p < .05$]. When support from friends and partner were analyzed separately, it was found that only partner support differentiated teens from adults. Not surprisingly, adults reported more support from their spouses or boyfriends [$t(309) = 2.34, p < .05$]. There were no differences between the groups in total social support.

Interrelationships Among Prenatal Variables

The correlational matrix reflecting the intercorrelations of prenatal adolescent maternal factors is shown in Table 4.5. As seen, there were uniform significant correlations between measures within areas of functioning, including the domain of cognitive readiness (Parenting Attitudes, Parenting Style, and Knowledge of Child Development), IQ (Block Design and Vocabulary), socioemotional adjustment (externalizing behavior problems, internalizing behavior problems, and social competence) and social support (friends/partner, siblings/mother and extended family). These correlations indicate that the measures we used to index each construct exhibited the anticipated interrelationships. The correlations between the IQ subscales as well as between socioemotional adjustment scales (internalizing and externalizing) are similar to those reported in the literature.

Table 4.5 also provides the reader a first glance at a theme is reiterated throughout this book: The various domains of psychological development are often modestly interrelated. For example, the data in Table 4.5 show the significant intercorrelations between measures of cognitive readiness (Parenting Attitudes, Style, and Knowledge) and the measures of two other important constructs in our model—IQ (Block Design and Vocabulary) and socioemotional adjustment (internalizing and externalizing behaviors). Higher scores on the Cognitive Readiness scales were associated with higher scores on the IQ subtests as well as lower (less problematic) scores on the internalizing and externalizing scales. Significant intercorrelations also existed between the measures of social support (friends/partner, sibling/mother, and extended family) and social com-

TABLE 4.5

Correlations Between Prenatal Maternal Variables

| | Cognitive Readiness | | | Intelligence | | Socioemotional | | | Social Support | | |
	Parenting Attitude	Parenting Style	Parenting Knowledge	Block Design	Vocab	Internalizing	Externalizing	Social Competence	Friend/ Partner	Siblings/ Mother	Extended Family
Parenting attitude	1.00	—	—	—	—	—	—	—	—	—	—
Parenting style	.33**	1.00	—	—	—	—	—	—	—	—	—
Parenting knowledge	.35**	.43**	1.00	—	—	—	—	—	—	—	—
Block design	.31**	.29**	.36**	1.00	—	—	—	—	—	—	—
Vocabulary	.26**	.37**	.39**	.49**	1.00	—	—	—	—	—	—
Internalizing	-.16**	-.15*	-.20**	-.16*	-.03	1.00	—	—	—	—	—
Externalizing	-.09	-.13*	-.19**	-.08	-.04	.68**	1.00	—	—	—	—
Social competence	-.00	.06	.00	.02	-.07	-.08	-.14*	1.00	—	—	—
Friend/partner	.10	-.04	.05	.00	.08	-.06	-.12*	.16**	1.00	—	—
Siblings/ mother	.01	.02	-.08	-.03	-.07	-.06	-.07	.28**	.15*	1.00	—
Extended family	-.05	-.02	-.16	-.05	-.05	-.01	-.06	.18**	.20**	.39**	1.00

*p < .05. **significant at p < .01.

petence, with greater support associated with greater competence. Interestingly, greater social support from friends/partner was also associated with fewer externalizing problems.

Summary

In general, adolescent mothers possessed fewer prenatal cognitive and socioemotional resources to support their role transition than adult mothers. Limitations in verbal intelligence, cognitive readiness for parenting, and social competence were apparent, as well as higher rates of internalizing and externalizing problems. The pattern of social support was also different from adult mothers, with teens receiving greater support from family and friends and less from their partners.

MATERNAL STATUS
WHEN CHILDREN WERE 6 MONTHS OLD

Adolescent mothers have been thought to put their children at risk for developmental problems because of their parenting behaviors. In this section, we examine multiple facets of the adolescent parenting experience, including its cognitive, affective and behavioral components. Descriptive data for the various measures of parenting are provided for the teen and adult samples in Table 4.6.

The three Cognitive Readiness subscales, given prenatally, were readministered at 6 months. Results from independent sample t tests comparing adult and adolescent cognitive readiness at 6 months are reported in Table 4.6. Comparisons of a summary measure of cognitive readiness (summed z scores of the three scales) revealed that adult mothers continued to be generally more prepared for parenting than teen mothers 6 months into their parenting roles. Analyses of individual cognitive readiness measures indicated differences on the Parenting Attitudes Questionnaire, with adults showing more positive attitudes than teens. As during the prenatal assessment, this difference was reflected only on the role reversal subscale. Although there were no overall differences on the Parenting Style scale at 6 months, analysis of individual subscales revealed, as at the prenatal assessment, that adult mothers' showed significantly greater empathy and responsiveness and less authoritarian attitudes than adolescent mothers. Differences between the adult and adolescent samples in Knowledge of Child Development were no longer present at 6 months.

TABLE 4.6

Adult and Adolescent Mothers' 6-Month Parenting Measures

Measure	Adolescent		Adult		t
	Mean	(SD)	Mean	(SD)	
Parenting Attitudes	61.66	(7.55)	66.58	(7.96)	2.96**
	(n = 166)		(n = 24)		
Role reversal	23.91	(5.61)	29.83	(5.98)	4.79**
Child-centeredness	37.78	(4.80)	36.75	(3.76)	1.01
Parenting Style	99.38	(14.65)	105.35	(15.05)	1.82
	(n = 166)		(n = 23)		
Respons./empathy	29.51	(5.94)	33.04	(5.09)	2.73**
Punishment	34.54	(6.47)	34.96	(7.23)	.29
Abuse/neglect	20.81	(3.08)	21.50	(2.57)	1.05
Authoritarianism	14.54	(2.33)	15.88	(2.13)	2.46**
Knowledge	24.27	(4.98)	27.12	(7.15)	1.92[a]
	(n = 163)		(n = 40)		
Information	10.99	(2.62)	12.36	(3.48)	1.88[b]
Expectancy	13.30	(3.24)	14.76	(4.42)	1.59[c]
Cognitive Readiness (Total)	-.02	(2.35)	1.65	(3.02)	3.07**
	(n = 161)		(n = 23)		
Maternal Interaction	39.23	(10.14)	49.39	(9.51)	4.79**
	(n = 167)		(n = 26)		
Parenting Stress	244.54	(38.56)	218.54	(35.15)	3.11**
	(n = 161)		(n = 24)		

*$p < .05$. ** $p < .01$.

[a]separate variance estimate used: df = 1,27.68.
[b]separate variance estimate used: df = 1,28.27
[c]separate variance estimate used: df = 1,28.06

The MIS was employed to evaluate videotapes of parenting behavior taken during structured mother–child interactions at 6 months. The MIS is a global rating scale designed to capture qualitative as well as quantitative dimensions of parenting interactional style. Higher scores on the MIS indicate more appropriate and sensitive interactions. A comparison between adolescent and adult samples revealed that adult mothers demonstrated more appropriate parenting interactions than teen mothers (see Table 4.6). When t tests were conducted, comparing teen and adult mothers on the 11 individual items of the MIS, teen and adult mothers were found to differ in all areas except control. Adult mothers interacted more with their children, paid more attention to their activities, were more flexible, more verbal, more positive, and more in tune with their children's emotions, and provided more praise, encouragement and appropriate instruction. Not surprisingly, the overall quality of adult mothers' interactions was also rated as superior.

Finally, the PSI was administered to assess parenting affect; higher scores on the PSI indicate greater parenting stress. A comparison between the adolescent and adult mother samples indicated that adult mothers experienced less parenting stress than adolescent mothers. Whereas the adult mean falls between the 45th and 50th percentile, the teen mean falls at the 75th percentile, the upper limit of the normal range.

In summary, the data analyses indicated that at 6 months postpartum, adolescent mothers were both cognitively and behaviorally less supportive and responsive in their orientation toward, and interactions with, their children and more stressed by their parenting role than adult mothers.

Stability and Change in Adolescent Mothers' Cognitive Readiness and Social Support

Given the potential for increased stress, new learning opportunities, and unexpected challenges associated with the adolescents' transition into motherhood, we examined how this transition affected their cognitive readiness for parenting. Both the stability and mean change in cognitive readiness from the prenatal period to 6 months after birth were analyzed. Stability refers to changes in the rank order of individual mothers in cognitive readiness across these two time periods, whereas mean change refers to differences in the sample means across time.

Pearson product correlations were calculated to estimate stability; results from these analyses are shown in Table 4.7. Each of the Cognitive Readiness scales, as well as the individual subscales comprising each scale, showed for the most part moderate stability over time, as did the overall measure of cognitive readiness. Despite this stability, the size of the correlation coefficients also suggests a fair amount of instability in the adolescent mothers' cognitive readiness during the transition period.

Repeated measure t tests of prenatal and 6-month data were also conducted to assess mean changes in teen mothers' cognitive readiness (see Table 4.7). In general, these analyses indicated that adolescent mothers showed positive changes in their cognitive orientation to parenting: Teen mothers became significantly more appropriate and positive in their parenting attitudes when their children were 6 months, with both attitudes about role reversal and child-centeredness undergoing positive

TABLE 4.7

Stability and Mean Changes in Maternal Cognative Readiness
From Prenatal to 6-Month Postpartum Assessments for the Adolescent Sample

Measure	Stability Coefficients	Mean t	Change N
Parenting Attitudes	.62**	4.68**	154
Role reversal	.52**	2.48*	
Child-centeredness	.57**	4.26**	
Parenting Style	.64**	2.43*	155
Respons./empathy	.63**	2.02*	
Punishment	.58**	2.61**	
Abuse/neglect	.45**	.10	
Authoritarianism	.54**	1.86	
Knowledge	.63**	3.85**	151
Information	.34**	3.88**	
Expectancy	.53**	1.44	
Cognitive Readiness Total	.76**	.78	148

* $p < .05.$ ** $p < .01.$

changes. Similarly, parenting style improved with time; this change was due to a reported increase in the mothers' responsiveness and empathic awareness, as well as a preference for a less punitive parenting style. Teens' scores on the abuse/neglect and authoritarianism subscales did not change significantly over time. Finally, adolescent mothers demonstrated an increase in their general knowledge of child development; this change reflected a gain in information, but not a change in expectancy about the timing of developmental milestones. Despite these important gains, adolescent mothers remained significantly less cognitively prepared for parenting at 6 months than adult mothers.

Perceived closeness and emotional support from mother, friends, and the primary partner were reassessed at 6 months postpartum. Statistical comparisons confirmed that the adolescent mothers' perceptions of support from each source declined significantly from the prenatal period. During the prenatal period, the teen moms reported considerable closeness and emotional support from their mothers (over 4 on the 5-point scale); in contrast, their perceptions of support had declined (2.5 on the 5-point scale) at 6 months [$t(115) = 11.27$, $p < .0001$]. Similar results were found for support from the primary partners. Pregnant adolescents reported substantial support from their partners (3.9) which declined significantly to 2.4 at 6 months postpartum [$t(114) = 8.03$, $p < .001$]. Although perceived support from friends also showed a significant decline, this change was less than for the other sources of support (from 3.7 to 2.9) [t (114) = 5.14, $p < .901$].

Interrelationship Among Maternal Measures at 6 Months

Correlations between 6-month adolescent maternal measures are shown in Table 4.8. The three Cognitive Readiness scales (Parenting Attitude, Style, and Knowledge) were again significantly intercorrelated; parents who were well prepared in one domain tended to demonstrate greater readiness in the other domains as well. In addition, there were lower but significant correlations between each of the three cognitive readiness measures and behavioral ratings on the MIS. In all cases, greater cognitive readiness to parent was associated with more appropriate parenting interaction. Finally, mothers who experienced less stress in their parenting parenting roles scored higher on all three cognitive readiness scales and had more appropriate interactions with their children. Thus, overall, the correlations indicate a close and possibly mutually interactive relationships among the three indices of quality of parenting—cognitive readiness, observed interactions, and stress. Although the direction of influence is unknown, mothers who experience greater stress may do so because they are less cognitively and behaviorally prepared to parent and/or conversely their parenting stress may inhibit the development of their cognitive and behavioral capacity for parenting.

TABLE 4.8
Correlations Between Adolescent Maternal Measures at 6 Months

	Parenting Attitudes	Parenting Style	Knowledge	MIS	Parenting Stress
Parenting Attitudes	1.00	—	—	—	—
Parenting Style	.49**	1.00	—	—	—
Knowledge of Child Development	.44**	.61**	1.00	—	—
MIS	.38**	.33**	.33**	1.00	—
Parenting Stress	-.27**	-.38**	-.33**	-.17*	1.00

* $p < .05$. ** $p < .01$.
Note. MIS = Maternal Interaction Scale.

MATERNAL STATUS: 1 YEAR AFTER BIRTH

Maternal functioning and social supports were evaluated at 1-year post-partum. The MCRS (Roth, 1980) was employed to assess maternal attitudes important at this stage of development including: acceptance and rejection of the child, overprotection, and overindulgence. Comparisons with normative data indicated that adolescent mothers tended to be at normative levels in acceptance and rejection but they were found to be more overprotective (an expression of anxiety in terms of prolonged infantile care, prevention of development of independent behavior, and an excess of control) as well as overindulgent (providing excessive gratification with lack of parental control). Although the mothers are average in accepting, they are also nonaccepting in their overprotectiveness and overindulgence. This parenting profile is thought to adversely impact children's socioemotional development as well as adaptive skills (Roth, 1980).

Parenting behavior at 1-year postpartum was assessed using a slightly modified version of the MIS. Mothers and children were videotaped while interacting for 5 minutes in a free-play situation with toys. Eleven parenting characteristics were each rated and then summed for a total score. Adolescent mothers demonstrated overall improvement in their parenting behavior from the 6-months postpartum period [$t(97) = 3.04, p < .01$]. Examination of specific subscales indicated that the teens of 1-year-old infants showed more flexible behavior, provided stimulation at a more appropriate rate, were more motivating and more responsive to their infants' emotions than they were 6 months earlier. Stability of parenting behavior from 6 months to 1 year was low ($r = .29, p = .004$).

Intercorrelations between the parenting measures were moderate. The MIS was significantly and negatively correlated with overprotection ($r = -.19$), whereas it was positively correlated with acceptance ($r = .33$). As expected, the four subscales of the MCRS were also correlated with each other (with a range from .22 to .48).

Examination of social support data indicated that approximately 63% of the adolescent mothers were living with their mothers at 1-year postpartum and 21% lived with a partner. Although teens living with their mothers perceived more support from them than teens living with a partner, this difference only approached significance. As expected, teens living with a partner perceived significantly more support from that partner than a nonresidential partner or their friends. Perceptions of support from both mothers and from partners, but not from friends, increased from 6 months to 1 year.

MATERNAL STATUS: 3 AND 5 YEARS AFTER BIRTH

Three and 5 years after the birth of the first child, the quality of maternal functioning was again evaluated. The mothers' job status, educational attainment, marital status, family size, SES and use of public assistance were assessed. In addition, information was gathered regarding their intellectual functioning, socioemotional adjustment, and parenting.

Demographics

Demographic data for adolescent mothers, 3 and 5 years after the birth of their children, are presented in Table 4.9. At both time points, less than half of the sample of mothers was working. A substantial percentage of mothers was, however, still attending school, 26% at 3 years and 20.9% at five years. Three years after the birth of their children, only 56% of the sample had completed high school; at 5 years this number rose to 65%. A sizable number of mothers reported obtaining more than 12 years of education; at 3 years 17.8% of mothers had had some additional schooling, and that percentage increased to 21.2% at the 5-year interview.

Marital status changed little during this time period, with only a small percentage of mothers married at 3 and 5 years, 10% and 15%, respectively. Although only a few mothers were pregnant at the time of the 3- and 5-year assessments, approximately 50% had had at least one additional child by the time their firstborn was 3 years old. At 5 years, the majority of the sample (approximately 76%) had at least one other child, with about 33% having two or more additional children. Average scores on the Hollingshead Index indicated that mothers were of low SES at both assessments: A large proportion of the sample, 69.2% of mothers at 3 years and 64.3% at 5 years, reported receiving support from one or more government agencies, most commonly Medicaid and/or food stamps. At both 3 and 5 years, only a small proportion of mothers reported receiving any help from the child's biological father, 8.8% and 12.3%, respectively.

Intelligence

Maternal intelligence was reassessed with the WAIS–R at 3 and 5 years. The average estimated full-scale IQ scores were 85.80 (SD = 11.91) at 3 years and 85.64 (SD =12.02) at 5 years, with means at both time points falling nearly one standard deviation below the norm. The average Block Design scaled scores at 3 and 5 years, 8.55 (SD = 2.99) and 8.71 (SD = 2.98) respectively, fell at the lower end of the average range, whereas mean Vocabulary performances at both time periods, 6.39 (SD = 1.92)

TABLE 4.9
Maternal Demographic Data at 3 and 5 Years

	3 Years (n = 146)	5 Years (n = 139)
Working	41.1%	49.6%
Attending school	26.0%	20.9%
Percent completing high school	56.1%	65.0%
Percent completing more than 12 years of school	17.8%	21.2%
Years of school	11.51 (1.29)	11.74 (1.42)
Marital status		
Single	83.6%	76.3%
Married	10.3%	15.1%
Divorced	3.4%	5.0%
Separated	2.7%	3.6%
Number of other children		
0	49.3%	24.5%
1	41.1%	43.2%
2	8.9%	27.2%
3	.7%	5.2%
Hollingshead (SES)	63.63 (5.48)	63.77 (6.23)
Percent receiving public support	69.2%	69.3%

and 6.21 (SD = 1.92), were over a full standard deviation below the norm. Mothers scored significantly higher on the Block Design subtest than on the Vocabulary scale at both 3 years [$t(142)$ = 9.70, $p < .01$], and 5 years [$t(136)$ = 11.08, $p < .01$].

The distribution of IQ scores at 3 and 5 years reported in Table 4.10 are similar across time. Between 25% and 33% of mothers had scores in the normal range. Roughly 33% of the sample fell in the low average range, and approximately 25% were classified as having borderline intelligence. A substantial percentage of the mothers were also classified as being intellectually in the mildly mentally retarded range (8.4% at 3 years and 7.3% at 5 years). In contrast, a very small percentage of mothers had scores in the high average range (4.2% and 2.9% at 3 and 5 years, respectively). There were no scores in the superior or very superior ranges of intelligence at either time point. Comparisons with the prenatal assessment of maternal IQ suggests that scores were stable over time. This issue is addressed further in a later section.

TABLE 4.10
Distribution of 3- and 5-Year Maternal IQ Scores

IQ Classification	IQ Range	3 Years		5 Years	
		Frequency	Percent	Frequency	Percent
Very superior	140–169	0	0	0	0
Superior	120–139	0	0	0	0
High average	110–119	6	4.2	4	2.9
Normal	90–109	38	26.6	41	29.0
Low average	80–89	50	35.0	48	35.0
Borderline	70–79	37	25.9	34	24.8
Mentally retarded	30–69	12	8.4	10	7.3
Total		143		137	

Socioemotional Adjustment

The general hypothesis that adolescent mothers would experience adjustment problems during their transition to parenthood was confirmed. At 3 and 5 years, maternal psychological well-being was assessed by the BDI, the SEI, the STAI, and the Life Stress Scale of the PSI (see chap. 3 for a complete description of these measures and Table 4.11 for mean scores).

TABLE 4.11
Descriptive Data for Maternal Measures of Socioemotional Adjustment

Time	Measure	Mean	SD	N
3 years	Depression	8.86	6.67	146
5 years	Depression	8.33	7.44	141
3 years	Self-esteem	16.83	4.68	144
5 years	Self-esteem	17.24	4.34	140
3 years	State anxiety	33.87	9.28	145
5 years	State anxiety	33.54	9.75	140
3 years	Trait anxiety	39.83	9.49	144
5 years	Trait anxiety	37.38	9.81	138
3 years	Life stress	16.18	9.49	143
5 years	Life stress	17.91	12.00	139

TABLE 4.12
Distribution of Beck Depression Inventory Scores According to Severity Rating

Severity Rating	Score Range	3 Years		5 Years	
		Frequency	Percent	Frequency	Percent
Minimal	0–9	91	62.3%	93	66.0%
Mild depression	10–16	39	26.7%	33	23.4%
Moderate depression	17–29	14	9.6%	10	7.1%
Extremely severe depression	30–63	2	1.4%	5	3.5%

The distribution of scores by severity ratings on the BDI is shown in Table 4.12. As seen, the distribution at 3 and 5 years is fairly similar. At both time points, the majority of adolescents scored between 0 and 9, indicating minimal to no signs of depressive symptoms. However, a significant minority, more than 33% of the sample, reported some level of depression, the majority in the mild range, although approximately 10% fell in the moderate to severe range.

The SEI, adult form, was used to evaluate maternal self-esteem. Higher scores indicate greater self-esteem. Compared to a similar age norm group, the average scores of the adolescent mothers at both 3 and 5 years (see Table 4.11) fell at the 33rd percentile, suggesting lower self-esteem in this sample of adolescent mothers (Coopersmith, 1981).

Both state and trait anxiety were also assessed with STAI. Higher scores on this scale indicate greater anxiety; raw scores above 34 place respondents in the top 50th percentile for state anxiety (Spielberger, 1983). At 3 years, 42.8% of the sample placed at or above the 50th percentile, and at 5 years 41.4% placed at or above the 50th percentile, suggesting that our sample was reasonably similar in state anxiety to other women their age. Trait anxiety scores were higher than state anxiety: 74.3% of adolescent mothers placed at or above the 50th percentile at 3 years. This percentage was lower at 5 years, with 63% of the sample scoring at or above the 50th percentile. Thus, this sample was somewhat higher in trait anxiety when compared to a norm group of women of a similar age.

Life stress at 3 and 5 years was indexed using the Life Stress Scale of the PSI. There was considerable variability in the scores on this measure. Scores of 17 or higher indicate a high level of stress (90th percentile). At 3 years, nearly 45% of adolescents had stress levels of 17 or higher, when

10% would be expected based on the norm. At 5 years 48.2% scored 17 or higher.

In summary, the analyses of socioemotional adjustment data indicated that more adolescent mothers were experiencing lower self-esteem and greater depression, trait anxiety, and stress than would be expected for young women of their age. In general, these psychological problems do not bode well for either their future adjustment or that of their children.

Parenting Quality

Parenting quality was also assessed at both 3 and 5 years through the MIS and the abbreviated version of the CAPI. These scores are not interpretable in themselves without a comparison group or normative information. However, mothers' interactions with their 3-year-old toddlers were significantly better than interactions with their 1-year-old infants on the extent of interaction, reciprocal control, verbalness, motivation, and overall quality. Validity and stability information are further discussed in the next sections as well as in chapters 5 and 7.

Interrelationships of Maternal Measures

The correlation matrix depicting associations among maternal measures at 5 years is presented in Table 4.13. Although not presented, the 3-year correlational matrix showed an almost identical pattern of relationships among those measures administered at both times. At 5 years, as expected, the two WAIS–R subtests (Vocabulary and Block Design) were significantly and positively correlated, as were the various socioemotional measures (BDI, SEI, STAI). In addition, the measures of intelligence were negatively correlated with the BDI, indicating that higher performance on the WAIS–R subtests was associated with lower depression. At the 3-year evaluation, higher WAIS–R Block Design scores were also associated with higher self-esteem. These correlations, consistent with those reported for the prenatal assessments (see Table 4.5), again suggested numerous interrelationships between maternal cognitive and socioemotional functioning. Table 4.13 also shows that higher (more problematic) CAPI scores were associated with lower Vocabulary and Block Design scores, lower self-esteem, greater depression, and higher anxiety. Finally, higher (better) MIS scores were associated with higher WAIS–R subtests and lower BDI scores.

TABLE 4.13

Correlations Among 5-Year Maternal Measures

	Vocabulary	Block	Depression	Self-Esteem	State Anxiety	Trait Anxiety	Life Stress	CAPI	MIS
Vocabulary	1.00	—	—	—	—	—	—	—	—
Block	.48**	1.00	—	—	—	—	—	—	—
Depression	-.21*	-.18*	1.00	—	—	—	—	—	—
Self-esteem	.12	.03	-.59**	1.00	—	—	—	—	—
State anxiety	-.06	-.15	.43**	-.45**	1.00	—	—	—	—
Trait anxiety	-.04	-.13	.64**	-.61**	.64**	1.00	—	—	—
Life stress	.00	-.03	.06	-.13	.06	.12	1.00	—	—
CAPI	-.47**	-.28**	.38**	-.38**	.24**	.28**	.03	1.00	—
MIS	.34	.29	-.19*	.13	-.17	-.10	.07	-.15	1.00

$*p < .05.$ $**p < .01.$

Note. CAPI = Child Abuse Potential Inventory, MIS = Maternal Interaction Scale.

Stability and Change in Maternal Development Over Time

Several indices of maternal functioning were collected in repeated fashion at 3 and 5 years as well as across other time periods. Stability estimates for these data are presented in Table 4.14. As seen, the intelligence subtests showed moderate to high stability over time. Depression showed relatively low, but significant, stability from 3 to 5 years. Self-esteem exhibited moderate to high stability during this period, as did state and trait anxiety and life stress. Finally, CAPI scores showed moderate stability, whereas MIS stability scores were relatively low. It should be emphasized, however, that even where stability was high, there was a

TABLE 4.14
Stability and Mean Change of Maternal Characteristics

Measure	Time Period	Stability Coefficients	Mean t	Change N
Vocabulary	Prenatal – 3 Yrs	.67**	2.42*	144
	Prenatal – 5 Yrs	.63**	3.78**	137
	3 – 5 Yrs	.78**	1.36	121
Block Design	Prenatal – 3 Yrs	.75**	.51	143
	Prenatal – 5 Yrs	.78**	2.20*	135
	3 – 5 Yrs	.81**	3.16**	119
Estimated IQ	Prenatal – 3 Yrs	.80**	1.78	143
	Prenatal – 5 Yrs	.80**	.88	134
	3 – 5 Yrs	.84**	1.72	119
Depression	3 – 5 Yrs	.38**	1.74	125
Self-esteem	3 – 5 Yrs	.55**	1.30	123
State anxiety	3 – 5 Yrs	.49**	.54	123
Trait anxiety	3 – 5 Yrs	.46**	2.98**	120
Life stress	3 – 5 Yrs	.45**	2.43*	121
CAPI	1 – 3 Yrs	.70**	.66	102
	1 – 5 Yrs	.70**	.21	98
	3 – 5 Yrs	.64**	1.53	124
MIS	1 – 3 Yrs	.38**	2.12*	78
	1 – 5 Yrs	.32**	.31	85
	3 – 5 Yrs	.35**	1.94	104

* $p < .05.$ $p < .05.$

Note: CAPI = Child Abuse Potential Inventory, MIS = Maternal Interaction Scale.

great deal of variability. For example, a stability coefficient of .70 indicates that 51% of the variance ($1-.70^2 = .51$) is related to either true instability in the data and/or measurement error.

Changes in maternal IQ from the prenatal period to 3 and 5 years were also analyzed (see Table 4.14). There were no changes in estimated full-scale IQ scores over these time periods. However, there was a significant decrease in Vocabulary scores from the prenatal assessment to 3 years, as well as from the prenatal period to 5 years. At the same time, there was a significant increase in Block Design scores from the prenatal interview to 5 years, as well as from 3 to 5 years. However, the magnitude of these changes was small and of little practical importance. Trait anxiety decreased and life stress increased from 3 to 5 years. Finally, maternal interactional style improved from 1 to 3 years. Other areas of psychological functioning (depression, state anxiety, and self-esteem) and parenting (CAPI) did not undergo significant changes over time.

DISCUSSION

Although researchers have become increasingly aware of the negative consequences of early childrearing for the children of adolescent mothers, relatively little is known about the development of adolescent mothers and how they fare as they assume their new parenting roles. During pregnancy, mothers in the Notre Dame Parenting Project were for the most part unmarried, living in poverty, and reliant on their families of origin for instrumental and emotional support. In general, they were operating in the low to average range of intellectual functioning, showing signs of socioemotional maladjustment, and often cognitively unprepared to become parents.

More specifically, almost two thirds of the adolescent mothers fell below the normal range in their estimated IQ scores: 38% were operating in the low average range, 17% in the borderline range, and 9% in the mentally retarded range. These scores showed moderate to high stability over time, with a similar proportion of mothers falling below the normal range when they were tested 3 and 5 years later. It is noteworthy that the target sample had higher scores on the performance subtest (Block Design) of the WAIS–R, compared to the verbal subtest (Vocabulary); additionally, their vocabulary scores decreased over time whereas their Block Design scores increased. The depressed vocabulary scores in conjunction with the low-average Block Design scores are consistent with the overall low achievement and slow progress of the sample in completing high school. Not surprisingly, many participants had difficulty finishing high school requirements; 5 years after the birth of their first child more than one third of mothers had not received their diploma and few mothers had good jobs, with benefits.

The association between low IQ, low educational attainment, and early childbearing is intriguing. Results of past research have indicated an association between early parenthood and educational attainment, with young mothers completing fewer years of schooling (cf. Moore et al., 1981). Although Moore et al. suggested that early parenthood may be the setting event for school drop out, it seems equally likely, as suggested by Hotz et al. (1997), that low academic achievement, which is related to low intellectual functioning and poor self-esteem, provides a setting condition that can lead to early pregnancy and parenthood as well as to later psychological problems such as stress and anxiety.

Of the adolescent mothers in this sample, 34% reported behavior problems of either an internalizing and/or externalizing nature during pregnancy. Internalizing problems reflect fearful, inhibited, and over-controlled behaviors, whereas externalizing problems include aggressive, antisocial, and undercontrolled behaviors. Many mothers were experiencing socioemotional problems, particularly high life stress and depression at 3 and 5 years. At both time points, almost one half of the mothers were experiencing high stress levels, and around one third reported signs of depression. Although it is impossible to conclude that parenthood caused these socioemotional problems, it seems likely that untimed pregnancies played a contributing role in interaction with other factors such as poverty and poor educational success.

Further analysis of the socioemotional adjustment data suggested that the pregnant adolescents had a different pattern of social involvement than their nonpregnant peers. Pregnant adolescents were less involved than nonpregnant adolescents in interpersonal relationships; in particular, they had less frequent and/or less positive involvement with their peers and family. This finding has both theoretical and clinical significance in view of the fact that healthy social interactions during pregnancy can lead to positive social support during early childrearing, thus serving as a buffer against parenting stress. Although the data suggested that the social relationships with peers of the pregnant adolescents were restricted, it is not clear whether this restriction occurred because of their poor social skills and personal feelings of inadequacy or because their pregnancy disrupted normal social relationships. Results of a comparative analysis by Passino et al. (1993) of pregnant adolescents and adults in our study suggested the latter conclusion: Pregnant adolescents appeared as socially involved with their peers as pregnant adults.

Social support data indicated, however, that adult mothers, who were generally married, relied more on their spouses for support and social stimulation than on friends. In contrast, pregnant adolescents, who generally were single, have limited access to this support option, relying more, probably out of necessity, on their families of origin. Thus, adolescent mothers appeared to face a critical life event—their pregnancy and the birth of their first child—with reduced social support from their friends as well as without a traditional support source, a partner or spouse. They were often forced to rely on a "conflicted" source of support—their immediate families. Analyses of changes in social support from the prenatal to the 6-month assessment, revealed that supports were, in general, declining and less satisfactory, although some improvement in social supports occurred from the 6-month to 1-year assessment. Consistent with past research (Schinke, Gilchrist, & Small, 1979), Passino et al. (1993) found that pregnant adolescents in our study were less effective in problem solving than their nonpregnant peers. Thus, adolescent mothers seem doubly disadvantaged as they make their transitions into parenthood because of deficient social and personal coping resources. This view was reinforced by our analyses of the cognitive readiness data.

Compared to adult mothers, teen mothers appeared less cognitively ready to assume their parenting roles. During pregnancy, our evaluations indicated that the teen sample knew less about how children develop, had less realistic expectations about their children, preferred a parenting style that was more authoritarian and less empathetic, and believed children should fulfill their personal needs rather than vice versa, suggesting a tendency toward role reversal. These findings are consistent with the existing literature that indicates that adolescent mothers possess less precise knowledge about development and parenting and more negative, often punitive, attitudes about parenting than adult mothers (Field, Widmayer, Stringer, & Ignatoff, 1980; Roosa, 1983; Roosa & Vaughn, 1984; Sommer et al., 1993).

It is important to note, however, that although teen mothers, compared to adult mothers, appeared at risk for poor parenting because of their cognitive readiness, they appeared somewhat more cognitively prepared than the nonpregnant teen comparison group. Interestingly, pregnant adolescents had a more positive attitude about parenting than nonpregnant adolescents; however, they were not significantly different from their peer group in their knowledge about child development and appropriate parenting styles. These findings suggest that young girls who became pregnant are more interested in having children but are not that different from young girls who do not become pregnant in their readiness to parent. More importantly, these results suggest that adolescent mothers may be more at risk for parenting problems than adult mothers because of age-related cognitive immaturity.

Thus, the analyses of prenatal data indicate that adolescent mothers as a group were cognitively and socioemotionally disadvantaged shortly before the birth of their first child. Subsequent analyses, 6 months after the birth, suggested that once they became parents they were cognitively, behaviorally and emotionally challenged by their new roles. Although the teen mothers seem to have become more knowledgeable about parenting, they continued to be less appropriate than a sample of adult mothers on several parenting dimensions: role reversal, responsiveness, empathy, and authoritarianism. These data suggest that although adolescent mothers were adapting in a positive sense to their parenting role, they remained less mature in their approach to parenting than adult mothers.

Consistent with past theory and research (Brooks-Gunn & Fursten-berg, 1986; Epstein, 1980; McLaughlin, Sandler, Sherrod, Vietze, & O'Conner, 1979; Osofsky & Osofsky, 1970; Roosa et al., 1982; Sommer et al., 1993), it was expected that adolescent mothers, who were cognitively unprepared for parenting, would exhibit less optimal parenting skills than would adult mothers. Analysis of the data indicated that adolescent mothers as a group interacted less frequently and less appropriately with their children than adult mothers. Adolescent mothers were less appropriate in their responses to their children's affective behavior as well as in their rates of stimulation, flexibility, positiveness, motivation, and overall quality of mothering. These differences were not explained by either race or SES factors, which differentiated the two samples.

In addition to cognitive and behavioral limitations, adolescent mothers reported more stress in both the parent and child domains of the PSI than their adult counterparts; almost one half were also evaluated as experiencing high levels of life stress. Adolescent mothers reported feeling more socially isolated and restricted by their parenting responsibilities. These findings are consistent with past research and theory which suggested that adolescent mothers experience more stress than adult mothers (Brooks-Gunn & Furstenberg, 1986; Brown, Adams, & Kellam, 1981; Ventura, 1980) as well as with the observation that adolescent motherhood represents a strenuous developmental challenge because of its asynchronous nature (Hamburg, 1986; Ventura, 1980). Finally, correlational data indicated that the cognitive, behavioral, and affective domains of adolescent parents were interrelated, implying the existence of a dynamic system in which these domains reciprocally influence one another. In combination, the pattern of interrelationships before and 6 months after birth, suggested that adolescent mothers and their children were at elevated risk for future problems.

Analyses evaluating maternal status at 3 and 5 years were consistent with, and extended, past research that has suggested an association between early parenting and a constellation of less than optimal adult out-comes (Beardslee, Zuckerman, Amaro, & McAllister, 1988; Card & Wise, 1978; Hayes, 1987; Mott & Marsigliano, 1985), including poor vocational skills, less problem-solving capacity, and a tendency to become en-meshed in poverty. When their children had reached 3 years of age, a majority of adolescent mothers (59%) were not working, those who worked generally held part-time jobs, and only 56% had completed high school. Most of the mothers were not married and about one half (51%) had at least one other child. About 70% were receiving some type of public assistance. Five years after the birth of the first child, the picture was very similar. At this point, however, more than 80% of the mothers had at least one other child, and 33% had two or more additional chil-dren. Additionally, 3- and 5-year data showed multiple signs of socio-emotional adjustment problems in the adolescent sample, including low self-esteem, anxiety, high life stress, and depression.

The findings reported in this chapter contrast somewhat with the findings reported by Furstenberg et al. (1987) who reported that many adolescent mothers appear to be functioning reasonably well. These seemingly conflicting pictures may be cohort specific; for example, the sample of adolescent mothers that Furstenberg et al. (1987) recruited in the 1960s may have benefitted from the optimism and opportunities as-sociated with new programs of the Great Society and the War on Pov-erty, a better educational system, and more reliable social supports pro-vided by older grandparents. In contrast, many of the adolescent moth-ers in our sample were caught in the middle of welfare reform, which may have curtailed their financial assistance. The discrepancy in findings may also be related to the fact that our maternal evaluations occurred relatively early in their parenting careers, whereas Furstenberg's findings were more relevant to later maternal functioning. It is also quite possible that the results of Furstenberg and colleagues (1987) may have underes-timated the problems of adolescent mothers by not focusing on psycho-logical outcomes such as self-esteem, depression, anxiety and stress.

Several final points are in order with respect to our model of adoles-cent parenting that has guided this project (see chap. 2) versus Belsky's (1984) earlier model of adult parenting: (a) Cognitive readiness—a new construct—differentiated teen and adult mothers, including its three major components that were moderately interrelated; (b) the levels of personal adjustment and intelligence were initially low in the adolescent sample and did not change much during the first 5 years; (c) the struc-ture of social support seemed different depending on the age of the mother, with teens having less frequent support from partners and friends; and (d) work and marital status, important constructs in Belsky's model, were infrequent in the adolescent sample and justified our initial decision to exclude them from our model of adolescent parenting. We believe that each of these factors is essential in the development of intervention programs, as is discussed in chapter 10 on social policy.

In summary, these results indicate that pregnant adolescents manifested signs of socioemotional and behavioral adjustment problems, problematic social supports, low IQ and insufficient cognitive readiness for parenting. Six months after the birth of their first child, their parenting was characterized by less than optimal attitudes and knowledge, high stress, and behavioral problems. At 3 and 5 years, adolescent mothers tended to be undereducated, underemployed, and continued to have additional children. Socioemotionally, they often showed multiple signs of adjustment problems. As expected, however, there were considerable individual differences in maternal outcomes, with some mothers showing good overall adjustment, some showing generalized difficulties, and some manifesting problems in specific domains. Moreover, there was a great deal of individual instability, particularly in personal adjustment over time. In the next chapter, we examine reasons for these individual differences as we explore relationships among early and later maternal development.

5

Predicting Maternal Outcomes

with Mary O'Callaghan and Tammy L. Dukewich

Although adolescent mothers were shown to be less responsive and more stressed in parenting their infants than adult mothers—and continue to be depressed, anxious, and stressed 5 years later—there was considerable variability in their personal adjustment and parenting skills, with some mothers faring considerably better than others. In this chapter, we seek to understand the sources of their individual differences in the adjustment to parenthood, attempting to explain why some adolescent mothers coped better with their transition to adulthood than others. The specific focus is on identifying the predictors of three important maternal outcomes: (a) parenting at 6 months; (b) risk for child abuse at 1, 3, and 5 years; and (c) maternal adjustment at 3 and 5 years. To accomplish this goal we report new analyses as well as summarize strategic results from our past research.

ANTECEDENTS OF EARLY PARENTING

In the last chapter, as well as in previous publications (Passino et al., 1993; Sommer et al., 1993), we reported that adolescent mothers experienced higher levels of parenting stress and were less responsive and sensitive in their interactions with their infants than adult mothers. In order to develop effective early intervention programs, it is imperative that teen mothers who are at risk for maladaptive parenting be identified as early as possible. The dominant model for understanding the antecedents of competent and incompetent parenting has been provided by Belsky (1984). Four sources of influence on parenting are highlighted in this model: psychological resources, work and marital status, social support, and child characteristics. Although Belsky's (1984) model captures much of the variability in adult parenting, we felt that it provided an incomplete account of parenting and, in particular, failed to emphasize the roles that maternal intelligence and cognitive readiness might play in influencing adolescent parenting.

95

As a consequence, we proposed an expanded model in chapter 2 that contained two new constructs—IQ and readiness to parent—as well as several constructs in Belsky's (1984) original model of adult parenting—namely, social supports, personality, and infant characteristics. We included maternal intelligence based on the assumption that many adolescent mothers operate in a lower range of intelligence and on evidence that parental intelligence is related to the establishment of rich, stimulating language environments for children (Hart & Risley, 1995). Cognitive readiness was emphasized because research suggests that in order to parent effectively mothers need to know how children develop and they need to understand appropriate parenting practices. Because adolescent mothers often struggle with their own developmental crises, including a search for their own identity, we hypothesized that they would be less cognitively prepared for parenthood, especially if this role conflicted with the "required" tasks of adolescent development.

In the next section, we examine the validity of our model as well as several potentially related molar constructs, such as SES, to explain adolescent parenting. To provide a preliminary overview of the antecedents of early parenting practices, we first describe correlations between three sets of predictor variables (prenatal demographic information, prenatal maternal resources, and birth characteristics) and parenting effectiveness.

Demographic Predictors of Parenting

Correlations between three prenatal demographic variables (years of maternal education, SES, and age at childbirth) and parenting measures at 6 months are reported in Table 5.1. Each of these variables were positively correlated with scores on the MIS: Mothers who were older, had more education, and higher SES displayed better interactional skills with their infants. There were also several significant relationships between two of these demographic variables (schooling and SES) and postnatal cognitive readiness measures (including Parenting Attitudes, Style, and Knowledge): Mothers who had completed more years of education and those with higher SES reported a preference for more appropriate parenting styles. In addition, higher SES was associated with greater maternal knowledge about child development and, overall, better maternal preparation for parenting. There were no significant relationships between these prenatal variables and parenting stress.

TABLE 5.1

Correlations Between Prenatal Demographic Factors
and 6-Month Parenting Measures

| Demographics | MIS | 6-Month Parenting Measures | | | | |
		Parenting Attitudes	Parenting Style	Knowledge	Cognitive Readiness[a]	PSI
Years of education	.28**	.13	.17*	.13	.15	-.04
SES	-.23**	-.08	-.17*	-.20*	-.18*	.05
Age at childbirth	.19*	.06	.04	-.03	.04	.05

* $p < .05$. ** $p < .01$.

[a] Composite Score formed by summing standardized scores for the three Cognitive Readiness subscales.

Note. MIS = Maternal Interaction Scale, PSI = Parenting Stress Index

Maternal Resources and Parenting

Relationships between prenatal maternal psychological and social resources and 6-month parenting measures are shown in Table 5.2. Prenatal cognitive readiness (attitudes, style, knowledge, and composite) was the best overall predictor of postnatal (6-month) maternal functioning. In addition to predicting postnatal cognitive readiness, prenatal cognitive readiness was associated with more skilled interactions with infants (MIS) and lower parenting stress (PSI) at 6 months postpartum. Prenatal maternal intelligence was also a good predictor of parenting: Higher maternal IQs were related to more appropriate parenting interactions and better cognitive readiness, but not to parenting stress. In contrast, measures of maternal socioemotional adjustment (social competence, internalizing and externalizing behaviors, and total YSR) were good predictors of parenting stress, but at best were only modestly related to other parenting outcomes. More socially competent and adjusted mothers showed lower stress. In addition, social competence predicted maternal interactional skills: Mothers with greater prenatal social competence had higher maternal interaction skills. Those who reported a greater number of internalizing problems prenatally had a less positive parenting style at 6 months. Finally, total YSR scores were significantly related to Parenting Style, Knowledge of Child Development, and overall cognitive readiness to parent: Mothers reporting more behavioral problems had less optimal parenting attitudes and less parenting knowledge at 6 months. With one exception, prenatal social support was unrelated to 6-month parenting variables; perceived support from friends/partner was associated with lower stress.

TABLE 5.2

Correlations Between Prenatal Resources and 6-Month Parenting Measures

| Prenatal Maternal Variables | MIS | 6-Month Parenting Measures | | | | |
		Parenting Attitudes	Parenting Style	Knowledge	Cognitive Readiness[a]	PSI
Intelligence						
IQ	.20*.	.30**	.39**	.47**	.47**	-.14
Socioemotional						
Social Competence	.17*	.03	.12	.12	.10	-.30**
Internalizing	-.08	-.10	-.16*	-.12	-.15	.40**
Externalizing	-.13	-.06	-.16	-.14	-.14	.39**
Total YSR	-.13	-.12	-.19*	-.16*	-.18*	.43**
Cognitive Readiness						
Parenting Attitude	.32**	.62**	.38**	.36**	.57**	-.26**
Parenting Style	.41**	.47**	.64**	.40**	.61**	-.28**
Knowledge	.17*	.40**	.43**	.63**	.58**	-.28**
(Composite)	.40**	.65**	.64**	.60**	.76**	-.36**
Social Support						
Friend/partner	.14	.11	.13	.14	.15	-.25**
Sibling/mother	.07	.14	.05	-.06	.04	-.12
Extended family	.08	.07	-.04	-.16	-.04	.02

* $p < .05$. ** $p < .01$.

Note. YSR = Youth Self-Report, MIS = Maternal Interaction Scale, PSI = Parenting Stress Index.

[a] Composite score formed by summing standardized scores for the three Cognitive Readiness subscales.

Birth Characteristics and Parenting

Correlations between measures of infant characteristics (birth weight and gestational age) and 6-month parenting revealed no significant relationships. The lack of relationships between variables that defined these two constructs may be due to the fact that there were relatively few very low birth-weight infants in the sample; in turn infant health was likely related to good prenatal care and an absence of significant drug, alcohol, and tobacco problems during pregnancy. Finally, there were no gender-related differences in parenting at 6 months.

PREDICTING PARENTING: A MULTIVARIATE PERSPECTIVE

Regression Analyses:
The Importance of Cognitive Readiness to Parent

In order to determine the amount of variance in parenting at 6 months accounted for by maternal and infant characteristics, demographic variables (maternal age at childbirth, SES, years of education), prenatal maternal resources (IQ, social competence, total YSR score, cognitive readiness, and social support), gender, and birth status (a summary score of birth weight and gestational age) were entered simultaneously into regression equations. The results of these analyses are shown in Table 5.3. Prenatal and child variables accounted for 22% of the variance in the quality of maternal interactions (MIS), 47% of the variance in Parenting Attitudes, 47% of the total variance in Parenting Style, 36% of the variance in Knowledge of Child Development, 59% of the variance in overall cognitive readiness, and 30% of the variance in parenting stress.

With one exception, demographic variables (age at childbirth, SES, and years of education), infant status and gender did not account for unique variance in parenting outcomes, when prenatal maternal resources were entered first into the regression equations; the exception was maternal education which uniquely predicted the quality of maternal interactions. From a prediction standpoint, the regressions analyses and the data in Tables 5.1 and 5.2 indicate that prenatal maternal resources were the best predictors of 6-month parenting outcomes. These analyses also revealed that Cognitive Readiness was the best overall prenatal predictor of parenting, accounting for more total and unique variance in all outcomes than other predictor variables, except for parenting stress that was best predicted by socioemotional adjustment.

TABLE 5.3

Regression of 6-Month Parenting Measures on Prenatal Maternal
and Early Child Characteristics

Parenting Measures	R^2	F	df
MIS	.22	3.19**	(9.100)
Parenting Attitudes	.47	9.90**	(9.99)
Parenting Style	.47	9.77**	(9.99)
Knowledge	.36	6.15**	(9.100)
Cognitive Readiness	.59	15.43**	(9.98)
PSI	.30	4.73**	(9.98)

**$p < .01$.

Note. MIS = Maternal Interaction Scale, PSI = Parenting Stress Index

Evaluating The Model of Adolescent Parenting

Although the results just reported as well as studies like those of Passino et al. (1993)—who found that less well-adjusted pregnant teens reported greater parenting-related stress—and Sommer et al. (1993)—who found that more cognitively prepared mothers experienced less stress and better responsivity— suggest the importance of a variety of maternal characteristics for understanding adolescent parenting, the dynamic interrelationships among these variables as they affect parenting have not been systematically evaluated. For that reason, we examined the utility of the model proposed in chapter 2 for explaining variability in adolescent parenting (O'Callaghan et al., 1999). This model proposes that parenting in adolescent mothers is directly influenced by personal adjustment, cognitive readiness for parenting, social support, and the perception of child characteristics such as temperament. A key hypothesis is that cognitive readiness mediates the effects of social support, maternal intelligence, and personal adjustment on parenting. It is this mediational role of cognitive readiness that we claim is a particularly critical feature of adolescent parenting, although it may also play a role in accounting for variability in adult parenting, especially if the mothers are undereducated, living in poverty, and/or highly stressed.

To examine our model of adolescent parenting, data for four constructs (maternal cognitive readiness, socioemotional adjustment, intelligence, and social supports) were gathered during the last trimester of the mother's pregnancy, whereas data for two other constructs (perceived child characteristics and parenting) were obtained when the infants were 6 months of age. Multiple indicators were employed to define each construct:

1. Parenting quality was measured through the observational rating scale (MIS) that assessed the quality of maternal interactions as well as by a self-report measure of parental style.
2. Socioemotional adjustment (externalization and internalization) was assessed through Achenbach's (1991c) YSR inventory.
3. Intelligence was measured by the Vocabulary and Block Design subscales from the WAIS–R.
4. Perceived child characteristics were defined by measures of maternal perceptions of child temperament and child-induced stress.
5. Social support was indexed through maternal reports about the quality of emotional and instrumental assistance received from family and friends.
6. Finally, cognitive readiness was measured through assessments of maternal knowledge about child development and maternal attitudes about parenting.

Through the application of structural equation modeling (LISREL VIII), we assessed the causal paths hypothesized in our model of adolescent parenting. The results are presented in Fig. 5.1.

As predicted, cognitive readiness played a central role in determining parenting. The effects of two factors previously identified as important in parenting—socioemotional adjustment and intelligence—were found to exert their influence through cognitive readiness to parent. The results reported in Table 5.2 and by Passino et al. (1993) suggested that teenage mothers who have internalizing or externalizing problems are not as likely to parent effectively, with mothers focusing less attention on meeting their child's developmental needs and more on meeting their own personal needs. The results of the O'Callaghan et al. (1999) study extended these findings, suggesting that maternal socioemotional adjustment indirectly influences parenting behavior through its effect on cognitive readiness for parenting. There is an important implication of this finding for designing effective interventions: Changing parenting readiness may influence actual parenting practices only if adjustment problems, such as depression, have been adequately addressed.

The results also indicate that intelligence exerted an indirect influence on adolescent parenting via cognitive readiness. Past research has revealed that less intelligent mothers tend to show less sensitivity in their interactions with their children (Field, 1980; Jarrett; 1982, Roosa &

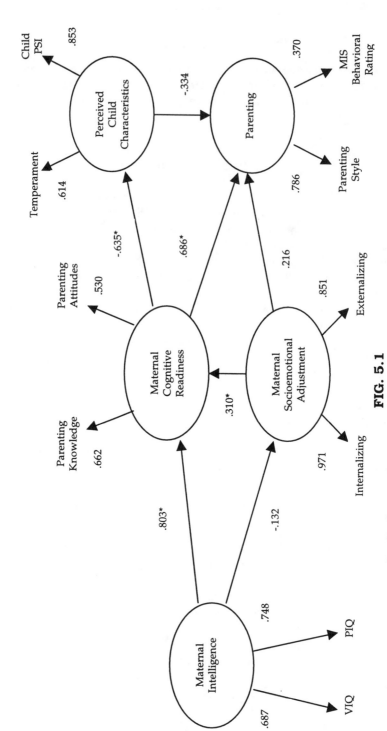

FIG. 5.1

Results of structural equation modeling: A central role for cognitive readiness

*Significant at .05 level

Vaughn, 1984; Sommer et al., 1993). The results of the O'Callaghan et al. (1999) study suggest, however, that this relationship is mediated through cognitive readiness, with less intelligent adolescent mothers displaying less accurate knowledge about child development and parenting practices as well as less appropriate parenting attitudes. Because of inappropriate attitudes and inadequate knowledge, adolescent mothers are less prepared to effectively parent their children at six months of age than adult mothers. In a sense, this is an optimistic finding: Although intelligence per se is difficult to change, cognitive readiness is much more malleable and can be targeted within an intervention framework to improve parenting.

It seems likely that mothers whose understanding of their children's growth and development is less detailed and sophisticated might also perceive "typical" infant behaviors as excessive, annoying, and/or manipulative. Our results generally support this hypothesis and also indicate that mothers who have greater knowledge about development, as well as more appropriate expectations regarding what childrearing actually entails, are not only more likely to have more positive perceptions of their infants but more effective interactions with them (see Fig. 5.1). It may be that women who are more cognitively prepared to parent have a more accurate understanding of the extent of work involved in caring for their infants and, as a consequence, are less stressed than mothers taken by surprise by the amount of time and effort required to parent. Support for this position is provided by our earlier research. Sommer et al. (1993) found that adolescent mothers less cognitively prepared for parenting experienced greater parenting-related stress and were less responsive to their children than more prepared mothers. Moreover, results of a study by Weed, Keogh, and Borkowski (2000) suggested that not only early parenting practices but also changes in parenting during the first 5 years were predicted by cognitive readiness and intelligence, with more cognitively prepared and intelligent mothers showing more positive changes in their parenting practices. In chaper 7, we show that deficiencies in cognitive readiness, manifested during the first year of parenting, not only negatively impacted parent–infant interactions but also hindered children's emotional and cognitive development during the preschool and early elementary school years.

Finally, two other findings from the O'Callaghan et al. (1999) study are noteworthy. Although the path from cognitive readiness to perceived child characteristics was significant, the latter construct did not influence parenting, as originally hypothesized (see Fig. 5.1). It is possible that the failure to find a direct relationship between perceived child characteristics and parenting (although marginally significant) may be related to the nature of adolescence as a unique stage of development. That is, the parenting practice of teen mothers, because of excessive egocentrism, may be less influenced by their perceptions of their children than typically occurs with adult mothers.

The results of O'Callaghan et al. (1999) also indicate that social support, as defined by maternal reports about emotional relationships and expected support, did not enter into the causal network related to parenting during the first year of life. This finding may be related to our choice of measures of social support. If alternative measures of support had been employed (such as maternal satisfaction with social supports), it is possible that this construct would have played a more important causal role. Recent research has, however, shown that social support is a more complex, and less predictable, construct among adolescent parents than among adult parents (cf. Spieker & Bensley, 1994). At times, support from family, especially the child's grandmother, is associated with diminished maternal involvement in childrearing. Either too little, or too much, support can have negative consequence on the young mothers' "commitments to parenting" and the occurrence of repeat pregnancies (cf. Apfel & Seitz, 1999)

ADOLESCENT MOTHERS AND CHILD ABUSE POTENTIAL

Adolescent parenthood not only places adolescent mothers at high risk for insensitive and ineffective parenting but also for punitive and abusive practices (Schellenbach, Whitman, & Borkowski, 1992). According to Bolton (1990), 36% to 51% of all abused children are raised by adolescent mothers. This estimate is especially striking because a much smaller proportion of all children (20%) are actually born to adolescent mothers. Nevertheless, Bolton's estimate makes sense given the numerous contextual similarities between adolescent parents and maltreating parents—such as poverty, social isolation, and a poor understanding of child development—which may, collectively, provide the foundations for the development of abusive or neglectful behaviors. Connelly and Strauss (1992) found that a mother's age at the birth of her first child was a significant predictor of the occurrence of physical abuse, even when other variables, such as income, race, and education were controlled. Furthermore, extensive analysis of data from the state of Illinois indicated that by age 5 children born to younger mothers (age 17 or younger) were about one and one-half more times likely to be victims of child abuse than to those born to older mothers (ages 20 and 21; Maynard, 1997).

Because many of the factors that place young parents at risk for child abuse and/or neglect are likely present before a child's birth or shortly thereafter, early identification of risk factors is especially important for prevention efforts. Research has identified numerous variables that differentiate abusive from nonabusive families. Belsky (1980) proposed that the causes and correlates of abuse can be divided into five major categories: psychological disturbances in parents, abuse eliciting characteristics of children, dysfunctional patterns of family interactions, stress inducing social forces, and abuse-promoting cultural values. Azar (1991), reviewing the research on the etiology of child maltreatment, identified similar factors embedded in five different models of abuse:

1. Perpetrator models suggesting that parental maladjustment is an important factor.
2. Child-based models focusing on the child's role in evoking abusive patterns.
3. Interactional models stressing the mismatch between parental expectations and children's behavior.
4. Contextual models emphasizing environmental stressors.
5. Social models suggesting society's validation of violence as instrumental in the development of child abuse and neglect.

In the Notre Dame Parenting Project, we were particularly interested in examining how prenatal maternal characteristics were related to child abuse potential, and providing a test of Azar's (1991) perpetrator model that emphasizes the causal role of psychological disturbances. In addition to maternal socioemotional adjustment, we analyzed maternal cognitive and social resources, parenting characteristics, and several child characteristics as additional potential causal factors of child abuse.

Child Abuse Potential and Cognitive Readiness

A short form of the CAPI was administered to mothers 1 year, 3 years, and 5 years postpartum. Average scores on the CAPI at these time points were 8.67 ($SD = 4.26$), 9.00 ($SD = 4.17$), and 8.66 ($SD = 3.95$), respectively. A repeated measures ANOVA conducted on CAPI scores at the aforementioned three time points revealed no significant changes in these scores over time. Moreover, the shortened CAPI showed significant stability; coefficients of stability were .71 ($N = 102$) between 1 and 3 years, .69 ($N = 98$) between 1 and 5 years, and .62 ($N = 124$) between 3 and 5 years. Because only subtest scores were obtained on the shortened version of the CAPI, normative clinical interpretations were not possible. However, in this chapter, as well as in chapter 7, we evaluate the validity of this instrument by examining its relationship with maternal adjustment as well as child development.

Table 5.4 provides a detailed picture of the relationships between teen mothers' scores on the CAPI and their prenatal characteristics, parenting characteristics, and their infant's birth characteristics. The data in this table reflect relationships at 1, 3, and 5 years. In general, the best predictors of child abuse potential were prenatal and postnatal cognitive readiness, prenatal IQ, and the quality of interactions at 6 months.

Interestingly, no significant relationships among maternal demographic variables and child abuse potential scores were found. However, lower birth weight was associated with higher CAPI scores at 3 and 5 years. Although this association could be interpreted as support for a child-based model of abuse (Azar, 1991), it could also be related to characteristics of adolescent mothers that prevented their seeking prenatal care and promoted prepartum stress. Surprisingly, and contrary to Azar's perpetrator model, prenatal socioemotional adjustment as measured by the YSR, was not a significant predictor of CAPI scores with one exception: High scores on the internalizing scale were significantly related to higher CAPI scores at 1 year. Finally, it is not surprising that social support variables were not correlated with CAPI scores, given the absence of significant paths from prenatal social support to parenting at 6-months postpartum.

In contrast, prenatal maternal IQ significantly predicted CAPI scores at 1, 3, and 5 years, with lower prenatal IQ scores associated with greater risk for child abuse. Moreover, all prenatal cognitive readiness measures (Parenting Attitudes, Style, and Knowledge) predicted CAPI scores at each of the three time points: Adolescent mothers who were less prepared for parenting were at greater risk for abusing their children. Similarly, mothers who had lower cognitive readiness scores at 6 months, as well as those who were less appropriate in their interactions with their children, were at greater risk for child abuse at each of the three time points. Finally, mothers with lower stress levels at 6 months had lower CAPI scores at both 1 and 5 years.

A series of regression analyses was performed to assess the amount of variance in CAPI scores across time predicted by the prenatal maternal and infant measures listed in Table 5.4, as well as child gender. To conserve power, several composites were formed, specifically of those measures used to index demographics, socioemotional adjustment, cognitive readiness, social support and child characteristics, and used as predictors. At 1 year, 47% of the variance in CAPI scores was accounted for by the early measures $[F (9,77) = 7.49, p < .01]$, at 3 years 40% $[F (9,82) = 6.09, p < .0 1]$, and at 5 years 38% $[F (9,82) = 5.55, p < .01]$. Cognitive readiness was the best maternal predictor of CAPI scores, as well as the only variable accounting for unique variance at each time point. Child gender, however, also accounted for a small amount of unique variance at 1 and 5 years. When SES was added to the regression model, it failed to account for unique variance.

TABLE 5.4

Prenatal Maternal and Early Child Predictors of Maternal Child Abuse Potential

	Predictors	Child Abuse Potential (CAPI)		
		1 Year	3 Years	5 Years
Demographics	Education	-.11	-.12	-.12
	SES	.14	.17	.09
	Age at childbirth	-.01	-.09	- .03
Prenatal Maternal Resources	IQ	-.42**	-.46**	-.42**
	Social Competence	-.06	-.08	-.12
	Internalizing	.20*	.07	.11
	Externalizing	.01	.03	.10
	Total YSR	.16	.08	.14
	Parenting Attitudes	-.31**	-.42**	-.36**
	Parenting Style	-.50**-	.43**	.37**
	Knowledge	-.42**	-.43**	- .37**
	Cognitive Readiness (Composite)	-.56**	-.55**	- .48**
	Friends/partner[a]	-.04	-.09	-.12
	Siblings/mother[a]	.03	.01	.07
	Extended family[a]	-.05	.09	-.09
Early Child Characteristics	Birth weight	-.17	-.21*	- .23*
	Gestational age	-.08	-.14	- .04
6-Month Parenting Measures	MIS	-.37**	-.33**	-.32**
	Cognitive Readiness (Composite)	-.55**	-.48**	-.48**
	PSI	.24*	.17	.25*

* $p < .05$. ** $p < .01$.

Note. YSR = Youth Self-Report, MIS = Maternal Interaction Scale, PSI = Parenting Stress Index.

[a] Source of Social Support.

The gender results were unexpected: Mothers of female children were found to display a greater potential for child abuse at 1 [$t(127)$= 2.05, $p < .05$], and 5 years [$t(138) = 2.69, p < .01$]. Furthermore, the mean CAPI score for mothers of girls was higher at three years, although not significantly different, from that for mothers of boys. Although girls appeared to be at greater risk of child abuse than boys, gender differences can be explained, in part, by preexisting maternal differences. The gender differences in the 1-year CAPI scores was no longer present once prenatal attitudes toward punishment were controlled through analyses of covariance. Controlling for these preexisting differences also reduced the gender effect on 5-year CAPI scores, although it was still marginally significant [$F (1, 127) = 3.50, p = .06$]. These analyses suggest the attitudes toward punishment were formed even before the children were born. It appears that those adolescents in our sample who held more punitive attitudes during pregnancy happened, by chance, to have girls rather than boys. More generally, these results indicate the importance of researchers controlling for preexisting prenatal attitudinal differences before assessing gender-related differences in the development of abuse.

A series of regression analyses was also conducted to determine the amount of variance in CAPI scores predicted from the 6-month parenting measures (MIS, postnatal cognitive readiness, and stress). At 1, 3, and 5 years, CAPI scores were regressed on 6-month MIS, PSI, and postnatal cognitive readiness scores. These parenting measures were found to account for a significant amount of variance in child abuse potential at all time points; specifically, at 1-year, 31% of the variance [$F (3,82) = 12.34, p < .01$]; at 3 years, 27% of the variance [$F (3,92) = 11.07, p < .01$]; and at 5 years, 23% of the variance [$F (3,92) = 9.11, p < .01$]. Cognitive readiness was again the only unique predictor of CAPI scores at each time point. The results of these regressions, in conjunction with the data in Table 5.4, indicate that cognitive readiness, both prenatal and postnatal was the best predictor of maternal child abuse potential, accounting for both more total and unique variance.

We next examined whether cognitive readiness to parent might have a differential influence on CAPI scores, depending on the level of maternal stress. We hypothesized that less cognitively prepared mothers would have higher CAPI scores, especially under conditions of higher stress. This expectation was confirmed: 38% of the variance in 1-year CAPI scores was explained by parenting style, parenting stress, and the interaction between style and stress [$F (3,100) = 20.81, p < .0001$], suggesting that both factors need to be targeted in order to reduce the potential for early appearing abuse and neglect.

In summary, maternal cognitive readiness not only plays a critical, mediating role in parenting behavior, as revealed in the O'Callaghan et al. (1999) study, but also influences child abuse potential. Prevention programs, aimed at identifying mothers at risk for abuse and neglect, need to evaluate maternal knowledge about child development, attitudes toward the parenting role and their parenting style preferences—especially the tendency to use punishment. To the extent that these aspects of parenting are deficient, remedial steps need to be implemented as early as possible in the mother's parenting career. Without early intervention, the adolescent mother is likely to be overwhelmed by her parenting responsibilities, thereby increasing the likelihood of child abuse and/or neglect.

Predicting Child Abuse Potential:
The Mediational Role of Aggressive Coping

Wolfe (1987) described the psychological processes linked to the expression of anger and abusive parenting, emphasizing the importance of parental stress and the preference for verbally aggressive punitive parenting practices. He pointed out that during childhood and early adolescence, children normally learn to inhibit aggressive tendencies. Conflicting messages in our culture—that seem to endorse violence as an appropriate means for obtaining compliance from others and yet punish those who use it excessively or at the wrong place and time—can serve to complicate if not inhibit the development of normal regulatory processes. If such messages have greater impact on adolescent than adult parents, because they are under greater stress and still in the process of attitude formation, the internalization process related to the inhibition of aggression may be disrupted. This scenario may explain why adolescent parents tend to be more at risk for child abuse than adult parents.

In a project by Dukewich et al., (1996), four major classes of risk factors for child abuse (maternal psychological adjustment, infant characteristics, social supports, and parenting preparation) were examined as predictors of child abuse potential in teenage mothers. A major goal was to evaluate the hypothesis that the psychological propensity for aggressive coping mediates the relationship between maternal and child risk factors and an early indicator of maltreatment (performance on the CAPI).

To examine the role of propensity for aggression in child abuse, we used data from the Notre Dame Parenting Project at three time points: Prenatally, 6 months after birth, and 1 year postnatally (Dukewich et al., 1996). Three components of a maternal risk composite were assessed prenatally: social support, socioemotional adjustment, and preparation for parenting. The index of social support contained a measure of financial support (SES) and a maternal self-report measure of the quality of emotional support received from mother, father, siblings, partner, extended family, and friends. A global measure of psychological adjustment was obtained using the YSR (Achenbach, 1991c). The third risk construct—preparation for parenting—was assessed via two self-report questionnaires from our cognitive readiness inventory that measured the mother's knowledge and expectancies about child development and her beliefs about her parenting role (child-centeredness and role reversal). A fourth component of the risk composite, child temperament, was assessed during an interview conducted approximately 6 months after birth. Measures of parenting stress, assessed through the PSI, and parenting style, evaluated through a questionnaire in the cognitive readiness inventory, were used as indices of the psychological predisposition for aggressive coping construct at 6 months. Finally, when children were 1 year old, mothers completed the abbreviated version of the CAPI (Milner, 1986).

Our results provided partial support for Belsky's (1980) and Azar's (1991) conceptualizations of child abuse. The four specific components evaluated by Dukewich et al. (1996)—social support, maternal socioemotional adjustment, parenting preparation, and child temperament— were significantly related to abuse potential in adolescent mothers. Consistent with results reported in the last section, componential analysis of the model's risk factors revealed that not all of the prenatal and early childhood constructs were equally effective in predicting abuse potential, confirming our expectation that some factors would be less salient in predicting maltreatment for adolescent mothers than for the general population. Whereas parenting preparation had a strong relationship with abuse potential—with less prepared teenage mothers having higher child abuse potential scores—and child temperament had a marginally significant relationship, social support and maternal psychological adjustment were unrelated to abuse potential.

Most importantly, one of the two components that defined the predisposition for aggressive coping construct—parenting style—was found to mediate the relationship between the maternal risk factors and abuse potential. The finding that the predisposition for aggressive coping construct acted as a mediator in predicting abuse potential is consistent with the notion that a mother's preference for punishment as childrearing technique provides an important link in understanding the relationship between prenatal maternal risk factors (particularly parenting preparation) and abuse potential: Pregnant adolescents who possessed less knowledge about how children develop and inappropriate attitudes about their parenting role tended to endorse punitive parenting practices during infancy; this endorsement, in turn, mediated the effect of maternal knowledge and attitudes on abuse potential at 1 year.

Although parental endorsement of a punitive parenting style, which is often causally implicated in the development of abusive parenting, accounted for the observed mediational relationship, perceptions of stress—also frequently associated in past research with abuse—did not act as a mediator. However, as pointed out in the previous section, mothers who were less cognitively prepared for parenting and experiencing greater stress had higher CAPI scores. Thus, it appears that even though parenting stress does not mediate the influence of maternal cognitive readiness on child abuse potential, it does appear to moderate this influence.

These results, in combination, indicate that although stress does not directly influence the expression of abusive behavior, it sets the stage for aggressive behavior to occur, with tolerance for punitive parenting practices providing the critical additional ingredient necessary for evoking physical abuse. Based on these results, it would seem appropriate that intervention programs, designed to prevent child abuse, should begin early—optimally before children are born—and be directed at increasing maternal knowledge about child development and the parenting process, at modifying maternal attitudes about punishment as an acceptable parenting technique, and at decreasing the stress mothers are experiencing.

PREDICTING THE TRANSITION TO ADULTHOOD

As pointed out in the last chapter, relatively little is known about the changing life patterns of adolescent mothers; still less is known about how the early characteristics of adolescent mothers shape their later lives. The results presented in chapter 4 emphasized that when their children had reached 5 years of age, adolescent mothers were generally operating in the low average range of intellectual functioning, with many demonstrating clinical levels of depression, anxiety, and low self-esteem. They were generally unmarried, with two children and unemployed. Although most had completed high school, they were typically not pursuing additional education or job training in a systematic, planful way. These findings are consistent with past research that indicates that early parenting is associated with a constellation of less than optimal developmental outcomes for teen mothers and a tendency to become trapped in poverty (Beardslee et al., 1988; Card & Wise, 1978; Hayes, 1987; Mott & Marsigliano, 1985).

Although these data characterize adolescent mothers in general, our data also indicates that there were striking individual differences in maternal outcomes, with some mothers showing good overall functioning, some showing generalized difficulties, and others manifesting problems in specific areas. To the extent that early precursors of later maternal adjustment problems can be identified, the possibility of developing effective, targeted prevention programs is increased. In the next section, we examine the early antecedents of maternal functioning 3 and 5 years after the birth of the teen's first child.

Early Correlates of Later Maternal Adjustment

Correlational analyses between prenatal maternal characteristics, early parenting characteristics, and maternal outcomes at 3 and 5 years were conducted. Because the patterns in the correlational matrices were similar between maternal predictors and outcomes at three and 5 years, only data at 5 years are presented. As can be seen in Table 5.5, the best overall predictors of 5-year outcomes were Block Design, prenatal Cognitive Readiness (especially the knowledge subscale), the Internalizing scale from the YSR, and 6-month Cognitive Readiness.

Signs of depression at 5 years postpartum were associated with lower Block Design, lower Cognitive Readiness (both prenatal and postnatal) and higher Internalizing scores. In addition, mothers with higher self-esteem had better cognitive readiness (prenatal and postnatal), more satisfactory socioemotional adjustment, more social support from extended family, and lower parenting stress. State anxiety was associated with lower Block Design, Cognitive Readiness, and adjustment scores. Trait anxiety was predicted by poor Block Design performance and greater internalization, whereas life stress was predicted only by internalization.

In order to determine the total variance explained by the set of predictor variables, 5-year maternal outcomes were regressed on prenatal maternal and 6-month parenting measures. Prenatal IQ, the prenatal Cognitive Readiness, Social Competence, total YSR, total social support, and 6-month MIS and stress were entered simultaneously into regression equations to predict each maternal outcome. The maternal variables were associated with a significant amount of variance in maternal depression [$R^2 = .17$, $F(7,79) = 2.29$, $p < .05$], as well as self-esteem [$R^2 = .17$, $F(7,78) = 2.34$, $p < .05$]. The specific predictors of depression were maternal adjustment, Cognitive Readiness, and IQ, whereas self-esteem was predicted by these same prenatal variables plus social competence and stress at 6 months. It should be noted, however, that neither prenatal nor 6-month variables contributed uniquely to these results.

TABLE 5.5
Correlation of Prenatal Measures and 6-Month Parenting
with 5-Year Maternal Adjustment

| | | | 5-Year Measures | | |
Measures	Beck Depression	Coopersmith Self-Esteem	State Anxiety	Trait Anxiety	Life Stress
Intelligence					
Vocabulary	-.13	.10	-.06	-.06	-.04
Block Design	-.25**	.17	-.17*	-.19*	.02
Cognitive Readiness					
Parenting Attitudes	-.05	.09	-.05	.02	.02
Parenting Style	-.26**	.17	-.13	-.14	-.01
Knowledge	-.29**	.21*	-.22*	-.09	.03
Composite	-.27**	.20*	-.18*	-.10	.01
Socioemotional Adjustment					
Social Competence	-.11	.21*	-.14	-.14	-.05
Internalizing	.31**	-.31**	.26**	.36**	.22*
Externalizing	.10	-.20*	-.18*	-.10	.08
Social Support					
Friend/partner	-.05	.03	.09	.09	.15
Mother/siblings	-.04	.10	.04	.03	.01
Extended family	-.16	.19*	.02	-.13	-.03
6-month Parenting Measures					
MIS	-.14	.14	.00	-.02	-.04
PSI	.18	-.33**	.07	.13	-.04
Cognitive Readiness Composite	-.22*	.29**	-.10	-.08	-.06

*p < .05. **p < .01.

Note. MIS = Maternal Interaction Scale, PSI = Parenting Stress Index.

Maternal Perceptions, Resources, and Later Outcomes

Guided by our model of parenting and using data from the Notre Dame Parenting Project, Mylod, Whitman, and Borkowski (1997) examined relationships among prenatal maternal resources, mothers' early perceptions of parenting, and later maternal outcomes. Several specific hypotheses were investigated: Mothers with greater resources during pregnancy were expected to have more positive perceptions of their parenting roles and experiences as well as their children's dispositions. In addition, it was predicted that mothers with more positive perceptions about their parenting roles would experience more favorable developmental outcomes. Finally, the extent to which the influence of maternal resources on later maternal outcomes was mediated by maternal perceptions about parenting was explored.

Data collection occurred on three occasions: prenatally, when children were 6 months old, and again when children were 3 years of age. Composite scores for maternal personal resources (intelligence, cognitive readiness for parenting, social supports, and socioemotional adjustment) and 6-month maternal perceptions (mothers' perceptions of parenting stress and their children's temperament) were formed. At 3 years, several maternal composite indicators of life adjustment were formed, including a demographic composite (educational attainment, subsequent children, employment, and marital status), a personal adjustment composite (self-esteem, anxiety, and depression), a cognitive ability composite (Vocabulary and Block Design), and a parenting composite (the quality of mother–child interactions and child abuse potential).

Support was found for the hypothesis that the prenatal resources of adolescent mothers would subsequently influence personal perceptions as well as perceptions about their children. An overall significant relationship was found between prenatal maternal resources and maternal perceptions at 6 months postpartum. When the resource composite was subanalyzed, results indicated that, with the exception of social support, maternal resource variables (cognitive ability, cognitive readiness for parenting, and socioemotional adjustment) were each correlated with maternal perceptions: Mothers with lower intellectual ability, less cognitive preparation for parenting, and poorer socioemotional adjustment perceived their children as more difficult and their parenting task as more stressful.

At a more global level, the hypothesis that composite resources and composite perceptions would predict maternal functioning when the children were 3 years of age was also confirmed. Resources and perceptions were, however, found to relate differentially to maternal outcomes. Whereas the composite of prenatal maternal resources predicted later maternal cognitive ability, socioemotional functioning, abuse potential, and maternal interactional style, the composite of postnatal perceptions only predicted three of these outcomes (maternal cognitive ability, abuse potential, and maternal interactional style) but also the demographic composite. The prenatal maternal resource predictors accounted for unique variance in later maternal intelligence, personal functioning, abuse potential, and maternal interactional style, whereas the maternal perception composite accounted for unique variance in maternal interactional style and demographic outcomes. Thus, prenatal resources and postnatal perceptions were differentially associated with the various outcomes.

Interestingly, maternal perceptions were found to mediate the association between prenatal maternal resources and parenting, suggesting that resources and perceptions are dynamically linked in influencing parenting: Mothers with fewer cognitive resources perceived their children as more difficult; in turn, these parental perceptions were associated with maladaptive parenting behavior. This finding is consistent with Nover et al. (1984) contention that adult interactions with children are based as much on the parent's perceptions and expectations about children's behaviors as on children's actual characteristics.

Surprisingly, no significant relationships were found among any of the prenatal maternal resources and maternal demographic outcomes. Life course outcomes were predicted only by maternal perceptions. It may be that mothers who were stressed by their parenting role saw fewer options for themselves, educationally and vocationally. Their perceptions may in turn have led to lower expectations about their future opportunities and to increase reliance on others for support.

DISCUSSION

In summary, the results reported in this chapter suggest that the life trajectories of teenage mothers are established early and that the course of development can be predicted using information about early appearing maternal characteristics, such as maternal IQ (especially Block Design performance), cognitive readiness (especially knowledge and style), and internalizing behaviors (especially depression). These results are generally compatible with the conceptualizations of Belsky's (1984) model of parenting and with our model of adolescent parenting (see chap. 2), both of which were formulated to provide insights into the types of maternal resources that influence parenting practices. The results reported in this chapter also suggest the general utility of our adolescent parenting model for understanding individual differences. The model appears to explain not only early parenting practices but also child abuse potential and later maternal adjustment. Finally, the results support Hill's (1958) ABCX model, which suggests that life adjustment is not only a function of a mothers' resources but also of her perceptions of potentially stressful events. Indeed, maternal stress perceptions emerged in our data analyses as both a moderator and a mediator of the impact of prenatal maternal resources on life course development and change.

Of all the constructs in our model, cognitive readiness for parenting was shown to have broad-based importance. For instance, examination of the antecedents of 6-month parenting indicated that the best predictor of the behavioral, cognitive, and affective components of maternal functioning was prenatal cognitive readiness. Results of the O'Callaghan et al. (1999) study suggested that cognitive readiness mediated the impact of two important maternal variables—IQ and socioemotional adjustment—on parenting during the first year of life. Prenatal cognitive readiness was also the best predictor of child abuse potential at 1, 3, and 5 years. Results by Dukewich et al. (1996) suggested that one component of cognitive readiness, parenting style, which reflected the parents' endorsement of punishment as an acceptable and sometimes desirable parenting practice—was a particularly sensitive indicator of later abuse potential. More specifically, those pregnant adolescents who were less prepared for parenting tended, once they became parents, to prefer punishment as a childrearing technique; in turn, this preference was associated with increased abuse potential during the first 5 years of life.

Finally, our results showed that cognitive readiness was a major predictor of later maternal functioning. For instance, adolescent mothers who possessed greater prenatal personal resources—including greater cognitive readiness, higher intelligence, and better socioemotional adjustment—fared better as they entered young adulthood than adolescent mothers with fewer resources. Based on these results, the development of a risk index that includes information about these maternal and social variables, and particularly maternal cognitive readiness, should prove useful in identifying mothers most at risk for long-term developmental problems. Such analyses are undertaken in chapter 8, as we search for factors associated with vulnerable and resilient mothers and children.

The findings presented in this chapter have emphasized the importance of preparing adolescent mothers for their transition to adulthood by helping them to better understand the required parenting tasks as well as the potential difficulties and obstacles they may confront as parents. Prenatal interventions directed at improving knowledge concerning how their children will develop and how to parent more actively and sensitively should help young mothers develop more accurate perceptions of the appropriateness of their children's behavior and better strategies for coping with, and facilitating, their development. Moreover, helping mothers gain control over two important domains—stress and parenting—should improve their overall sense of self-esteem and self-efficacy as well as reduce their potential for abuse and neglect. Because adolescent mothers are more prone to experience depression, it is important to address this condition during pregnancy, or soon after, and to continue necessary supports in order to maintain gains achieved through early interventions as mothers enter into their adult parenting roles. These new roles become even more complex as additional children are born, relationships change, government assistance declines, and the challenges of parenting preadolescent children—often in the context of poverty and crime—increase. In short, early interventions need to program techniques that maintain gains through the creation of new life-styles, clearer visions and realistic hopes for the future, enhanced self-agency, and more effective support systems.

6

Developmental Delays in Children of Adolescent Mothers

with Mary O'Callaghan and Christine C. Willard

Children born to adolescent mothers are likely to experience more adverse developmental outcomes than those born to adult mothers. Developmental problems in children with teenage mothers seem to appear early and often endure throughout childhood and adolescence (Furstenburg et al., 1987). Problems may appear in cognitive, socioemotional, adaptive, and/or academic functioning. Comprehensive projects, such as those conducted in New York City (Belmont et al., 1981) and Great Britain (Record, McKeown, & Edwards, 1969) as well as the National Perinatal Project (Broman, 1981), and NLSY suggest that the age of mothers predicts later deficits in their offspring, even when factors such as SES are held constant.

Delays and problems in child functioning often appear early. Culp, Osofsky, and O'Brien (1996) found that 1-year-old infants of adolescent mothers had fewer vocalizations than infants of adult mothers. Sandler (1979) found lower developmental assessment scores among 9-month-old infants of adolescent mothers compared to a control group of infants of adult mothers. Maracek (1979) reported that infants of adolescent mothers performed less well than infants of adult mothers on the Bayley Scales of Infant Development at 8 months of age, the SBIS at 4 years, and WISC at 7 years. In an early longitudinal study of children born to teenage mothers, less than 5% of the sample scored above average on the SBIS, whereas a disproportionate number (25%) scored below an IQ of 79 (Hardy, Welcher, Stanley, & Dallas, 1978). Broman (1981) found shorter gestational ages, lower birth weights, and poorer Apgar scores in newborns, as well as lower IQs, higher rates of mental retardation, delayed motor development, and higher frequencies of deviant behaviors among

119

the 4-year-old children of teenage mothers. A higher incidence of cerebral palsy and battered child syndrome was also noted.

Belmont et al. (1981), using multiple regression analyses, found a small but consistently positive relationship between maternal age and children's IQs in three different data sets, especially notable because a variety of social and demographic factors associated with IQ, including age and race of child, family size, parent educational level, family income, caretaker status, employment, residential area, and teenage mother status, were controlled: As age of the teen mothers increased, so did their children's IQs. In a recent analysis of data from the NLSY and the National Study of Children, Moore, Morrison, and Greene (1997) found that younger adolescent mothers typically provided a less stimulating home environment for their children and that the children were delayed cognitively relative to children born to older mothers, even after controlling for SES. They further reported that the negative association between cognitive development and age was stronger within the African-American population and that subsequent children born to women who were adolescent mothers were similarly disadvantaged.

Socioemotional problems in children of adolescent mothers have been less widely reported. Although research has not extensively explored the socioemotional and behavioral competencies of children of adolescent mothers, the available evidence suggests that development in these domains is adversely affected (Dubow & Luster, 1990; Furstenberg, Brooks-Gunn, & Morgan, 1987). Furstenberg (1976) described children parented by teenagers as sometimes unable to complete preschool inventories because of severe physical and/or psychological handicaps. Maracek (1979) found that young children of adolescent mothers were overly conforming and uncommunicative, whereas older children were often hostile and resentful of authority. Aggressiveness, impulsiveness, and distractibility have also been found in children with teenage mothers (Hechtman, 1989).

Several studies have employed the CBCL or an abbreviated version of the CBCL (the Behavior Problem Index) to assess the socioemotional adjustment of children of adolescent mothers. Dubow and Luster (1990) using data from the NLSY reported that children of adolescent mothers had elevated scores on both Total Behavior Problems and Antisocial Behavior Problems, compared to the normed data from the general population. In a more recent study, Spieker, Larson, Lewis, Keller, and Gilchrist (1999) reported that 33% of a sample of 180 six-year-old children of adolescent mothers scored in the clinical range (above the 84th percentile) on the CBCL and 36% in the clinical range (above the 84th percentile) according to the TRF. Surprisingly, Moore et al. (1997) reported that children born to mothers under the age of 18 had fewer behavior problems than those born to 18- and 19-year-old mothers; this finding may be due to greater family support and involvement among younger mothers.

Another way to understand socioemotional dysfunction is to examine attachment patterns in children of adolescent mothers. Although studies of attachment in disadvantaged families have sometimes utilized samples containing a high proportion of single and adolescent mothers (e.g., Egeland & Farber, 1984), only a few studies have explicitly addressed the issue of attachment in infants with adolescent parents. Frodi et al. (1984) found that only 53% of the infants they studied were classified as securely attached to their adolescent mothers. Although this proportion of securely attached infants is less than the 70% expected in a middle-class sample (Ainsworth et al., 1978), it did not differ appreciably from the 55% secure rate found in another low SES sample (Vaughn, Egeland, Sroufe, & Waters, 1979). Relatedly, Lamb, Hopps, and Elster (1987) found that attachment classification in infants of teen versus adult mothers was significantly different, with more infants of teens in the "distal" subgroups (A1 through B2) than in the "contact seeking" subgroups (B3 through C2).

More recently, two major studies on attachment in children of adolescent mothers were conducted, both using the disorganized (D) classification. Spieker and Bensley (1994) studied 197 adolescent mother–infant pairs. When compared to the distribution for normative, low-risk U.S. samples, they found significantly more insecurely attached infants (50%) and more infants in the "distal" subscategories than would be expected in an adult sample. The proportion of insecure attachment was comparable to samples of low SES, high-risk families in which some of the cases are known to be maltreating or neglectful. In another study of children of adolescent mothers, Ward and Carlson (1995) found that 51% of the children were insecurely attached, with a high percentage being either avoidant (21.8%) or disorganized (18%).

To the best of our knowledge, the Notre Dame Parenting Project is the first study to examine adaptive behavior in children of adolescent mothers. We anticipated children would have particular difficulties in the communication and social areas due to related cognitive and socioemotional problems. It has been estimated that up to 10% of infants born to adolescent mothers will be diagnosed as mentally retarded prior to adolescence (Broman, 1981). This incidence level is approximately three times greater than for the population as a whole. Because the diagnosis of mental retardation requires not only intellectual deficits, but adaptive behavior limitations as well, understanding the development of adaptive behavior in children with teenage mothers is crucial.

Early socioemotional dysfunction, in combination with diminished early intellectual-cognitive capacities, would seem to set the stage in children of adolescent mothers for multiple developmental and academic problems once they enter school. A review of the psychological and academic histories of children born to teenage mothers indicates that differences between children of teenage and adult parents become increasingly evident as development unfolds. Brooks-Gunn and Furstenberg (1986) found higher levels of academic and behavioral problems in children of teen mothers, especially in middle and secondary school where more than 50% of these children repeated a grade or showed disruptive behaviors.

Moore et al. (1997), reporting on data from the NLSY and controlling for SES and other background factors, concluded that children of adolescent mothers were more likely to repeat a grade and less likely to be described as "the best in the class." In a related analysis Haveman, Wolfe, and Peterson (1997) reported that being born to an adolescent mother reduces a youth's chances of graduating from high school, over and above other background factors. Not all the data, however, is consistent with these conclusions; Dubow and Luster's (1990) analysis of the achievement data indicated children with adolescent mothers performed within the average ranges in math (PIAT Math) and reading (PIAT Reading Recognition and Reading Comprehension).

In summary, numerous investigators have found cognitive, socioemotional, adaptive, and achievement-related problems in children of adolescent mothers. These children, and their developmental problems likely challenge teenage mothers who find parenting of even "typically developing" children to be often difficult and demanding. If adolescent mothers do not possess the internal coping resources, and the external supports, required to handle challenging children (e.g., those with ADHD), their parenting practices may exacerbate existing developmental delays or produce new problems such as estrangement from the nuclear family.

CHILD DEVELOPMENT IN THE NOTRE DAME PARENTING PROJECT

In this chapter, we describe the development of the children of adolescent mothers in the Notre Dame Parenting Project. In contrast to studies of adolescents mothers and children in large urban studies, our sample of children have mothers who are on average older, less disadvantaged socioeconomically, less involved in drugs and alcohol, and more likely to remain in school until obtaining a diploma. Our study also differs from previous projects in the comprehensiveness of its developmental analysis. The data reported in this section were obtained at birth and when children were 6 months, 1, 3, and 5 years of age. At these various time points we examine outcomes related to physical, intellectual, adaptive, academic, and sociooemotional development. Additionally, we evaluate interrelationships among these various domains at each time point, as well as determine the stability of functioning within each domain. We also examine how early and later child development are related, within and between multiple domains of development. At the end of this chapter, we take a preliminary look at how a segment of the sample is performing academically when they reach 8 years of age.

Birth Characteristics

As a group, infants in the sample were healthy at birth. Their weight ranged from 1,670 to 5,018 grams (3.68–11.06 pounds) and averaged 3,205 grams (7.06 pounds). There were 25 infants (9% of sample) weighing below 2,500 grams (a conventional cutoff for determining low birth weight) but no *very* low birth weight babies (less than 1,500 grams). Their gestational ages ranged from 32 to 44 weeks, averaging 39.56 weeks. There were 21 infants (8% of sample) born before 37 weeks, a conventional cutoff for classifying preterm infants. Apgar scores averaged 7.7 at 1 minute (range of 1–10) and 8.9 at 5 minutes (range of 4–10). The average birth characteristics of these children are similar to those children of adult parents, although their distributions for these characteristics are somewhat more negatively skewed.

Motor, Cognitive, and Language Development

In this section we present data describing the motor, cognitive, and language functioning of the children during the first 5-years of their life, as reflected in their performance on the Bayley Scales of Infant Development, the SBIS (Form L-M), the PPVT-R, the DVMI and the Math and Reading subscales of the PIAT. Table 6.1 presents these various developmental outcomes at 6 months, 1 year, 3 years, and 5 years. Based on the Bayley assessments, mental and motor development appeared normal at 6 months and 1 year. However, 3- and 5-year assessments indicated marked deficiencies in intellectual, language, visual-motor, and academic readiness.

Bayley. At 6 months of age, cognitive functioning was assessed using the Bayley Scales of Infant Development. The mean scores of the

TABLE 6.1
Descriptive Data for Indices of Cognitive Development

Time	Measure	Mean	SD	Range	N
6 months	Bayley Mental	101.79	17.61	67 – 150	141
1 year	Bayley Mental	99.29	16.41	45 – 131	119
6 months	Bayley Motor	106.35	15.47	64 – 138	139
1 year	Bayley Motor	107.40	15.86	45 – 143	115
3 year	Stanford–Binet	81.85	13.02	52 – 110	143
5 year	Stanford–Binet	87.06	13.75	38 – 125	143
3 year	PPVT–R	76.05	15.28	40 – 118	142
5 year	PPVT–R	74.52	18.39	40 – 117	144
5 year	DVMI	87.82	13.18	60 – 127	141
5 year	PIAT–Math	87.89	14.73	65 – 122	142
5 year	PIAT–Reading	97.04	15.07	65 – 135	142

Note. PPVT–R = Peabody Picture Vocabulary Test–Revised, DVMI = Developmental Test of Visual Motor Integration, PIAT = Peabody Individual Achievement Test.

children on the Mental and Motor Scales were respectively, 101.79 and 106.35 (see Table 6.1). These data indicate that the majority of infants fell within the normal range of development. The Bayley was repeated at 1 year; mean scores on Mental (99.29) and Motor (107.40) scales again suggested that the children were developing normally.

Stanford–Binet. Although the majority of infants fell within the normal range on the Bayley at 6 months and 1 year, assessments of intelligence at 3 and 5 years, using the SBIS, showed increasing evidence of intellectual delays in our sample (see Table 6.1). The average 3-year Stanford–Binet score was 81.85 (SD = 13.02), with individual scores ranging from 52 to 110. The distribution of IQ scores according to traditional

TABLE 6.2
Distribution of 3- and 5- Year Stanford-Binet IQ Scores

		3-Year		5-Year	
IQ Classification	IQ Range	Frequency	Percent	Frequency	Percent
Very superior	140 – 169	0	0	0	0
Superior	120 – 139	0	0	1	.7
High average	110 – 119	1	.7	6	4.2
Average	90 – 109	38	26.6	49	34.3
Low average	80 – 89	40	28.0	50	35.0
Borderline	70 – 79	36	25.2	24	16.8
Extremely low	30 – 69	28	19.6	13	9.1

classification criteria is shown in Table 6.2. Using this classification, 19.6% of the sample fell into the mentally retarded range, 25.2% were classified as borderline, 28% scored in the low average range of intelligence, and only 26.6% were in the normal range. One child fell into the high average range, whereas none scored at the superior or very superior levels.

At 5 years, the average Stanford–Binet IQ was 87.06 (SD = 13.75), with scores ranging from 38 to 125. Note that the mean IQ increased over the 2-year interval, as did the range and standard deviation. Compared to 3-year data, there were fewer but still a striking percentage of children in lower IQ categories at 5 years (see Table 6.2): Nine percent of the children scored in the mentally retarded range, 16.8% fell in the borderline category, and 35% were in the low average range. In contrast, only 34% of the children fell in the normal range of intelligence, 4.2% scored in the high average range, and one child was classified as superior.

PPVT–R. The majority of the children displayed receptive language delays at 3 and 5 years. Language development was assessed using the PPVT–R, a measure of receptive vocabulary. This test is standardized with a mean of 100, and a standard deviation of 15. The average PPVT–R score at 3 years, 76.05 (SD = 15.28), was more than one and one-half standard deviations below the normative mean. Scores ranged from 40 to 118; however, the distribution was markedly skewed toward the lower end of the scale. As seen in the breakdown in Table 6.3, 59.2% of the children scored below the 10th percentile. The mean and distribution of PPVT–R performance at 5 years was nearly identical to those at 3 years. Again, the majority of children (60.4%) scored below the 10th percentile (see Table 6.3)

TABLE 6.3
Distribution of 3- and 5-Year PPVT–R Scores by Percentile Range

Percentile	Range	3-Year		5-Year	
		Frequency	Percent	Frequency	Percent
90th	≥119	0	0	0	0
75th	110–119	2	1.4	3	2.1
50th	100–110	7	4.9	8	5.6
25th	90–100	19	13.4	17	11.8
10th	81–90	30	21.1	29	20.1
Below 10th	<81	84	59.2	87	60.4

DVMI. In addition to delays in the intellectual and receptive language areas, many children were evaluated as having visual-motor integration deficiencies. The DVMI was employed to assess visual-motor coordination at 5 years of age. The sample mean was 87.82 (SD = 13.18), compared to a mean of 100 (SD = 15) for the standardization group. Although scores ranged from a low of 60 to a high of 127, most children fell in the lower end of the distribution, with 39.7% of the sample scoring below the 10th percentile. Only 4.9% scored at or above the 75th percentile (see Table 6.4)

Socioemotional Development

In this section, we evaluate the children's socioemotional functioning, including data regarding temperament, behavioral interactions, attachment, and behavioral problems over the first 5 years of life. In general, analyses indicated that a substantial percentage of children were rated as difficult in temperament at 6 months of age, insecurely attached at 1 and 5 years and depressed-withdrawn at 3 and 5 years.

TABLE 6.4
Distribution of 5-Year DVMI Scores by Percentile Range

Percentile	Range	Frequency	Percent
90th	>119	2	1.4
75th	110-119	5	3.5
50th	100-110	24	17.0
25th	90-100	29	20.6
10th	81-90	25	17.7
Below 10th	<81	56	39.7

Temperament. Clinical ratings were obtained on the Revised Infant Temperament Questionnaire (RITQ) at 6 months, as well as for BSQ at 3 and 5 years. Whereas a high percentage of the children were perceived by their adolescent mothers as difficult in temperament at 6 months, this percentage was reduced considerably by 5 years (see Table 6.5). At 6 months, approximately 60% of our sample fell into the difficult classification, whereas only 4.3% were considered easy. The remainder of the sample were classified as slow-to-warm and average, 19% and 15.9%, respectively. These ratings are quite significant when compared with past research (Carey & McDevitt, 1978; Thomas & Chess, 1977) that has found 10% to 12% of 6-month-old infants falling into the difficult category and 37% to 40% in the easy category.

TABLE 6.5
Temperament Classification by Age

Classification	6 Months		3 Years		5 Years	
	N	Percent	N	Percent	N	Percent
Easy	7	4.3	18	12.3	21	14.8
Average	26	15.9	88	60.3	77	54.2
Slow to warm	31	19.0	14	9.6	20	14.1
Difficult	99	60.7	26	17.8	21	14.8

At 3 years, the percentage of children categorized as difficult dropped dramatically to 17.8% of the sample (see Table 6.5). The majority of 3-year-olds (60.3%) fell into the average category. At 5 years, the distribution was similar to that at 3 years; 14.8% of the sample were classified as difficult and 54.2% were classified as average. The percentage of children in the difficult classification was still elevated when compared to Carey and McDevitt (1978) findings of 10% for 3- to 5-year-olds.

Interactional Behavior. Behavioral data on infant responsivity were collected in the context of mother–child interactions during toy play when infants were 6 months of age. The three child items from the MIS—responsivity, activity, and mood—were summed to derive a general interaction score. At 6 months, infants of adolescent mothers were not significantly different from infants of adult mothers.

Attachment. Attachment status was measured using the Ainsworth Strange Situation paradigm at 1 year of age. As indicated in Table 6.6, only 37.6% of the sample was securely attached to their mothers, with the largest percentage of these (29%) in the B2 category. For insecure infants, 18% fit the type A pattern (insecure-avoidant), and 4% were classified as insecure-resistant (Type C). Most striking is the finding that the largest proportion of the sample showed a disorganized (Type D) attachment profile, with 41% of the sample falling into this category.

Attachment status at 5 years was measured by the Preschool Attachment Assessment System (Cassidy & Marvin, 1992). As seen in Table 6.6, 43% of the children were securely attached to their mothers. Of the 57% insecurely attached, the majority were avoidant (36% of the sample), 16% were insecure-other and disorganized, and 5% were resistant.

For the 77 dyads for whom we had attachment ratings at both 1 and 5 years, consistency of attachment classification from 1 year (avoidant, secure, resistant, and disorganized) to 5 years (avoidant, secure, and disorganized plus insecure-other) was evaluated. The chi-square analysis, was significant at the .03 level of confidence. The major findings are that 56% of the avoidant children remained avoidant at 5 years, and 62.5% of securely attached infants were still secure at 5 years, whereas all three children resistant at 1 year were classified at 5 years as securely attached. Only 23.5% of the disorganized at 1 year remained classified as insecure-other or disorganized at 5 years: 56% became avoidant and the remaining 26% were classified as securely attached at 5 years.

TABLE 6.6
Attachment Classification at 1 Year and 5 Years

Attachment Categories		1 Year Frequency	Percent	5 Years Frequency	Percent
A1	Insecure (avoidant)	10	7.6	14	11.8
A2	Insecure (avoidant)	14	10.7	29	24.4
B1	Secure	5	3.8	29	24.4
B2	Secure	38	29.0	0	0.0
B3	Secure	3	2.3	15	12.6
B4	Secure	2	1.5	4	3.4
C1	Insecure (resistant)	3	2.3	2	1.7
C2	Insecure (resistant)	2	1.5	4	3.4
D	Disorganized	54	41.2	7	5.9
I-O	Insecure-Other	*	*	12	10.1
		$N = 131$		$N = 116$**	

Note. Attachment ratings for only 77 children are available at both times.

* Insecure-other not coded at 1 year.

** Three additional children were classified at 5 years as secure-other ($N = 119$).

Behavioral Problems. The CBCL was given when children were 3 and 5 years of age. A substantial percentage of the children were evaluated as having behavioral problems at both time points. The percentages in the normal, borderline-clinical, and clinical categories are presented in Table 6.7. As shown, the majority of children at 3 fell in the normal range on the Internalizing and Externalizing subscales. However, a high percentage, 36.9%, were in the borderline-clinical and clinical ranges for internalizing problems, and 35.5% scored in these ranges for externalizing problems. At 5 years, the proportion of children in the normal range of behavioral functioning increased. Nevertheless, 24.5% of the sample remained in the borderline-clinical and clinical ranges for internalizing

TABLE 6.7
Distribution of 3- and 5-Year CBCL Scores

| | 3-Year | | | | 5-Year | | | |
| | Internalizing | | Externalizing | | Internalizing | | Externalizing | |
Range	N	Percent	N	Percent	N	Percent	N	Percent
Normal	89	63.1	91	64.5	105	75.5	119	85.6
Borderline	35	24.8	8	5.7	8	5.8	8	5.8
Clinical	17	12.1	42	29.8	26	18.7	12	8.6

problems, and 14.4% were in these ranges for externalizing behaviors. The cutoff for borderline-clinical category is at the 82nd percentile whereas the cutoff for clinical category is at 90th percentile. Therefore, at 3 years, the number of children displaying internalizing and externalizing problems exceeded expectations. At 5 years, externalizing problems decreased to within normal limits, but internalizing problems remained elevated.

Adaptive Behaviors

Standard scores for adaptive behaviors, as measured on VABS, suggested that the children had increasing delays, particularly at 5 years of age (see Table 6.8). The subscale and composite VABS scores have a mean of 100 ($SD = 15$). The mean adaptive behavior composite for the sample at 3 years was 91.78 ($SD = 10.99$), with a range between 70 and 122. Average scores for the subscales of communication, daily living, socialization, and motor skills ranged from 87.75 to 99.81. Analysis of 5-year data revealed a lower mean adaptive behavior composite score of 85.48 ($SD = 10.23$), with scores ranging from a low of 60 to a high of 116. The adaptive behavior composite mean score at 5 years is nearly one standard deviation below the mean, indicating that many of the children were not keeping pace with their peers in behaviors considered to be developmentally adaptive.

TABLE 6.8
Descriptive Data for VABS

Time	Domain	Mean	SD	Range	N
3 years	Communication	99.81	10.94	62–132	147
5 years	Communication	88.10	7.97	72–113	115
3 years	Daily living skills	97.67	11.35	69–133	147
5 years	Daily living skills	89.60	10.40	59–121	115
3 years	Socialization	87.75	10.09	61–113	145
5 years	Socialization	86.20	10.47	54–121	115
3 years	Motor skills	91.48	12.11	63– 24	147
5 years	Motor skills	93.34	16.26	42–124	108
3 years	Composite score	91.78	10.99	70– 22	147
5 years	Composite score	85.48	10.23	60–116	115

Academic Functioning

Academic readiness was assessed at 5 years using the Math and Reading subscales of the PIAT. The average Math subscale score was 87.89 (SD = 14.73), with a range from 65 to 122. The distribution of scores for this subscale is summarized in Table 6.9. Nearly half of the children (45.5%) scored below the 10th percentile. Only 9.1% scored at or above the 75th percentile.

Performance on the Reading subtest of the PIAT was substantially higher than on the Math subtest; the mean score was 97.04 (SD = 15.07), close to the mean of 100 for the standardization sample. Scores ranged from 65 to 135. Thus, as seen in Table 6.5, many children showed preliminary signs of deficiencies in math at age 5, whereas their reading achievement scores were only slightly skewed in a negative direction. These scores should be interpreted, however, in the context of the structure of the PIAT, a test that for 5-year-olds assesses the precursors of reading and math rather than achievement per se.

TABLE 6.9
Distribution of 5-Year PIAT Math and Reading Scores by Percentile Range

Percentile	Range	Math Frequency	Math Percent	Reading Frequency	Reading Percent
90th	> 119	3	2.1	15	10.5
75th	110–119	10	7.0	20	14.0
50th	100–110	21	14.7	11	7.7
25th	90–100	26	18.2	48	33.6
10th	81–90	18	4.0	34	23.8
Below 10th	< 81	65	45.5	15	10.5

Interrelationships Among Variables

In this section, relationships between indices of development when children were 6 months, 3 years, and 5 years of age are described. Correlational analyses were conducted to determine the extent to which measures within a domain (e.g., math and reading achievement) as well as between domains (e.g., IQ and achievement) were interrelated. When children were 6 months of age, these indices included the Bayley Mental and Motor Scales and Revised Infant Temperament Questionnaire. As expected, Bayley Motor scores correlated positively with Bayley Mental scores ($r = .63$, $p < .01$). Interactive behavior also correlated positively with both Motor ($r = .20$, $p < .01$) and Mental ($r = .20$, $p < .01$) Bayley scales. Temperament, however, was not significantly correlated with the other measures.

At 1 year of age, intercorrelations were examined between the Bayley Mental and Motor Scales, interactive behavior, and attachment security. The correlation between the Motor and Mental scales remained significant ($r = .48$, $p < .01$). In addition, securely attached infants scored somewhat higher on the Motor scale of the Bayley ($r = .20$, $p < .05$), and were observed to have more appropriate interactive behavior ($r = .28$, $p < .01$), than insecure or disorganized infants. Higher scores on Mental development were also correlated with interactive behaviors ($r = .24$, $p < .05$).

Because the pattern of intercorrelations between 3-year variables was quite similar to those at 5 years, only 5-year data are described (see Table 6.10). The measures of IQ, adaptive behavior, language, visual-motor integration, and achievement were all significantly intercorrelated, and

TABLE 6.10
Intercorrelations of Child Measures at 5 Years

	Stanford–Binet	VABS	PPVT–R	BSQ	CBCL	DVMI	Math	Reading
Stanford–Binet	1.00							
VABS	.45**	1.00						
PPVT–R	.75**	.40**	1.00					
BSQ	-.10	-.34**	-.13	1.00				
CBCL	-.07	-.20*	-.06	.53**	1.00			
DVMI	.59**	.29**	.40**	-.13	-.19	1.00		
PIAT–Math	.67**	.24*	.60**	-.16	-.10	.60**	1.00	
PIAT–Reading	.55**	.27**	.42**	-.10	-.12	.56**	.55**	1.00

*$p < .05$. **$p < .01$.

Note. VABS = Vineland Adaptive Behavior Scale, PPVT–R = Peabody Picture Vocabulary Test–Revised, BSQ = Behavioral Style Questionnaire, CBCL = Child Behavior Checklist, DVMI = Developmental Test of Visual Motor Integration, PIAT = Peabody Individual Achievement Test.

in the expected positive direction. In contrast, measures of behavioral problems (CBCL) and temperament were correlated only with each other and with adaptive behavior. Children with easier temperaments had fewer externalizing and internalizing behavior problems and higher adaptive behavior scores; adaptive behavior and adjustment problems were negatively associated. Also, adaptive behavior (one of the criteria for defining mild mental retardation), was positively associated with language, achievement, and intelligence (the second component for defining mental retardation).

Relationship Between Gender and Child Development.

Gender differences in child outcomes were explored at 6 months, 1 year, 3 years, and 5 years of age. In general, gender differences were not noticeable in the majority of the analyses. At 6 months, male and female infants were compared on mental and motor development, behavioral interactions, and temperament measures. Girls were found to be more responsive in their interactions than boys [$t(1, 163) = 1.94$, $p = .05$]; no other differences were found at this time. At 1 and 3 years, no gender differences in IQ, language, temperament, adaptive behavior, or emotional/behavior problems were found. At 5 years, males and females were again compared on these same measures as well as on visual-motor integration and math and reading achievement. The only difference between boys and girls that emerged was in temperament: Females were perceived as having more difficult temperaments than males [$t(1, 140) =$ 1.97, $p = .05$]. Because of the total number of tests conducted, the aforementioned significant differences should be taken as only suggestive.

CHILDREN WITH MULTIPLE PROBLEMS

Separate analyses were performed to explore the extent to which children had multiple developmental and behavioral problems at 3 and 5 years. Cutoffs were established for four different domains (intelligence, socioemotional, adaptive, and preacademic); next children were classified on the basis of having, or not having, a problem in each domain. Only children with complete data in all areas were included.

Children were considered to have a problem in the cognitive domain if the average of their IQ and PPVT–R scores was below 84.5 (scores of 84 for the Stanford–Binet and 85 for the PPVT–R fall one standard deviation below the mean). A cutoff of 60 was used to index problems in socioemotional adjustment as assessed on the CBCL; T scores at or above 60 on this measure indicate functioning in the borderline-clinical or clinical range. For VABS, composite scores below 85 (one standard deviation below the mean) were considered problematic. Finally, children who scored below 85 on either the reading and math scales of the PIAT (or one standard deviation below the mean) were considered to have problems in the domain of school readiness.

The major findings from these analyses at three years were that almost three quarters of the children (72.4%) children displayed delays or problems in at least one domain of development and close to one half (44.1%) had multiple problems. There were three possible domains in which children with complete data ($N = 124$) could have exhibited problems: intellectual, socioemotional, and adaptive behavior; preacademic data was not collected at 3 years. Nine percent of the sample demonstrated dysfunction in all three domains, 35.1% showed problems in two, 28.4% had one, and 27.6% showed no evidence of problems in any of the three areas. Cross-tabulations were then performed to determine the most common patterns in children with multiple problems. Results indicated that 29% of the children had problems in both the cognitive and socioemotional domains; 22% of the children exhibited simultaneous problems in adaptive behavior and cognitive development; and 11% of the sample evidenced problems in the adaptive behavior and socioemotional domains.

Four domains of child functioning were assessed at 5 years: the three areas evaluated at 3 years plus school readiness (PIAT). There were 131 children with complete data at age 5. Of these, 78% experienced problems in at least one domain and again close to one half (47.3%) had multiple problems. More specifically, 10.7% of the children had problems in all four domains, 19.8% exhibited dysfunction in three areas, 16.8% in two areas, 30.5% in one area, and 22% showed no sign of delay or dysfunction in any domain. Cross-tabulations were again performed to determine the most common pattern in children with more than one problem. Results indicated that 36% of the children simultaneously exhibited problems in intelligence and adaptive behaviors; 29% showed dysfunction in the intelligence and academic domains; 21% evidenced simultaneous delay in academic and adaptive behavior, 18% had problems in both the intelligence and socioemotional domains; 17% exhibited dysfunction in both the adaptive behavior and socioemotional areas, and 15% had coexistent problems in academic and socioemotional functioning.

STABILITY AND THE PREDICTION OF DEVELOPMENT

Stability and Change in Development Over Time

Stability scores for measures of intelligence, socioemotional, and adaptive functioning are shown in Table 6.11. Stability coefficients reflect the extent to which the rank order of each individual's score remains constant in rank over time. All the measures showed significant stability across time; most notable are the coefficients between 3- and 5-year measures of intelligence, language (PPVT-R), temperament, behavioral problems (CBCL) and communication. Despite the stability in the aforementioned measures, the size of the stability coefficients suggests that considerable instability was also present in these measures. To the extent that this instability is not due to errors in measurement, this finding indicates that individuals showed considerable change in their rank orders over time.

TABLE 6.11

Stability Estimates for Measures of Intellectual/Language,
Socioemotional, and Adaptive Behavior Development

Measure	Time Period	Stability Coefficient (r)	Mean t	Change N
Intellectual/Language				
Bayley Mental	6 Months–1Year	.27*	.17	86
Bayley Motor	6 Months–1Year	.41**	1.06	84
Stanford–Binet	3 Years–1Year	.68**	6.18**	125
PPVT–R	3 Years–1Year	.63**	.32	125
Socioemotional				
Temperament	6 Months–3 Years	.40**	3.51**	106
Temperament	6 Months–5 Years	.27**	1.88	105
Temperament	3 Years–5 Years	.51**	1.12	126
CBCL	3 Years–5 Years	.54**	1.51	118
Adaptive Behavior				
Communication	3 Years–5 Years	.51**	13.56**	123
Daily living skills	3 Years–5 Years	.29**	7.64**	123
Socialization	3 Years–5 Years	.25**	1.52	123
Motor skills	3 Years–5 Years	.26**	.77	118
Composite score	3 Years–5 Years	.44**	6.60**	123

*$p < .05$. **$p < .01$.

Note. PPVT–R = Peabody Picture Vocabulary Test–Revised, CBCL = Child Behavior Checklist.

    Simple comparisons were also performed to determine if the children's measures of intelligence, language, behavioral adjustment, and adaptive behavior changed on average over time (see Tables 6.1, 6.8, and 6.11). There were no significant differences between 6-month and 1-year Bayley Mental or Motor scores. The difference between 3-and 5-year Stanford-Binet scores was significant; children at 5 years of age had higher IQ scores than at 3 years of age. However, there was no significant change in receptive language, as measured by the PPVT–R. There was a significant change in temperament from 6 months to 3 years, with children perceived as becoming less difficult. Changes in behavioral adjustment on the CBCL were examined from 3 to 5 years. Although there was no overall change in CBCL total scores, there was a significant reduction in internalizing behavior problems $[t(117) = 6.79, p < .01]$; the reduction in externalizing scores approached significance. The composite score for the VABS was significantly lower for 5-year-old children in comparison with 3-year-old children. More specifically, children declined over time in the acquisition of Communication Skills and Daily Living Skills but not Socialization or Motor Skills (see Table 6.11). In summary, these results suggest the occurrence of both positive and negative changes in functioning across time. Whereas IQ scores increased and internalizing problems and temperamental difficulties decreased over time, the development of adaptive behaviors slowed.

Antecedents and Consequences of Changes in Temperament

Although there was stability in the children's scores across all domains from 3 to 5 years, the size of the relationships indicated a fair amount of instability, with the greatest instability occurring in the temperament and adaptive behavior areas. This instability may be either a function of true change and/or measurement error. To the extent that real change is occurring, research is needed to understand the determinants as well as the consequence of these variations. For example, understanding the role that temperament changes from 6 months to 3 years play in future development may be especially important for children of adolescent mothers who are at risk for multiple delays. Using our data set, O'Callaghan (1996) examined both the antecedents and consequences of temperament changes in order to gain insights into the process through which dysfunctional development occurs. Results indicated that prenatal maternal adjustment was significantly related to temperament changes from 6 months to 3 years, with mothers who perceived themselves as having fewer behavioral problems being more likely to judge their child as becoming "easier." In addition, 3-year IQ significantly predicted changes in temperament from 3 to 5 years, with higher IQ children becoming "easier." There was also evidence that changes in temperament were related to later child development, with children who were viewed as becoming less difficult in their temperament being also seen as exhibiting fewer signs of behavioral problems at 5. This is just one example of change in one domain, future research needs to focus on the antecedents and consequences of changes in other developmental areas.

Predicting Child Outcomes From Early Measures

Correlational analyses were conducted between birth status variables and 6-month child outcomes; between 6-month and 1-year child variables as predictors of 3-year child outcomes; and between 6-month, 1-year, and 3-year child variables as predictors of 5-year child outcomes.

Birth Status and 6-Month Outcomes. Relationships between variables reflecting birth status (i.e., weight, gestational age, and Apgar scores) and developmental outcomes at 6 months (i.e., behavioral interactions, temperament, and mental and motor development) were examined. Birth weight predicted both mental development and motor performance; babies who were heavier at birth tended to have higher Bayley scores at 6 months. Gestational age was also positively correlated with child interactions and development at 6 months; babies born closer to term showed greater responsivity, were more active, and performed better on both the mental and motor subtests of the Bayley. Finally, 5-minute Apgar scores were related to temperament; higher Apgar scores, which indicate more optimal birth status, were associated with more difficult temperament. It appears that more active, robust infants were viewed by the teens mothers as more difficult.

Predictors of 3- and 5-Year Child Outcomes. Six-month (Bayley, temperament, and behavioral interaction) and 1-year (Bayley, attachment, and behavioral interactions) data were correlated with 3-year child outcomes (Stanford–Binet, PPVT–R, VABS, and CBCL). For the purpose of these analyses, continuous scores for temperament were employed in all cases. Six-month Bayley Mental scores were significantly related to 3-year Stanford–Binet IQ, PPVT–R, and adaptive behavior scores. Better performance on the Bayley was associated with higher IQ, better receptive language, and more advanced adaptive skills at 3 years. In contrast, 6-month Bayley Motor performance was related only to 3-year Stanford–Binet performance, with higher Bayley Motor scores predicting higher IQ scores. Most importantly, temperament ratings at 6 months predicted every aspect of 3-year functioning: Children perceived as having more difficult temperaments at 6-months had lower IQ scores, poorer receptive language development, fewer adaptive behavior skills, and more internalizing and externalizing problems.

The relationship between 6-month measures and 5-year outcomes, which in addition to 3-year outcomes included visuomotor integration and achievement scores, were also examined. Temperament was the only 6-month measure associated with 5-year outcomes: Difficult temperament at 6 months was associated with lower IQs, lower receptive language scores, and poorer math performance.

The Mental Development Index of the Bayley, obtained at 1 year was significantly associated with all areas of 3-year development: Children who performed well on the Bayley at 1 year had higher IQ scores, better language development, more adaptive behavior skills, and fewer internalizing and externalizing problems at 3 years. The Psychomotor Development Index of the Bayley was also related to Stanford–Binet performance and Vineland scores. Higher psychomotor scores and more appropriate interactive behavior at age 1 were associated with higher IQ scores and better behavioral adaptation at age 3. Attachment did not predict 3-year outcomes.

Bayley Mental scores at 1 year also predicted 5-year Stanford–Binet, PPVT–R, Vineland, DVMI, and PIAT math outcomes, with higher Bayley scores related to better outcomes on all of these measures. Children who did well on the Motor portion of the Bayley also had higher Stanford–Binet, PPVT–R and Vineland scores at age 5. Infants observed to have more appropriate interactive behaviors at age 1 also scored higher on the Stanford–Binet, Vineland, and PIAT math at age 5. Finally, attachment at 1-year predicted Vineland and PPVT–R scores at 5 years, with securely attached infants showing better receptive language and adaptive skills than insecure or disorganized infants.

Table 6.12 shows intercorrelations among the child measures administered at 3 years and 5 years. As indicated earlier, those measures that were administered at both times (the Stanford–Binet, PPVT–R, Vineland, and CBCL) showed moderate stability over time. The best overall 3-year predictors of 5-year academic outcomes and visual-motor integration were Stanford–Binet, PPVT–R, and Vineland scores. However, with only one exception (IQ), these 3-year measures did not predict 5-year outcomes on the CBCL. In contrast, examination of the predictive efficacy of the CBCL indicated that either one or both of its subscales (Internalizing and Externalizing) predicted all of the 5-year outcomes except reading.

Summary. Birth status variables were significantly, albeit weakly, correlated with 6-month child outcomes. The best early (6-month and 1-year) predictors of later (3- and 5-year) child development were 6-month temperament and 1-year Bayley mental scores. When 3-year predictors of 5-year outcomes were examined, adaptive behavior (VABS), and especially Stanford–Binet IQ and receptive language (PPVT–R), were good predictors of most 5-year outcomes, except for internalizing and externalizing behaviors. Three-year internalizing and externalizing scores predicted all 5-year outcomes except reading.

TABLE 6.12

Correlations Between 3- and 5-Year Child Measures

3-Year Measures	5-Year Measures							
	SBIS	PPVT–R	VABS	CBCL Internalizing	CBCL Externalizing	DVMI	PIAT Math	PIAT Reading
SBIS	.68**	.67**	.57**	-.12	-.20*	.39**	.57**	.40**
PPVT-R	.62**	.63**	.38**	-.06	-.13	.36**	.50**	.33**
VABS	.47**	.40**	.44**	-.08	.01	.26**	.27**	.24**
CBCL Internalizing	-.21*	-.19*	-.26**	.44**	.47**	.24**	-.16-	.09
CBCL Externalizing	-.22*	-.24**	-.18	.31**	.49**	-.07	-.26**	-.07

*p < .05. **p < .01.

Note. SBIS = Stanford-Binet Intelligence Scale, PPVT-R = Peabody Picture Vocabulary Test-Revised, VABS = Vineland Adaptive Behavior Scale, CBCL = Child Behavior Checklist, DVMI = Developmental Test of Visual-Motor Integration, PIAT = Peabody Individual Achievement Test.

SCHOOL FUNCTIONING:
DEVELOPMENTAL PROBLEMS CONTINUE

Although our school data set was not complete, we conducted preliminary analyses of the academic functioning of children who had reached 8
years of age. Analyses were performed on the data for 83 children; that
is, approximately 80% of the potential sample at age 8 was represented.
No significant differences were found between the sample available at
age 8 and the entire 5-year sample on pre-reading and pre-math
achievement measures (PIAT data). Descriptive statistics for the children's academic functioning at age 8 are presented in Table 6.13.

TABLE 6.13
Descriptive Statistics for Children's Academic
and Behavioral Functioning at 8 Years of Age

Measure	Mean	SD	Range	N
WISC–III(est)	88.27	16.05	56.00–124.00	83
PPVT–R	85.27	16.89	40.00–120.00	83
PIAT–R Reading	88.56	18.65	55.00–131.00	82
PIAT–R Math	86.55	15.69	59.00–126.00	82
School performance (TRF)	2.75	0.89	1.00–5.00	74
TRF Internalizing	51.62	10.33	36.00–77.00	72
TRF Externalizing	55.90	9.56	39.00–78.00	72
TRF Total	54.72	9.51	35.00–76.00	74
Vineland Adaptive Behavior Scales	79.35	8.96	58.00–104.00	82

Note. WISC-III = Wechsler Intelligence Scale for Children–Third Edition, PPVT–R =
Peabody Picture Vocabulary Test–Revised, PIAT–R = Peabody Individual Achievement
Test–Revised, TRF = Teacher Report Form.

Children's IQs, based on a shortened form of the WISC–III, were again nearly a standard deviation below the population mean, generally in the low average range, and their adaptive behaviors were classified in the moderately low level of functioning. The children were almost one standard deviation below the mean on the PPVT–R, indicating below average language skills. Teacher ratings of socioemotional functioning (TRF of the CBCL) indicated 47% of the children demonstrated significant problem behavior; 22% had internalizing problems and 36% had externalizing behavior problems. Teacher's ratings of school performance indicated that children were performing significantly below grade level ($M = 2.75$), where an average rating would be 3.0 [$t(73) = 2.48$, $p < .05$]. Confirming teachers' judgments, PIAT–R scores for reading and math were nearly one standard deviation below the mean, further reflecting the below average performance of the sample in achievement. It should be noted that scores on these two achievement tests were significantly related ($r = .73$, $p < .001$). There were also high correlations between school performance as rated by teachers (TRF) and the PIAT–R Reading ($r = .70$, $p < .001$) and PIAT Math ($r = .66$, $p < .001$) scores. In addition, 8-year PIAT–R reading and math scores were significantly correlated with 5-year PIAT reading readiness ($r = .53$, $p < .001$) and math readiness scores ($r = .51$, $p < .001$), indicating moderate stability in achievement from kindergarten to the second grade in these important domains.

Teachers were surveyed to gather information on the children's classroom placements, using the TRF. Most of the sample (97.2%) were in regular classrooms. Although the majority were in the second grade (84.5%), a few children were in first (5.6%) and third (9.9%) grades. Three of four children in the first grade had repeated a grade due to poor academic progress. Although most students were in regular education classes, 35.7% had been referred for special services, whereas a small percentage (2.8%) were in special or alternative classrooms.

In order to better understand children's school performance, six diagnostic categories were formed based on IQ, achievement, receptive language, and adaptive behavior data:

1. Children with mild mental retardation.
2. Children with learning disabilities.
3. Children with below average IQs and low achievement.
4. Children with below average IQs performing average in school.
5. Children with average IQs with low achievement.
6. Children with average IQs performing average in school.

Mild mental retardation (MR) was defined as having an IQ less than 75 and adaptive behavior deficits (a score less than 75) on two or more subscales of the Vineland. Students were considered to have a potential learning disability if they had an achievement score on either the PIAT–R math or reading that was 18 or more points lower than their IQ, taking into account regression to the mean (Sattler, 1994); in addition their IQs needed to be 85 or above. For the purpose of this classification scheme, average IQ was defined as a score of 85 or greater on the WISC–III; low IQ was defined below 85. In addition, children were considered average achievers if all of their scaled scores on the PPVT–R, PIAT–R reading, and PIAT–R math were 85 or greater; conversely, low achievement was defined by a score below 85 on one or more of these measures.

Using this classification system, surprisingly high frequencies of children with "potential" learning disabilities (LD) and mild MR were detected. These prevalence data are presented in Fig. 6.1. Only 22.9% of the sample had average IQs and were performing adequately in all school areas; interestingly, 4.8% of children had low IQs but average academic performance. Thus, approximately 28% of the sample were at, or near, grade level. With respect to the children having academic problems, the incidence of LD and mild MR were unusually high: 20.5% and 18.1%, respectively. The identified prevalence of these disabilities for the second grade in the school district from which the majority of the sample was drawn was 4% for LD and 2.6% for mild MR (see Fig. 6.1). The other two categories had less frequent occurrences: 14.5% of the children exhibited low achievement in at least one academic area but had average IQ, and 19.3% had low IQ and low achievement (but failed to meet the IQ and adaptive behavior criteria for mild MR). Thus, the children of adolescent mothers appeared to experience a multitude of problems in their classrooms and showed a greater need for special services in school than other children of their age.

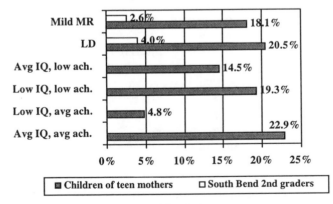

FIG. 6.1
Achievement- and IQ-related diagnostic categories.

Although all of the students classified as LD were participating in regular education programs, 43.8% had been referred for special services. For children classified as mildly mentally retarded, 80% were participating in a regular education program; 20% were in special education or alternative classrooms. Only 30% of the classified children in regular classrooms had been referred for special services.

Differences between the behavioral adjustment of children in the six aforementioned diagnostic categories were evaluated using the T scores from the TRF of the CBCL. There were no significant differences between diagnostic groups on either the Externalizing or Internalizing scales; however, there was a significant difference for TRF total scores [$F(5,68) = 3.78, p < .01$]. Post-hoc analyses using the Tukey HSD test indicated that the children with average IQs and adequate school achievement were rated as significantly better adjusted ($M = 48.67$) than both children with mild MR ($M = 59.42$) and children with low IQ and low school achievement ($M = 60.77$). On average, children with mild MR were in the borderline-clinical range for behavior problems as were children with low IQ and low school achievement. These findings suggest that the more serious achievement and IQ-related problems were often accompanied by socioemotional adjustment problems. This type of comorbidity likely further compromises children's chances for future success and happiness.

GENERAL SUMMARY AND DISCUSSION

In general, the children of adolescent mothers appeared to be physically healthy at birth, as evidenced by their average gestational ages, birth weights and Apgar scores, as well as low incidence of congenital problems. At 6 months and 1 year of age, Bayley IQ scores also suggested that the children were functioning mentally and physically in normal ranges. Moreover, comparative analyses failed to reveal differences in responsivity, activity, and mood between children of adolescent and adult mothers.

From a maternal perspective, however, a majority of the infants at 6 months of age were perceived as having a difficult temperament. In addition, at 1 year, a majority of the infants showed disorganized or other insecure patterns of attachment, with only 37% of children classified as securely attached. This proportion of securely attached infants is lower than that typically observed even in low SES samples (Vaughn et al., 1979; Ward & Carlson, 1995) as well as in other studies with children of adolescent parents (Spieker & Bensley, 1994). In short, although infants appeared physically healthy and developing adequately mentally and motorically during their first year of life, they showed signs of being at risk for socioemotional problems because of their temperament and attachment patterns. When the infants reached 3 and 5 years of age, there was more evidence of emerging developmental problems in the intellectual, socioemotional, adaptive and academic domains. A large percentage of children were operating in the borderline and mentally retarded ranges of intellectual functioning: 45% at 3 years and 26% at 5 years, with only a small percentage scoring in the above average range. Even more problematic, many children showed serious signs of delayed language development and visual motor integration problems, with around 80% of children falling at or below the 10th percentile on the PPVT–R at both 3 and 5 years of age, whereas 57% of the children were in this same range at 5 years of age on the DVMI. Academically, 50% and 34% of 5-year-old children were in the 10th percentile or below on the math and reading portions of the PIAT. At age 8, less than 30% of the children were performing satisfactorily in the second grade, and nearly 40% met traditional criteria for LD or mild MR diagnoses. Despite these problems, the majority of children had not been identified as needing special services nor were they receiving adequate attention in most classrooms.

Upon examining socioemotional functioning at 3 and 5 years, the percentage of children with difficult temperaments was found to drop dramatically from the time of the 6-month assessment. However, a high percentage of children was evaluated as having either internalizing problems (37% at 3 years and 24% at 5 years) and/or externalizing (35% at 3 years and 14% at 5 years) problems. Children also displayed deficiencies in the adaptive behavior domain: The mean composite score on the VABS, which assesses communication, daily living, socialization and motor skills, decreased from 3 to 5 years to one standard deviation below the population mean. A particular slowing was noted in the development of communication and daily living skills, the two areas of adaptive behavior in which they were evaluated as functioning best at 3 years. Additionally, 60% of the children were below the 10th percentile in receptive language.

Perhaps the most revealing finding is the number of children who displayed one or more problems in the intellectual, socioemotional, adaptive, and academic domains. At 3 years, 72% of the children had at least one developmental problem and 44% had more than one. At 5 years, 78% of the children had at least one problem whereas 48% had multiple problems. Children at 3 years with multiple problems most commonly displayed cognitive deficiencies and signs of emotional dysfunction. At 5 years, children with multiple problems most commonly exhibited deficiencies in cognitive and adaptive behavior domains, although "comorbidity" was found in other combinations of developmental delays.

Analyses of the early predictors of later child outcomes indicated that birth status (e.g., birth weight) predicted 6-month measures of child development. Six-month temperament was a particularly good predictor of 3- and 5-year child outcomes, as was the Bayley at 1 year, with children who displayed an easier temperament and higher mental development showing better development in language, socioemotional, and adaptive behavior domains as well as early reading and math achievement. Three-year IQ and language scores were generally good predictors of 5-year math and reading readiness, and the internalizing–externalizing components of socioemotional adjustment at age 3 predicted a broad range of intellectual, adaptive, and academic readiness outcomes at age 5, although the latter relationships were not as strong as the former between IQ, language, and 5-year outcomes.

Another set of findings that should be highlighted are the significant interrelationships between children's functioning across multiple domains. With only a few exceptions, significant concurrent relationships existed between children's intellectual, socioemotional, adaptive, and achievement scores at 5 years. Similar relationships existed between these measures across time from 3 to 5 years. Based on these results, the pattern of development in children of adolescent mothers is perhaps best viewed from a systemic perspective, with the various domains of child functioning (cognitive, socioemotional, and behavioral) not only interconnected but quite possibly reciprocally interacting. This perspective implies that problems and delays in one domain may have profound implications for what happens subsequently in other domains. It is interesting to speculate that problems in adaptation and intelligence may share a common mediational deficit—immature self-regulation in social and cognitive domains (cf. Borkowski & Dukewich, 1996).

In an examination of academic achievement in the second grade, more than 70% of the children of adolescent parents had problems of low achievement, LD, or MR. Although some had been referred for special services, most of those who were identified as being in need of services were not receiving them. Moreover, children with MR as well as children with low IQs and poor achievement had significantly poorer socioemotional adjustment than children with higher IQs and average achievement. Although the 8-year evaluation provided a bleak picture of future academic success, a substantial number of children (nearly 30%) seemed to be performing at a satisfactory level, or only slightly below. In the next chapter, we identify early maternal characteristics that predict, and likely causally influence children's development during the preschool years, in order to understand more about the antecedents of the developmental delays.

In summary, these findings provide considerably greater detail about the nature, scope, and sequence of developmental problems in children of adolescent mothers than previous research (Broman, 1981; Brooks-Gunn & Furstenberg, 1986; Hechtman, 1989). More specifically, our results indicate that a sample of children of adolescent mothers, while physically normal at birth, manifested an increasing array of problems at 1, 3, and 5 years of age, including insecure attachment, low IQ, language delays, visual-motor integration difficulties, internalizing and externalizing behaviors, adaptive behavior difficulties, and signs of future academic problems. Although the children showed some improvement in their IQ scores from three to five-years of age and a reduction in behavior problems, they still manifested, as a group, substantial deficiencies in these as well as other areas. In fact, close to 50% of the children showed delays or problems in multiple domains at 5 years, whereas only a relatively small percentage were free of problems. Their problems were increasingly notable when academic difficulties and adjustment problems surfaced in Grade 2. At age 8, 70% of the children were experiencing academic difficulties, the causes likely related to earlier appearing vocabulary, intellectual, adjustment, and socioemotional problems.

Although our sample of children seemed less impoverished than those studied by other investigators, they nevertheless appeared to show even more developmental delays. It is not clear whether these outcomes are a function of our more intense and comprehensive measurement system and/or related to the fact that the sample was born in the mid-1980s and early 1990s—decades of great prosperity for many, but also a time of deepening poverty for increasing numbers of people as federal and state assistance for the poor diminished. Whatever the case, the high prevalence of language delays, visual-motor integration problems, and behavior problems in our sample at 5 years, and the poor academic achievement at 8, portend serious personal and academic challenges as the children proceed through the elementary grades.

7

Predicting Child Development

with Mary O'Callaghan

As indicated in chapter 6, most children in our sample showed intellectual, linguistic, socioemotional, and/or adaptive behavior deficiencies. Indeed, many were deficient in multiple domains, providing further evidence of the problematic developmental trajectories first identified by Broman's (1981) and later by Brooks-Gunn and Furstenberg's (1986) longitudinal studies of children with adolescent mothers.

In this chapter, we examine the relationship of early maternal functioning and later child outcomes, searching for the important predictors of children's developmental delays. Although information is available regarding specific maternal predictors of development in children of adolescent mothers, little is known about the relative importance of these predictors in combination or their precise association with long-term development (cf. Furstenberg et al., 1987). Such information is valuable not only for understanding how maternal characteristics influence child development but also for the early detection and treatment of behavioral problems during the preschool years. The search for early maternal antecedents of later child development is guided by our model of adolescent parenting, as described in chapter 2. In addition to the maternal and social support constructs contained in this model, we assess how other important variables—including child abuse potential and child attachment security—are related to later development. Thus, we search for early as well as later predictors of development in children with adolescent mothers.

PREDICTORS OF DEVELOPMENTAL DELAYS

In our model of adolescent parenting, we hypothesized that four important characteristics of adolescent mothers—immature cognitive readiness for parenting, low IQ, inadequate social supports, and socioemotional maladjustment—place their children at risk for a variety of develop-

149

mental delays through their influence on parenting: Maternal intelligence was expected to predict children's intellectual-linguistic functioning as well as school achievement (math/reading) through direct transmission from mother to child as well as because more able mothers tend to create more stimulating environments for their children (Bouchard & McGue, 1981; Yeates, MacPhee, Campbell, & Ramey, 1983). Cognitive readiness was hypothesized to influence intelligence, language, and achievement based on the assumption that more cognitively prepared mothers will utilize this knowledge to interact with their children with greater sensitivity and responsivity (Whitman et al., 1987). In contrast, relationships were expected between the socioemotional adjustment of teen mothers and their social supports and a variety of personality-related child outcomes because of the purported roles these antecedent factors play in influencing maternal stress and parenting consistency, which in turn affect children's social, emotional, and behavioral development (Passino et al., 1993).

Although previous research has suggested the important role of maternal intelligence, cognitive readiness for parenting, social support, and socioemotional adjustment in accounting for individual differences in child development, few investigators have systematically utilized multivariate methodologies to assess their relative and combined impact on different domains of child development. Using our data set, we examine relationships between maternal factors (prenatal characteristics, demographic characteristics, and parenting practices) and intellectual-linguistic, socioemotional, and adaptive child outcomes at 3 and 5 years of age.

Prenatal Maternal Characteristics and Child Development

In order to evaluate the impact of prenatal and demographic maternal factors on later child development, child outcomes measures at 3 and 5 years were regressed on the variables listed in Tables 7.1 and 7.2. Because of the number of predictor variables in relation to sample size as well as for conceptual reasons, several variables were combined when multiple regression analyses were conducted to increase power and to form more broad-based constructs. Specifically, a construct, maternal socioemotional adjustment, was created by subtracting Social Competence from the total YSR score. Support from friends/partner, mother/siblings, and extended family were combined to create a social support construct. Education level was subtracted from Hollingshead scores to create a more specific index of SES related to income. For all constructs, standardized scores were used in the creation of composite scores. For each regression analysis, maternal IQ, socioemotional adjustment, cognitive readiness, and social support were entered simultaneously. Subsequently, age of mother at childbirth and SES were entered in separate steps to determine if these demographic variables explained variance in the child development beyond that already accounted for by the prenatal maternal predictor variables contained in our adolescent parenting model.

Three-Year Development. Correlations between prenatal maternal variables and 3-year child development are shown in Table 7.1. Maternal IQ was related to all domains of development at 3 years except adaptive behavior: Mothers with higher IQs had 3-year-old children with higher IQs, easier temperaments, fewer behavior problems on the CBCL, and better receptive language skills as measured by the PPVT–R. Maternal socioemotional adjustment predicted 3-year socioemotional, language, and temperament outcomes in children: Mothers with higher YSR scores (i.e., poorer adjustment) had children who were perceived as having more difficult temperaments and more behavior problems as well as evaluated as having less well developed language skills. The global measure of cognitive readiness was the only measure that predicted child functioning in all domains at three years: Adolescent mothers who were more cognitively prepared for parenting had children with higher IQs, easier temperaments, fewer behavioral problems, better adaptive behavioral skills (Vineland), and more advanced language development. Greater social support from friends and partners was associated with easier child temperament whereas support from the family was associated with lower IQs and language scores. Among the demographic variables, only SES was related to later child outcomes. Mothers from higher SES backgrounds had children whose IQs and PPVT–R scores were higher at 3 years; SES did not, however, account for unique variance in any of the subsequent regression analyses.

Regression analyses revealed that 11% of the variance in 3-year IQ [$F(5,101) = 2.41$, $p < .05$], 13% of the variance in language development [$F(5,101) = 2.94$, $p < .05$], 20% of the variance in temperament [$F(5,103) = 5.28$, $p < .01$], and 26% of the variance in socioemotional adjustment [$F(5,99) = 6.99$, $p < .01$], were accounted for by the set of maternal characteristics. These characteristics were not, however, significant predictors of adaptive behavior, as measured by the Vineland scales, although as indicated in Table 7.1, cognitive readiness was significantly correlated to this measure. In all of the significant regression analyses, cognitive readiness was the most consistent predictor. Not surprisingly, maternal IQ was the strongest predictor of children's IQ and vocabulary, whereas maternal adjustment was most highly associated with child adjustment.

TABLE 7.1
Correlations Between Prenatal Maternal Characteristics
and 3-Year Child Outcomes

Variables	3-Year Outcomes				
	IQ	BSQ	CBCL	VABS	PPVT–R
Education	.13	-.05	-.04	.02	.13
SES	-.21*	.16	.13	-.06	-.21*
Age at childbirth	.02	.02	-.04	-.05	.11
Intelligence	.36**	-.19*	-.18*	.13	.37**
Cognitive readiness (Composite)	.25**	-.21*	-.26**	.21*	.25**
YSR Social Competence	.09	-.13	-.01	.15	-.12
YSR Total Problems	.05	.26**	.37**	-.09	-.20*
Social Support					
Friends/partner	-.01	-.20*	-.14	.05	.03
Mother/sibling	-.15	.01	.11	.07	-.13
Extended family	-.17*	.09	.10	-.01	-.20*

*p < .05. **p < .01.

Note. BSQ = Behavior Style Questionnaire, CBCL = Child Behavior Checklist, VABS = Vineland Adaptive Behavior Scale, PPVT–R = Peabody Picture Vocabulary Test–Revised, YSR = Youth Self-Report.

Five-Year Outcomes. Correlations between prenatal and demographic maternal characteristics and child functioning at 5 years are presented in Table 7.2. In general, the pattern is similar to those at 3 years. Maternal IQ again emerged as the major predictor of intellectual and language outcomes as well as academic achievement and visual-motor integration. Maternal socioemotional functioning was the best predictor of child behavior adjustment. It is interesting to note, however, that cognitive readiness was nearly as good a predictor of IQ, language and achievement as maternal IQ.

TABLE 7.2
Correlations Between Prenatal Maternal Characteristics
and 5-Year Child Outcomes

				5-Year Outcomes				
Variables	IQ	BSQ	CBCL	VABS	PPVT–R	DVMI	PIAT Math	PIAT Read
Education	.22**	-.12	-.03	.07	.22**	.20*	.18*	.18*
SES	-.23**	.28**	.13	-.11	-.14	-.19*	-.20*	-.21*
Age at childbirth	.16*	-.05	.08	-.01	.20*	.17*	.15	.08
Intelligence	.37**	-.13	-.17	.17*	.44**	.26**	.35**	.22**
YSR Social Competence	-.06	-.14	-.12	.09	-.04	-.03	.03	.01
YSR Total	-.11	.25**	.26**	.06	-.06	-.14	.12	-.17*
Cognitive readiness (Composite)	.36**	-.12	-.07	.11	.37**	.15	.29**	.19**
Social Support								
Friend/partner	-.09	-.05	-.07	.10	.02	-.03	-.03	-.02
Mother/sibling	-.01	.06	.12	-.15	-.10	.04	-.09	-.01
Extended family	-.17*	-.01	-.02	-.15	-.17	-.16	-.17	-.08

$*p < .05.$ $**p < .01.$

Note. BSQ = Behavior Style Questionnaire, CBCL = Child Behavior Checklist, DVMI = Developmental Test of Visual-Motor Integration, PIAT = Peabody Individual Achievement Test, VABS = Vineland Adaptive Behavior Scale, PPVT–R = Peabody Picture Vocabulary Test – Revised, YSR = Youth Self-Report.

As indicated in Table 7.2, prenatally measured maternal IQ and cognitive readiness predicted most measures of children's functioning at 5 years, with the exception of socioemotional functioning (temperament and adjustment): Children with higher IQ mothers had higher IQs themselves, better adaptive behavior, superior receptive language skills, better visual-motor integration (DVMI), and higher pre-math and pre-reading performance. More cognitively prepared adolescent mothers also tended to have children who demonstrated higher IQs, superior language ability, and better math and reading readiness. In contrast, maternal YSR was correlated with temperament, adjustment, and pre-reading achievement: Mothers who were less socioemotionally adjusted prenatally had children at 5 years with more difficult temperament, more behavior problems, and lower reading skills. Finally, social support measures were related to only a single child outcome: Greater social support from the extended family was associated with lower children's IQs.

Table 7.2 also indicates that the number of years of education completed before childbirth predicted child intelligence, language, and visual-motor integration: Mothers with more education had children with higher IQs , better receptive language, better visual motor integration skills, and higher math–reading achievement. SES was related to 5-year development: Mothers from more disadvantaged backgrounds had children with lower IQs, more difficult temperaments, poorer visual-motor integration skills, and lower math and reading achievement. There were also significant relations between maternal age at childbirth and children's intelligence, language, and visual-motor integration: Older mothers had children with higher IQs, superior visual motor integration, and better developed language skills. In general, demographic variables were not as good predictors of 5-year child outcomes as the endogenous maternal prenatal variables (IQ, cognitive readiness, and socioemotional adjustment), nor did they account for unique variance in any of the multiple regression analyses.

The pattern of results for the 5-year regression analyses was similar to that at 3 years. In conjunction, prenatal maternal variables accounted for 19% of variance in 5-year IQ scores [$F(5,104) = 4.98$, $p < .01$], 30% of the variance in 5-year socioemotional adjustment (CBCL) [$F(5,101) = 8.57$, $p < .01$], 20% of the variance in receptive language development (PPVT-R) [$F(5,105) = 5.27$, $p < .01$], and 13% of the variability in math achievement [$F(5,103) = 3.15$, $p < .05$]. It should be noted that the variance accounted for in child outcomes by the set of maternal predictors was for the most part greater at 5 than at 3, especially for child IQ and language. Early maternal characteristics were not significantly associated in the multiple regression analyses with temperament, adaptive behavior, visual-motor performance, or reading achievement at 5 years.

Implications. These results, as well as those reported by Sommer et al. (2000), who also used data from the Notre Dame Parenting Project, suggest that the paths of influence on children's development are different depending on the domain under consideration. Maternal IQ was found to be the best single predictor of intelligence and receptive language. In contrast, prenatal maternal socioemotional functioning was the best predictor of socioemotional adjustment. Maternal cognitive readiness proved to be a good overall predictor of child functioning, predicting more outcomes at 3 years than any other maternal variable and the only predictor of adaptive behavior. Moreover, cognitive readiness predicted most child outcomes almost as well as maternal IQ.

We suspect that mothers with higher intelligence are likely to develop a broader knowledge base about their children's development and to utilize this knowledge as they parent, thereby facilitating their children's cognitive-intellectual growth (C. Miller et al., 1996; O'Callaghan et al., 1999). Cognitive readiness to parent is, however, a more appropriate target for early intervention than maternal IQ because its three components (knowledge about child development, parenting style, and parenting attitudes) are malleable and capable of being remediated through focused early interventions.

Social supports from the extended families also correlated, albeit negatively, with both children's IQ and language outcomes. This somewhat surprising finding may be related to unique status of teen mothers. The reality is, for many adolescent mothers, that they are not the primary caregiver of their infants; often the baby's grandmother plays a significant role in rearing her grandchild. In addition, other members of extended family such as aunts, cousins, and grandfathers sometimes provide advice, directives, and care. In this regard, Spieker and Bensley (1994) and Contreras, Mangelsdorf, Diener, and Rhodes (1995) showed that a "supportive" grandmother can sometimes hinder rather than help the emergence of good parenting skills in adolescent mothers. Although grandmother support might be expected to be beneficial, it may not always be useful to, or welcomed by, teenage mothers, causing family conflict, in part because such support may seem controlling and as preventing the development of a sense of self-efficacy and independence and, hence, a barrier in the path toward adulthood. In essence, support from grandmothers can seem as a throwback to preadolescence, unless given with an attitude that encourages the emergence of parenting skills: "The child is yours, and you have the major responsibility for parenting, but I'm here to help you in any way needed."

As hypothesized, children with fewer behavioral problems and easier temperaments tended to have mothers who were also well adjusted. Subanalyses of the maternal components of children's adjustment at 3 years by Sommer et al. (2000) suggested that internalizing problems in the mothers were a more important source of influence on child functioning than externalizing problems. This finding is consistent with research by Leadbeater, Bishop, and Raver (1996), who found that pregnant adolescents experiencing somatic or depressive symptoms have a tendency to rear children with internalizing and/or externalizing problems (cf. Leadbeater & Bishop, 1994). The relation between maternal personal adjustment, especially depression, and children's adjustment can be understood within the context of research suggesting that maternal psychological resources contribute to individual differences in parenting availability, nurturance, and competency (Stevens, 1984; Vondra & Belsky, 1993), which in turn influence children's socioemotional development.

The pattern of results predicting temperament at ages 3 and 5 was similar to those for behavior problems, and supportive of our original hypotheses: Better adjusted mothers perceived their children as having easier temperaments. In addition, anticipated social support from partners and close friends contributed significantly and positively to maternal perceptions of easier temperaments when children were 3 years of age. Overall, adaptive behaviors were not predicted well by the set of four maternal predictors. Contrary to our expectations, maternal socioemotional adjustment and social supports failed to predict adaptive behavior. Only maternal cognitive readiness predicted Vineland scores at age 3: Mothers who expressed a preference for a more empathetic parenting style tended to have children with more advanced adaptive skills, perhaps because empathetic mothers are likely to be more physically as well as psychologically available to their children. At 5 years, Vineland scores were predicted by maternal IQ, with the children of higher IQ mothers having more skilled adaptive behaviors.

Parenting and Child Development

In addition to examining the influence of prenatal maternal characteristics on child development, we also evaluated how maternal parenting characteristics affected child functioning at 3 and 5 years.

Three-Year Development. Correlations between maternal characteristics assessed at 6 months and child outcomes at 3 years are shown in Table 7.3. Mothers who experienced more stress at 6 months had children perceived as having more difficult temperaments, poorer adjustment (higher CBCL scores), and a less skillful adaptive behavior repertoire as assessed by the VABS. Children of mothers with higher cognitive readiness had higher IQs, less difficult temperaments, better behavioral adjustment, and more advanced language development. Finally, children of mothers with better interactive skills as assessed through the MIS had higher IQs.

Each of the major developmental markers at 3 years of age was then regressed on 6-month parenting measures, which included cognitive readiness, parenting stress, and interactional style (MIS). Taken together, the three predictors accounted for 9% of the total variance in 3-year IQ scores [$F(3,92) = 3.13$, $p < .05$], 11% of the variance in children's tem-

TABLE 7.3
Correlations Between 6-Month Maternal Characteristics
and 3-Year Child Outcomes

	3-Year Outcomes				
Maternal Variables	IQ	BSQ	CBCL	VABS	PPVT–R
Parenting Stress	-.14	.29**	.30**	-.25*	-.19
MIS	.20*	-.07	-.06	.17	.10
Cognitive Readiness (Composite)	.25*	-.25**	-.29**	.13	.26**

* p <. 05. ** p <. 01.

Note. BSQ = Behavior Style Questionnaire, CBCL = Child Behavior Checklist, VABS = Vineland Adaptive Behavior Scale, PPVT–R = Peabody Picture Vocabulary Test – Revised, MIS = Maternal Interaction Scale.

perament [$F(3,93)$ = 3.88, p < .05], 14% of variance in behavioral adjustment scores [$F(3,91)$ = 4.76, p < .01], 9% of the variability in adaptive behavior skills [$F(3,94)$ = 3.01, p < .05], and 9% of the variance in language development [$F(3,91)$ = 3.09, p < .05].

The results of the regression analyses, in conjunction with correlational data in Table 7.3, indicate that parenting stress and cognitive readiness were the best predictors of developmental outcomes. Although both significantly predicted temperament and adjustment, parenting stress was the only significant predictor of adaptive behavior, whereas cognitive readiness was the sole predictor of receptive language. Parenting stress accounted for unique variance in the three major child outcomes (temperament, behavioral adjustment and adaptive behavior), whereas cognitive readiness accounted for unique variance in two important outcomes (behavioral adjustment and language).

Five-Year Child Development. Table 7.4 contains correlations between 6-month maternal characteristics and child outcomes at 5 years. Mothers who demonstrated more positive interactional styles had children with higher IQs, better receptive language, and higher achievement in math and reading. Greater cognitive readiness was associated with higher IQs, more advanced receptive language, and better math and reading performance. Greater maternal stress at 6 months was related to more difficult child temperament at 5 years.

TABLE 7.4
Correlations Between 6-Month Maternal Characteristics
and 5-Year Child Outcomes

Maternal Variables		5-Year Outcomes						
	IQ	BSQ	CBCL	VABS	PPVT–R	DVMI	PIAT Math	PIAT Read
Parenting Stress	-.08	.27**	.14	-.09	-.10	-.01	-.07	-.12
MIS	.31**	-.06	-.09	.09	.20*	.19	.27**	.24**
Cognitive Readiness (Composite)	.27**	-.13	-.16	.07	.23*	.16	.31**	.17

*p < .05. **p < .01.

Note. BSQ = Behavior Style Questionnaire, CBCL = Child Behavior Checklist, DVMI = Developmental Test of Visual-Motor Integration, PIAT = Peabody Individual Achievement Test, VABS = Vineland Adaptive Behavior Scale, PPVT–R = Peabody Picture Vocabulary Test – Revised, MIS = Maternal Interaction Scale.

Next, regression analyses were used to explore relationships between adolescent mothers' parenting abilities at 6 months and child development at 5 years. Each of the 5-year outcome measures was regressed on the 6-month parenting variables (cognitive readiness, parenting stress, and interactional style). Six-month parenting factors accounted for a significant amount of the variance in IQ, 13% [$F(3,95) = 4.81, p < .01$], as well as 13% of the variance in math performance [$F(3,92) = 4.65, p < .01$]. Cognitive readiness accounted for unique variance in two outcomes (IQ and math achievement), whereas interactional style accounted for unique variance in only IQ. In contrast to 3-year analyses, parenting stress was not a major predictor of 5-year outcomes, its only significant correlation being with temperament. SES explained additional variance for a single outcome at 5 years, child temperament.

Summary. Cognitive readiness was the best overall predictor of 3- and 5-year outcomes. In contrast, parenting stress—a relatively good predictor of 3-year outcomes—predicted a single outcome at 5 years, temperament. Conversely, maternal interactional style was a better predictor of 5-year than 3-year outcomes. These latter two findings show the changing and differential impact of early occurring, parenting-related variables on child outcomes at various developmental stages. More research is needed to determine how changes in parenting practices exert their influence on different domains of child development.

Gender Differences in the Prediction of Developmental Outcomes

A series of regression analyses was also conducted to determine whether there were gender differences in the prediction of child development. Specifically, 5-year outcomes, (PPVT–R, VABS, CBCL, Temperament, DVMI, PIAT–Math, and PIAT–Reading scores), were regressed separately on the interactions between gender and a number of important maternal variables including prenatal cognitive readiness, behavioral adjustment, and social competence as well as postnatal cognitive readiness and maternal interactional style. Significant gender differences were found when examining the effects of social competence and cognitive readiness on child outcomes. Specifically, a significant gender by social competence interaction predicted VABS scores [$F(1,122) = 3.9, p = .05$]. For girls, greater maternal social competence was associated with higher VABS scores, whereas there was no relationship for boys. A gender by social competence interaction also predicted reading achievement [$F(1,124) = 4.3, p = .05$]. For girls, there was a positive relationship between maternal competence and 5-year reading, whereas for boys this relationship was negative. Gender was also found to moderate the effects of prenatal and 6-month cognitive readiness on VABS scores. For girls only, greater prenatal and postnatal cognitive readiness was associated with better adaptive behavior [$F(1, 124) = 5.42, p < .05$ and $F(1,98) = 5.48$, $p = .05$, respectively]. Finally, girls with mothers having better cognitive readiness scored higher on the math portion of the PIAT at 5 years [$F(1,124) = 3.93, p < .05$]; this relationship did not hold for boys. In short, more often than not gender did not interact in the prediction of major outcomes. When gender proved significant, it tended to emerge mainly in the predicting of adaptive behavior and achievement.

Three-Year Maternal Characteristics and 5-Year Outcomes

Correlations between maternal characteristics at 3 years postpartum and child outcomes at 5 years are reported in Table 7.5. Maternal IQ was a significant predictor of functioning in all domains of child development: Higher maternal IQ was associated with higher child IQ, less difficult temperament, better behavioral adjustment, more advanced adaptive skills, greater language proficiency, higher DVMI scores, and better performance in both math and reading. In addition, mothers who reported more depressive symptoms had children with poorer behavioral adjust-

TABLE 7.5
Correlations Between 3-Year Maternal Characteristics
and 5-Year Child Outcomes

3-Year Maternal Measures	5-Year Outcomes							
	IQ	BSQ	CBCL	VABS	PPVT–R	DVMI	PIAT Math	PIAT Read
IQ	.37**	-.33**	-.20*	.21*	.42**	.30**	.37**	.33**
Beck Depression	-.12	.14	.17*	-.12	-.08	-.22*	-.13	-.10
Self-Esteem	.09	-.15	-.27**	.15	.05	.07	.12	.16
State Anxiety	-.14	.14	.25**	-.18*	-.08	-.13	-.15	-.02
Trait Anxiety	-.16	.26**	.26**	-.24**	-.17*	-.14	-.12	-.09
Life Stress	.21*	.04	.15	.12	.21*	.03	.22*	.03

$*p < .05.$ $**p < .01.$

Note. BSQ = Behavior Style Questionnaire, CBCL = Child Behavior Checklist, DVMI = Developmental Test of Visual-Motor Integration, PIAT = Peabody Individual Achievement Test, VABS = Vineland Adaptive Behavior Scale, PPVT–R = Peabody Picture Voca~ry Test – Revised.

ment and visual-motor integration. Higher maternal state anxiety was related to poorer child behavioral adjustment and deficits in adaptive behavior, whereas maternal trait anxiety predicted a wider range of child outcomes, including more difficult temperament, poorer behavioral adjustment and adaptive behavior, and less developed receptive language. Conversely, high maternal self-esteem predicted better behavioral adjustment in the child. Surprisingly, mothers who reported more life stress at 3 years had children who had higher IQs, better language development, and higher scores on the math readiness test. This result seems difficult to explain, particularly as in chapter 4 it was noted that life stress was not found to impact maternal outcomes. However, it may be that certain stressors are serving as an impetus to change a situation or associated with changes that have a positive influence in the long run (moving to a better environment or changing to a better job situation).

To complete the analyses of the effects of adolescent mothers' influence on their children's development, a series of regressions were run in which each 5-year child outcome was regressed on 3-year maternal IQ, depression, self-esteem, state and trait anxiety, and life stress scores. Nineteen percent of the variance in children's IQ scores at 5 years was attributed to 3-year maternal factors [$F(6,112)$ = 4.39, $p < .01$], 15% of the variance in child temperament [$F(6,111)$ = 3.31, $p < .01$], 18% of the variance in child CBCL scores [$F(6,108)$ = 3.92, $p < .01$], 24% of variance in receptive language development [$F(6,113)$ = 5.91, $p < .01$], 13% of the variance in visuomotor integration [$F(6,111)$ = 2.73, $p < .05$], 19% of the variance in math [$F(6,111)$ = 4.31, $p < .01$], and 12% of the variance in reading [$F(6,111)$ = 2.62, $p < .05$]. Adaptive behavior was the only outcome at 5 years not predicted by 3-year maternal characteristics. Maternal IQ was the single variable to account for reliable amounts of unique variance in child outcomes; those outcomes were IQ, receptive language, visuomotor integration, math achievement, and reading achievement.

MATERNAL CHILD ABUSE POTENTIAL AND CHILD DEVELOPMENT

As we have seen, children raised by adolescent mothers are at risk for a variety of developmental problems including deficits in intellectual ability, delays in receptive language, slowed development of adaptive behavior, socioemotional maladjustment, and academic problems. Abused children show many of these same developmental difficulties (Lynch & Roberts, 1982). For example, Hoffman-Plotkin and Twentyman (1984) found that the average IQ of abused children was approximately 20 points lower than nonabused children. Other researchers have found that by age 9, the reading levels of abused children were severely delayed (Oates, Peacock, & Forrest, 1984).

Although cognitive and language deficits have been noted in abused children, behavioral and emotional problems are generally the critical indicators of maltreatment. Frequently identified problems in abused children include an impaired ability to inhibit aggressive impulses and physical aggression toward peers and adults (cf. Wolfe, 1987). Egeland and Sroufe (1981) found that maltreated children, as young as 2, showed more anger, aggression, frustration, and noncompliance when interacting with their mothers compared to children who were not maltreated. In clinical contexts, abused children, especially boys, had a higher incidence of conduct disorders than is typically observed in the general population (National Research Council, 1993). Abused children are also more likely than nonabused children to be socially withdrawn, depressed, and to feel helpless (cf. Wolfe, 1987).

One obvious explanation for the similarities between the children of adolescent parents and abused children is that teenage parents are at a greater risk for engaging in abusive parenting practices than adult parents. In a study of adolescent parenting practices, deLissovoy (1973) found that adolescent parents were more likely than older parents to use physically punitive techniques for gaining child compliance. Adolescent parents also frequently endorsed, in interviews, the use of severe physical punishments with their children. Bolton (1990) reported that although 20% of all children are born to adolescent mothers, the proportion of abused children raised by adolescent mothers is estimated to be between 35% and 50%. Furthermore, Connelly and Strauss (1992) found that the age of the mother at the birth of her first child significantly predicted the occurrence of child maltreatment—even when income, race, education, number of children, and age of the child were statistically controlled. Finally, our own analyses, reported in chapter 5 and also by Dukewich et al. (1996), suggested that teen mothers who were less cognitively prepared for parenting and who preferred using punishment as a childrearing technique showed a higher potential for child abuse.

Although children of adolescent mothers are likely to be at greater risk for being maltreated than children of adult mothers, it is important to remember that not all adolescent mothers abuse or neglect their children. For this reason, it is essential that those adolescent parents most at risk for child abuse be identified early in their children's lives. An assessment device that has been found useful for this purpose is the CAPI (Milner, 1986). Using data from the Notre Dame Parenting Project, Dukewich, Borkowski, and Whitman (1999) explored the validity of a shortened form of the CAPI for predicting developmental delays in the children of adolescent parents.

A detailed picture of the relation between maternal child abuse potential—as measured by the abbreviated form of the CAPI when children were 1, 3, and 5 years of age—and 5-year child developmental outcomes is presented in Table 7.6. As shown in Table 7.6, 1-, 3-, and 5-year CAPI scores are related to intellectual functioning, temperament, internalizing and externalizing problems, adaptive behaviors, receptive language and academic readiness, with higher abuse potential associated with more adverse outcomes.

Dukewich et al. (1999) also examined relationships between abuse potential and development in preschool children after controlling for problematic parenting orientation, defined by maternal knowledge and expectations about child development, child-centeredness or role reversal, and parenting style. Problematic parenting was assessed when children were 6 months of age; child abuse potential at 1, 3, and 5 years; and child development (intelligence, language, behavioral problems, and adaptive behaviors) at 3 and 5 years.

Because abuse potential and development were assessed at multiple times, the directionality of potential causal influences was able to be examined. It was found that early variations in mothers' child abuse po-

TABLE 7.6
Correlations Between Maternal Child Abuse Potential
and 5-Year Child Outcomes

	Child Abuse Potential (CAPI)		
5-Year Child Outcomes	1 Year	3 Year	5 Year
Intelligence			
Stanford–Binet	-.37**	-.40**	-.31**
PPVT–R	-.31**	-.34**	-.35**
DVMI	-.19	-.29**	-.17*
Socioemotional			
Temperament (BSQ)	.25*	.27**	.23**
CBCL total	.19	.22*	.26**
Internalizing	.20*	.19*	.22*
Externalizing	.21*	.17*	.24**
Adaptive			
VABS	-.23*	-.21*	-.16
Achievement			
PIAT–Math	-.40**	-.38**	-.23**
PIAT–Reading	-.39**	-.33**	-.22**

* $p < .05$. ** $p < .01$.

Note. BSQ = Behavior Style Questionnaire, CBCL = Child Behavior Checklist, DVMI = Developmental Test of Visual-Motor Integration, PIAT = Peabody Individual Achievement Test, VABS = Vineland Adaptive Behavior Scale, PPVT–R = Peabody Picture Vocabulary Test – Revised.

tential impacted subsequent child IQs and adaptive behaviors, but that the reverse did not hold. In addition, it was found that child abuse potential, assessed at 1 and 3 years, predicted children's intelligence and adaptive behavior at 3 and 5 years even when problematic parenting orientation was controlled. However, results also indicated that children's behavior problems (internalization and externalization) at ages 3 and 5 were better predicted by problematic parenting orientation than by abuse potential.

The results of the Dukewich et al. (1999) study carry implications for how the etiology of child maltreatment should be viewed. Abused toddlers have been found to exhibit behaviors that provoke irritability, rejection, and even aggression in adults other than their parents (Dodge,

Bates, & Pettit, 1990; George & Main, 1979). Researchers have also noted that abused children are sometimes revictimized when placed in foster homes (National Research Council, 1993), a finding that has sometimes been used to support the idea that children themselves evoke abusive parenting styles. Based on the results of the Dukewich et al. (1999) study and its longitudinal design, it appears that maternal characteristics—rather than, or in addition to, children's behaviors and characteristics—are a critical, if not the major component in the cycle of abuse. In short, the present findings provide an important piece in the "cause versus consequence" puzzle regarding roles of maternal characteristics versus child characteristics in parenting, and their influence on cognitive, socioemotional, and behavioral development.

A major implication of these findings centers on potential targets for intervention programs. The finding that there are different pathways in the development of intellectual, adaptive, and behavioral problems suggests that interventions need to address specific aspects of parenting. For example, the results suggest that decreasing abuse potential may improve adaptive behaviors and cognitive development, whereas the problematic parenting orientation of adolescent mothers needs to be targeted directly in order to reduce behavior problems such as aggression and depression. In conjunction, these results point to the need for broad-based interventions that are designed to improve parenting knowledge (e.g., about child development), parenting styles (e.g., about the unacceptability of punishment as a "typical" childrearing technique), and parenting practices (e.g., the need for teaching sensitive and responsive interactional styles).

ATTACHMENT SECURITY AND ITS DEVELOPMENTAL CONSEQUENCES

Due to the scarcity of longitudinal research on attachment in children of adolescent mothers, relatively little is known about the incidence of insecure attachment in this population, its precursors, or its developmental consequences. It is clear, however, that many of the factors predicting insecure attachment in children of adult mothers, such as insensitive parenting (Egeland & Farber, 1984), marital dissatisfaction (Goldberg & Easterbrooks, 1984), low self-esteem (Ricks,1985), and inadequate social support (Rutter, 1985), are common characteristics of adolescent parents, and likely antecedents of insecure attachment in their children. For this reason, we hypothesized—and indeed discovered—that insecure attachment occured more frequently among children of adolescent mothers than among children of adult mothers. It is our contention that the same characteristics that place adolescent mothers at risk for inadequate parenting, as well as for other developmental problems, also place their children at risk for cognitive and socioemotional delays, including insecure attachment. Nevertheless, the precise antecedents of attachment in children with adolescent mothers remain elusive (Ward & Carlson, 1995).

There are important social consequences related to insecure attachment. For instance, attachment security has also been linked to social competency with peers, with insecurely attached children showing impaired interactional skills and being rated less positively by other children (Arend, Grove, & Sroufe, 1979; Sroufe, 1983). Past research has also revealed a variety of socioemotional difficulties in children of teen mothers, including increased delinquency and behavioral problems (Furstenberg et al., 1987). Similar problems have been observed among children of adult mothers who are insecurely attached (Lyons-Ruth, Alpern, & Repacholi, 1991; Matas, Arend, & Sroufe, 1978; Troy & Sroufe, 1987). In contrast, insecure attachment does not seem to affect directly the cognitive abilities of children; however, it may have a negative impact on the way in which children approach a variety of learning tasks and, perhaps, on the development of social and cognitive self-regulation. For example, Matas et al. (1978) found that insecurely attached children did not differ from securely attached children in terms of their intelligence, but that during problem solving tasks they were significantly less enthusiastic, less persistent, and spent more time engaging in off-task behaviors. It is possible that insecure attachment, especially disorganized attachment, may influence problem solving through restricting the growth of self-regulation (cf. Borkowski & Dukewich, 1996).

In the next two sections, we examine a wide range of maternal and child variables as potential antecedents of infant attachment at 1 year and then evaluate how insecure attachment influences later development at 3 and 5 years.

Antecedents of Secure Attachment

Prenatal maternal variables (age, education, SES, IQ, socioemotional adjustment, cognitive readiness, and social support); parenting variables (mother–child interactions, stress, and cognitive readiness); birth characteristics (weight and gestational age); and 6-month child characteristics (temperament, Bayley scores, and infant responsivity) were correlated with attachment at 1 year. The attachment scores were based on the Ainsworth categorical scale and converted to a continuous variable using a 5-point range, where 5 indicated the most secure attachment. Specifically, a rating of B3 was scored 5; B1, B2, and B4 were assigned scores of 4; A2 and C1 were rated as 3; A1 and C2 as 2; and D (disorganized) was given a score of 1.

Results indicated that maternal education, prenatal cognitive readiness, and the quality of maternal interactions were significant predictors of attachment status: Mothers with more years of schooling tended to have more securely attached infants at 1 year ($r = .018$, $p < .05$) as did mothers who were more cognitively prepared for parenting during pregnancy ($r = .20$, $p < .05$), and mothers who demonstrated more appropriate parenting skills at 6 months ($r = .20$, $p < .05$).

Correlation coefficients were also computed between attachment and scores on the IPPA, which measured relationships between the adolescent mother and her mother in the areas of trust, alienation, and communication as well as overall attachment. Infants who were rated as more securely attached had adolescent mothers who reported less trust ($r = -.27$, $p < .01$) more alienation ($r = .30$, $p < .01$) and poorer communication ($r = -.30$) in their relationships with their own mothers. On the surface, these results may seem paradoxical. However, others have found that adolescents who heavily depend on grandmothers (as evidenced by good communication and trust) may find it difficult to move into their adult roles and to become active and responsive parents (cf. Contreras et al., 1995; Spieker & Bensley, 1994).

Developmental Consequences of Insecure Attachment

In order to analyze the consequence of attachment security on developmental problems during early childhood, we correlated attachment classifications with children's IQ, temperament, CBCL, Vineland, PPVT–R, and PIAT math and reading scores. The only significant relationship was between attachment and Vineland scores: More securely attached infants showed better adaptive skills at 5 years ($r = .27$, $p < .01$). Interestingly, regression analyses showed that attachment status accounted for a unique portion of the variance in the children's adaptive behaviors even after a variety of maternal characteristics, including maternal IQ and cognitive readiness, were controlled. This finding is generally consistent with research that indicates that insecurely attached children are less likely to react to problem situations with flexibility or resourcefulness and have difficulty utilizing adult assistance to meet their goals (Matas et al., 1978).

Next, we employed a different approach to examine the influence of attachment classifications on 3- and 5-year child outcomes as we explored whether race would moderate important relationships. Children were grouped into secure versus insecure subgroups, with participants including African-American and Euro-American adolescent mothers and their children; racial classification was based on the race of the mother.

Hispanic dyads were not included because there were too few in each attachment classification.

The influence of 1-year attachment on 3-year child outcomes (intelligence, receptive language, adaptive behavior, behavior problems, and temperament) and 5-year child outcomes (same outcomes plus visuomotor integration and math and reading achievement) was examined using a general linear model. The model consisted of four variables including maternal intelligence, race, attachment classification, and the interaction between race and attachment; race and attachment classification were dichotomous variables whereas maternal intelligence was a continuous variable.

Three-Year Analyses. Eighty-nine dyads were included in these analyses. Three of the five outcome variables (i.e., intelligence, adaptive behavior, and temperament) were significantly related to attachment status, after controlling for the effects of maternal intelligence and race. In each case, the expected benefit of a secure attachment relationship was found for the Euro-American dyads, but not for the African-American dyads. Securely attached Euro-American children had higher intelligence, more developed adaptive behavior, and easier temperaments than insecure Euro-American children. Outcomes for the African-American children were unrelated to attachment classification.

Five-Year Analyses. Seventy-eight dyads were included in these analyses. The general linear model accounted for significant variance in all of the 5-year outcomes, except for adaptive behavior and reading achievement. Although most of the variance accounted for was related to maternal intelligence, interactions between attachment and race were found to approach significance in predicting intelligence, temperament, visual-motor integration, and behavior problems ($p < .1$). In each case, these marginally significant interactions paralleled 3-year outcomes: Securely attached Euro-American children had higher intelligence and visual-motor integration scores, easier temperaments and fewer behavior problems than insecurely attached Euro-American children. Attachment classification was again unrelated to outcomes for African-American children.

Summary of Attachment Results

Analyses reported in chapter 6 revealed an unusually high percentage (63%) of insecure children, especially disorganized attachment. Results reported in this chapter suggested that mothers who were more educated and cognitively prepared for parenting tended to have more securely attached children. Based on results of the O'Callaghan et al. (1999) and Sommer et al. (2000) studies, both of which used data from the Notre Dame Parenting Project, it seems likely that cognitively prepared mothers have more positive and sensitive parenting skills, which in turn help promote secure attachment. The present results indicate that the relationship of a child's mother with her mother is also important: Adolescent mothers who had a trusting and open relationship with their mothers had children who were less securely attached. This finding may be related to the fact that adolescent mothers who cede their parenting responsibilities to their mothers are unlikely to acquire the parenting orientation and skills necessary for developing secure bonds with their infants. It might be expected, however, that their infants would be securely attached to the grandmothers. Unfortunately, we did not assess the attachment of infants to their grandmothers in our project.

Finally, these results extend the findings of past research on the positive consequences for children who display secure attachment (cf. Arend et al., 1979; Sroufe, 1983). The findings, however, appeared specific to children of Euro-American mothers; that is, securely attached Euro-American children had higher intelligence, better adaptive behaviors, and an easier temperament than insecure Euro-American children. It may be that the meaning of attachment as measured in the strange situation varies among ethnic and/or cultural groups. Also, it may be that the patterns of attachment children have with people other than mother varies with culture and ethnicity.

SUMMARY AND CONCLUSIONS

The findings reported in this chapter provide general support for the model we proposed in chapter 2, they emphasize the extent to which the lives of adolescent mothers and their children are interwoven, and also suggest the existence of multiple pathways through which adolescent mothers influence their children. Although maternal intelligence and cognitive readiness were generally good predictors of children's development across domains, these characteristics best predicted those child outcomes that were more cognitive in nature, including IQ, receptive language, and math and reading achievement. In contrast, maternal socioemotional adjustment best explained individual differences in temperament and adjustment.

The results in this chapter and those in chapter 5, however, also highlight the critical role that cognitive readiness plays in maternal and child development. Children's later adjustment, as well as that of their mothers, appears closely tied to the adolescent girls' preparation for parenting and their commitment to their parenting responsibilities. Mothers who are cognitively prepared for parenting are less stressed, more sensitive in their parenting roles, and have a lower potential for child abuse. They also have children who are more likely to be securely attached, more cognitively advanced, and better adjusted.

Several precautionary notes should be made regarding the generalizability of the results of these analyses and those reported in chapters 4, 5, and 6. Because there was a selective attrition of young mothers with higher levels of adjustment problems, our results may underestimate the actual extent of the problems for both mothers and children. Based on the methodology employed, it is also unclear whether the relationships we observed are unique to adolescent parents, or related more generally to all mothers living in poverty. The adolescent mothers in this study were of lower SES and generally had unstable or low-level jobs, characteristics of individuals whose lives are compromised by poverty. Much like their children, mothers were also as a group below average in intelligence and experiencing personal problems. It should be noted, however, that relatively few mothers reported the use of drugs, even moderate use of alcohol, during pregnancy; these reports are consistent with the fact that relatively few infants in our sample had medical problems at birth, such as low birth weight. Thus, the present results are particularly applicable to teen mothers in small towns and rural areas where poverty is less variable, medical care more accessible, and drug or alcohol problems less prevalent. Although the adolescent mothers and their children in the Notre Dame Parenting Project experienced many developmental challenges, the problems experienced by inner-city urban teenage mothers and their children, who are often trapped by more extreme poverty, are likely more numerous and of greater severity.

In addition, it is unclear to what extent the patterns of mother–child relationships are the same for African-American and Euro-American adolescent mothers. Because of the smaller size of the White subsample, the power to detect differential patterns across the ethnic groups was reduced considerably. The results are likely more descriptive of relationships that exist within the African-American population. Future research needs to examine more closely whether or not the conclusions we have reached in this project hold equally well across class, ethnicity, and race.

From an applied perspective, the importance of the findings reported in chapter 6 and in this chapter, center on the detection of early appearing cognitive and socioemotional problems in children born to adolescent mothers and in the identification of differential precursors of these problems. If not addressed adequately, early developmental problems will most likely lead to school failures, delinquency, and/or mild MR or LD. It is essential that children at risk for developmental problems be identified before such problems surface, or at least before they become ingrained and intractible. The ability to identify unique prenatal maternal factors that predict, and likely cause, cognitive and socioemotional delays in at-risk children has important implications for both prevention and intervention programs. Through understanding the maternal and socioenvironmental factors that influence the development of at-risk children, intervention programs—implemented early in each child's life, or prenatally—can be better designed to prevent or ameliorate cognitive and socioemotional deficits (cf. Ramey & Ramey, 1990). Based on our results, decreasing maternal socioemotional problems, building "positive" parenting skills, and facilitating the appropriate kind, timing, and amount of social support are likely essential in forestalling early child developmental delays.

8

Resiliency in Adolescent Mothers and Their Children

Autobiographical novels, such as *Angela's Ashes* (McCourt, 1998) and *I Know Why A Caged Bird Sings* (Angelou, 1983) document the development of extraordinary individuals who have overcome deprived or traumatic childhoods. In *Angela's Ashes*, Frank McCourt poignantly describes the trials of growing up in Ireland, cold and hungry, with a father who squandered his meager income on alcohol. Despite seemingly insurmountable odds, McCourt escaped the harshness of his early upbringing to fulfill his desire for a better life by becoming a writer. In *I Know Why the Caged Bird Sings*, Maya Angelou writes of being rejected by her mother and father, being raped as a child, and becoming pregnant at age 16. Angelou's other books describe her search for esteem and belongingness as a young woman, and her eventual fulfillment as an adult (Angelou, 1984, 1985a, 1985b). Individuals, like McCourt and Angelou, who confront significant obstacles as children, yet go on to establish successful adult lives, exemplify the concept of resilience.

Although autobiographical novels of resilient individuals have engaged our curiosity and evoked our admiration for years, the scientific study of resilient children only began to coalesce in the early 1980s. In a pioneering study, Garmezy et al. (1984) undertook Project Competence to explain why some children from disadvantaged backgrounds with low IQ scores, low SES, and family instability were able to show satisfactory achievement and socioemotional adjustment. In this chapter, we briefly examine research on resiliency in teen mothers and their children and then evaluate factors that distinguish resilient from nonresilient mothers and children using data and case histories from the Notre Dame Parenting Project.

171

RESILIENCY AND ADOLESCENT PARENTING

Resiliency has been defined in a variety of ways by theoreticians and researchers (Garmezy et al., 1984; Rutter, 1985; Werner & Smith, 1992; Zimmerman & Arunkumar, 1994). According to Zimmerman and Arunkumar resiliency refers to a process that disrupts the negative trajectory from risk to psychopathology, resulting in adaptive outcomes despite the presence of adversity. Resilience implies the existence of stressful or challenging circumstances. The stressors may be acute or chronic, biological, psychological and/or social. Although resilience is the process of successfully coping with and adapting to stressors, it is most often inferred by successful outcomes. For the purposes of this chapter, resiliency is conceptualized as positive developmental outcomes despite the risks and stressors associated with adolescent parenting. In contrast, children and adolescent mothers who lack resilience are referred to as *vulnerable*: Vulnerability implies that children, or their mothers, were susceptible to the risks and stressors associated with early childbearing, resulting in less-than-satisfactory developmental outcomes.

RISK AND RESILIENCY AMONG ADOLESCENT MOTHERS

Teenage childrearing poses numerous risks and challenges for the adolescent mother and her children and sometimes hardship and stress for the extended family as well as the community in which they live. Challenges include balancing the need for continuing education with the responsibilities of parenthood, being able to financially provide for a new baby, and meeting the physical and emotional needs of an infant while working through the normal developmental tasks of adolescence. Confronted with these challenges, some adolescent mothers are able to cope effectively, fulfilling their own developmental needs as well as those of their children. These mothers find ways to continue their education and support themselves economically, while still providing adequate care and stimulation to their children. Other resilient young mothers, like Maya Angelou, experience considerable turmoil and misdirection before eventually achieving success and resiliency. Still others are vulnerable to the stressors associated with early parenthood, and manifest signs of developmental distress, including depression, anxiety, and low self-esteem as the data in chapter 4 amply demonstrates.

Like their mothers, children of adolescents grow up in environments that provide a range of opportunities and obstacles. All face the challenge of being raised by a young, often inexperienced mother. Many live in poverty and lack a stable father figure. A smaller number face additional traumas of emotional, physical, or sexual abuse, or see their parents suffering from addictions and/or other emotional disturbances. Despite these risks, some children like Frank McCourt, exhibit resilience, overcoming the hardships of their early childhoods, and then move on to establish successful lives.

Given the risks and challenges posed by early childbearing, various factors appear to reduce the negative impact of "risks" in the development of mothers and children, increasing their self-esteem, ability to cope, and opportunities for successful adaptation (Rutter, 1989). For example, regardless of the age of the teen mother, low education at the time of childbirth has been identified as a risk factor for poor developmental outcomes in children. Conversely, graduating from high school provides a useful resource for adolescent mothers struggling to cope with their parenting role. In this chapter, we seek to understand the factors that account for resiliency in both adolescent mothers and their children, factors that help to protect or innoculate them from risk factors and assist them in compensating for preexisting problems.

Previous research with the adolescent mothers in the Notre Dame Parenting Project (Mylod et al., 1997) and other studies (Camp, Holman, & Ridgway, 1993; Furstenberg et al., 1987; Leadbeater & Linares, 1992; Linares, Leadbeater, Jaffe, Kato, & Diaz, 1992; McKenry, Browne, Kotch & Symons, 1990; Werner & Smith, 1992) have led to greater understanding of factors leading to adaptive maternal outcomes following pregnancy and early motherhood. For example, Mylod et al. (1997) found that higher cognitive ability and cognitive readiness for parenting during the prenatal period were predictive of later maternal psychosocial adjustment, and parenting. Relatedly, Leadbeater and Linares (1992) found significant relationships between early personal adjustment and later maternal outcomes. Their longitudinal study focused on depression and its impact on early childbearing in a sample of African-American and Puerto Rican poor, inner-city, adolescent mothers: Nondepressed adolescent mothers were more likely to return to school and exhibited more positive interactions with their infants.

Werner and Smith (1992) focused on stability and satisfaction of maternal relationships and work in examining resiliency in a subsample of 20 adolescent mothers from the Kauai study. Fifty percent of these adolescent mothers had established stable relationships with a partner, were employed, and satisfied with their work (Werner & Smith, 1992). Compared to other young mothers in the sample, resilient early childbearers had closer and more secure relationships with their own caregivers. In addition, they scored higher on measures of internal locus of control, socializing, capacity for status, responsibility, and flexibility. They also reported reliance on siblings and friends, rather than parents or relatives, as sources of child care and other types of support. Only 40% of the resilient early childbearers had additional children, compared to 80% of young mothers with less successful outcomes. In addition, early successes in careers and relationships were associated with later positive developmental outcomes during early adulthood (Werner & Smith, 1992).

In the Baltimore study, Furstenberg et al. (1987) focused on income and fertility as the outcomes of interest 17 years following adolescents' transition to motherhood. More successful mothers were economically secure, or had at least better incomes compared to the "working poor" or welfare recipients, and had limited further childbearing. The strongest predictor of welfare status at the follow-up was the education level of the adolescent mothers' parents, independent of the young mother's own educational status. Furstenberg et al. (1987) surmised that parents with more education had more effective economic and social resources to assist them in early childrearing. Teens who limited further pregnancies often participated in school and community intervention programs; these community supports may have compensated for other ineffective support systems. Furstenberg and his colleagues (1987), evaluating grade retention, academic problems, delinquency, and drug abuse as important outcomes for children of adolescent mothers in their Baltimore Project, concluded that positive outcomes were more likely if mothers were married, had graduated from high school, had limited their subsequent childbearing and were not on welfare.

The contributions of risk and protective factors to behavior problems and school achievement in children born to adolescent mothers were investigated by Dubow and Luster (1990). The sample included 721 children, ages 8 to 15, from the NLSY. Although these children were older than children in the Notre Dame Project, mothers in both samples were similar in terms of age at childbirth and race. Dubow and Luster (1990) concluded that "the risk of developing problems increased linearly with the number of risk factors to which the children were exposed" (p. 402). The three most problematic, maternal risk factors were poverty, low self-esteem, and age less than 17 at the time of childbirth. In contrast, four protective factors (i.e., verbal intelligence, child self-esteem, emotional support at home, and cognitive stimulation at home) were associated with better child socioemotional adjustment and higher achievement. These protective factors further interacted with risk status to affect specific outcomes. For example, an emotionally supportive home environment served as a protective factor for the socioemotional adjustment of children most at risk; both an emotionally and cognitively supportive home environment were important for successful school achievement.

In summary, past research suggests resilient adolescent mothers often have a secure and supportive relationship with their own mother; are raised in homes with adequate financial and emotional resources; are intellectually, cognitively, and physically prepared for childbirth; are supported by their partners, siblings, and friends; possess good mental health, positive self-esteem, and parenting skills; and delay their next pregnancies (East & Felice, 1996; Furstenberg et al., 1987; Leadbeater & Linares, 1992; Mylod et al., 1997; Werner & Smith, 1992). In the rest of this chapter, we explore the importance of many of these same variables for the resiliency of adolescent mothers and their children. Our results show that some variables are associated with resilience in both adolescent mothers and their children, whereas other variables are uniquely related to either the resiliency of either mothers or children.

RESILIENCY IN THE NOTRE DAME PARENTING PROJECT

Although past research has examined resiliency in adolescent mothers or in their children, it has not explored the dual relationship: between resilience (or vulnerability) in adolescent mothers and resilience (or vulnerability) in children. It seems likely, however, that resilient teenage mothers who are able to meet the developmental tasks of adolescence, establish their own identities, and form intimate relationships are more likely to have resilient children. Although it may seem logical to assume that resilient mothers raise resilient children, it is possible that there is a trade-off between the resiliency of mothers and that of their children. In this sense, the lives of mothers and their children would be "interwoven" in inverse relationships. For example, it may be that some adolescent mothers achieve vocational or educational success to the detriment of their children. That is, in order to finish school, or earn sufficient funds to support themselves and their children, some mothers neglect the physical and emotional needs of their children and/or relegate child care to their parents, other relatives, or community agencies. The consequences of this relinquishment of responsibilities may be positive or negative depending on the quality and consistency of care that others provide for the children, and the extent to which the young mothers successfully negotiate their own developmental transitions through adolescence into adulthood. In contrast, other mothers may sacrifice their own personal growth and fulfillment for the sake of their children. These adolescent mothers may feel the need to postpone their education or to restrict their social engagements in order to provide directly for the care of their children. The remainder of this chapter explores factors associated with resilient outcomes in the lives of adolescent mothers and their children in the

Notre Dame Parenting Project and introduces the reader to selected adolescent mothers and children who exemplified resilience.

Maternal Resiliency Index

In contrast to analyses presented in prior chapters that focused on the prediction of specific outcomes (e.g., cognitive or socioemotional functioning), resilience is considered here as a multidimensional construct (Kaufman, Cook, Arny, Jones, & Pittinsky, 1994). Our approach to developing a resiliency index reflects the variability in possible pathways to success for early childbearers. For many young mothers, a trade-off exists between working and finishing school. Work brings the income needed for self-sufficiency, but the type of jobs available without additional schooling limits their future earning potential. However, in order to finish school and acquire the prerequisites for career advancement additional financial support from family or welfare is needed. Although either working or further education may be associated with resilience, doing both may be difficult to achieve and may not always enhance successful adaptation. Resiliency is also related to socioemotional factors; the probability of succeeding in a work and/or in an educational setting is enhanced if the individual is socioemotionally adjusted. Conversely, depression, anxiety and low self-esteem can adversely affect educational achievement and job performance. However, strengths in two of these three areas may compensate for weakness in the third. For example, low depression and high self-esteem may attenuate the negative effects of high anxiety. For these reasons, our resiliency index includes multiple measures of achievement of valued social outcomes (i.e., school and work) as well as measures of positive socioemotional adjustment (i.e., low depression, low anxiety, and high self-esteem).

More specifically, maternal resilience was defined in terms of an index that was composed of seven social and socioemotional outcomes at 5 years postpartum (Weed et al., 2000): high school graduation, current educational endeavors, current job status, employment history, self-esteem, depression, and anxiety. Table 8.1 describes the specific criteria used to define each outcome. Young mothers received one point for reaching each outcome criterion. Those achieving at least five out of seven possible points were considered resilient whereas those with less than five points were considered vulnerable.

TABLE 8.1
Maternal Resilience Index

Outcomes	Criterion
Social	
High school graduation	Successful completion of 12th grade or GED
Current educational status	Attending high school, technical or regular college, or certification program
Job Status	Current full- or part-time employment
Employment History	Any combination of full- or part-time employment spanning at least 30 months (not necessarily consecutive)
Socioemotional	
Self-esteem	A score over 56 on Coopersmith's SEI (adult form)
Depression	A score less than 13 on the BDI
Anxiety	Less than 43 on the trait subscale of the STAI

Note. One point was awarded for each outcome achieved by 5 years postpartum. Adolescent mothers receiving at least 5 points were considered resilient; mothers with less than 5 points were considered vulnerable.

Child Resiliency Index

Three criteria were considered in the classification of the 5-year-old children as resilient: intelligence, adaptive behavior, and behavior problems. Children who scored within one standard deviation of the mean of 100 (i.e., over 84) on both intelligence and adaptive behavior and below the borderline-clinical cutoff on behavior problems were considered resilient, whereas children who failed to meet any one of these three criterion were considered vulnerable. Significant deficits in one or more of these three areas at age 5 may predispose the young child for educational failure or special class placement. In contrast, adequate performance in all three areas implies children are within the normal range of cognitive and behavioral functioning for their age levels.

Dyadic Classifications

Simultaneous consideration of the resiliency of both the mothers and children generates four possible combinations: resiliency in both the adolescent mother and her child; resiliency in the mother, with the child

TABLE 8.2
Cross Classification of Resiliency in Children and Mothers

| | Mothers | |
Children	Resilient (n = 47)	Vulnerable (n = 79)
Resilient (n = 39)	22 (17.5%)	17 (13.5%)
Vulnerable (n = 87)	25 (19.8%)	62 (49.2%)

experiencing vulnerability; vulnerability of the mother associated with resiliency of the child; and vulnerability in both mother and child. Chi-square analysis confirmed the hypothesis that the resilience of mothers was associated with resilience in children $[\chi^2 (1, N = 126) = 8.54, p = .003]$. Table 8.2 shows that two thirds of the mother–child dyads were in agreement on their resiliency classification. The majority of the congruent classifications were accounted for, however, by the fact that mothers classified as vulnerable had children who were also evaluated as vulnerable, whereas resilient mothers were almost equally likely to have children who were evaluated as resilient or vulnerable. The status of mothers and children from each of the four groups on the specific outcome criterion and on related 5-year outcomes (e.g., fertility, marital, and welfare status) is described next.

Resilient Mothers With Resilient Children. Nearly 18% of the adolescent mothers and their children in our sample met the criteria for resiliency. Figure 8.1 shows the social and socioemotional status of these resilient mothers compared to mothers from the other classifications. Five years postpartum, all but one of these 22 young women had graduated from high school, and 23% were continuing their education. Ninety-one percent were working and 68% had worked at least 30 months since their child was born. Most had improved their SES from their childhood. Only 41% still relied on any governmental assistance (most often Medicaid and/or food stamps). Twenty-three percent were married at the time of the 5-year interview, 18% had been divorced, and 59% had never been married. Thirty-six percent had no additional children, whereas 18% had two or more. These resilient adolescent mothers had high self-esteem and showed few signs of depression or anxiety.

The achievements of the resilient children of resilient mothers in comparison to children in the other resiliency classifications are shown in Fig. 8.2. By definition, they had at least average intelligence and adaptive behavior and had few behavior problems. Seventy-seven percent were male. The racial distribution of resilient children of resilient mothers was similar to the larger sample: 68% African American, 27% Euro-American, and 5% Hispanic.

Resilient Mothers With Vulnerable Children. Twenty percent of the dyads were categorized as having resilient mothers and vulnerable children. As shown in Fig. 8.1, of this group, 92% had graduated from high school and 48% were continuing their education. Of these resilient mothers, 84% were working and 52% had worked relatively steadily since giving birth. A slightly higher percentage of these mothers than resilient mothers with resilient children relied on governmental support (64%). Eighty percent were still single, while 16% were married. Thirty-six percent had no other children, whereas 24% had two or more additional children. Similar to resilient mothers with resilient children, they had high self-esteem and showed few signs of depression or anxiety.

Vulnerable children with resilient mothers had problems in at least one of three domains (i.e., intelligence, adaptive behavior, or socioemotional adjustment): 48% had problems in one domain, 44% in two domains, and 8% in all three domains. The type of problems was distributed fairly equally across the domains. Forty-four percent of the children were male. Sixty-four percent were African-American, 28% were Euro-American, and 8% were Hispanic.

Vulnerable Mothers With Resilient Children. Less than 14% of the dyads had vulnerable mothers and resilient children. Twenty-nine percent of the mothers had not graduated from high school; only 12% were working, and a similar percentage had worked at least 30 months since giving birth; 81% relied on governmental support. None of the mothers had successfully completed post-high school education. Eighty-two percent were still single at 5 years; 12% were married; 41% had one additional child, and 41% had two or more. Many of these mothers were struggling with low self-esteem, high anxiety, and/or depression.

Despite the vulnerability of their mothers, resilient children in the classification had at least average intelligence and adequate adaptive behavior, and they displayed few internalizing or externalizing problems (see Fig. 8.2). Only 35% of these children were male. Although the proportion of African-American infants in this category did not differ from that of the larger sample (65%), there were fewer Euro-American dyads (18%) and more Hispanic dyads (18%). Interestingly, 37.5% of all Hispanics in the sample were in this dyadic category.

180

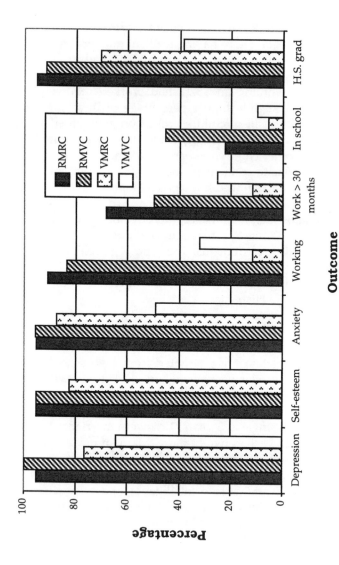

Outcome

FIG.8.1

Percentage of criteria variable in relation to maternal resilience groups.

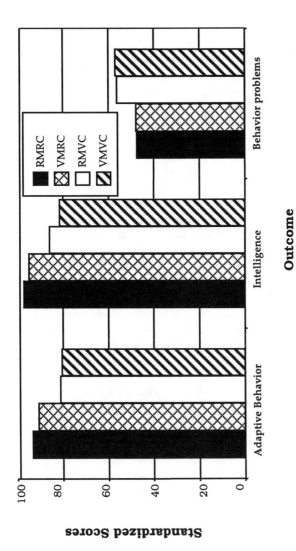

FIG. 8.2

Developmental outcomes and child resilience classification.

Vulnerable Mothers With Vulnerable Children. Forty-nine percent of mother–child dyads in our sample were considered vulnerable. As shown in Fig. 8.1, at 5 years postpartum, 61% of the mothers had not graduated from high school; only 10% were currently in school. Thirty-two percent were working, but only 26% had worked steadily after having a child. Eighty-five percent relied on assistance. Seventy-five percent had never married, whereas 17% were currently married. Eighty-three percent of these mothers had one to three additional children. They reported higher rates of depression and anxiety than mothers in any of the other groups, and approximately 39% had low self-esteem.

Vulnerable children with vulnerable mothers demonstrated low levels of adaptive behavior, and intelligence, and high levels of externalizing problems (see Fig. 8.2). Thirty-seven percent of vulnerable children met two out of the three resiliency criteria; 44% met only one of the criteria; and 19% failed to meet any of the criteria for resilience. Fifty percent of vulnerable children with vulnerable mothers were male. Seventy-one percent of this group were African American; 26% were Euro-American; only 3% were Hispanic.

Predictor Variables and Discriminatory Analyses

In this section, antecedent factors associated with the 5-year resiliency status of mothers and children from the prenatal period through 3 years postpartum are described. Using discriminatory analysis, we identified antecedent factors at each of four assessment periods (prenatal, 6 months, 1 year, and 3 years postpartum) associated with resiliency status in adolescent mothers and their children. Identification of these factors provides important information about the resiliency process from pregnancy through 5 years and suggests a strategy for interventions. Simultaneous consideration of the resiliency status of early childbearers and their children provides a dynamic glimpse into the interwoven developmental trajectories.

Discriminant analysis was employed to identify sets of variables that distinguished the four dyad types: resilient mothers with resilient children, resilient mothers with vulnerable children, vulnerable mothers with resilient children, and vulnerable mothers with vulnerable children. Whereas multiple regression analysis identifies the relative contribution of each of a set of predictor variables for a particular outcome, discriminant analysis yields a linear combination of the identified predictor variables (the discriminant function) that maximally discriminates among the groups. Predictor variables are selected that account for maximal separation between the four groups through a stepwise process. The accuracy of the discriminant function is assessed by comparing the classification of subjects based on chance to their classification via the discriminant analysis. Random classification of subjects into four groups yields a chance accuracy rate of about 25%. The degree to which the discriminant function improves the classification results over what would be expected by chance is evaluated through chi-square analysis.

Cognitive, socioemotional, and social support predictor variables included in the discriminatory analyses are listed in Table 8.3. In general, these predictor variables are similar, if not identical, to those included in regression analyses reported in earlier chapters. Child-Centeredness, however, was omitted from the cognitive readiness construct because it constituted a separate factor in a factor analysis of the six cognitive readiness subscales. The composite cognitive readiness score was based on a simple summation of responses across all items, with Parenting Style being more heavily weighted because this scale included more items.

In order to explore the process of resiliency over time, analyses were conducted separately at each time period, with significant predictors from prior analyses being carried forward. In this way, important prenatal, early, and later influences on resiliency status were identified. To further understand the magnitude of differences between the four resilience groups, based on the identified predictor variables at each step, a least-squared analysis of variance was used to compare the means of the four groups, after controlling for variables from prior steps in the discriminant analysis. Adjusted means of significant predictor variables for the four resiliency groups are shown in Tables 8.4 to 8.6.

Prenatal Predictors of 5-Year Resiliency Classification. Results of the discriminant analysis indicated that five prenatal variables—grade and age at the time of the pregnancy, cognitive readiness, emotional support from partner, and social competence—accounted for approximately 16% of the variance between the four groups (see Table 8.4). Fifty-three percent of the sample were correctly classified into resiliency categories based on these five prenatal variables [χ^2 (9) = 49.3, $p < .001$].

TABLE 8.3
Predictor Variables Included in Discriminant Analyses at Each Time Period

Variable	Prenatal	6-Month	1-Year	3 Years
Maternal characteristics				
Grade level	X			
Age	X			
SES	X			X
Intellectual resources				
Maternal intelligence	X			X
Parenting				
Cognitive readiness	X	X		
Parenting stress		X		
Maternal interaction		X		X
MCRS – acceptance			X	
MCRS – over protection			X	
MCRS – over indulgence			X	
MCRS – rejection			X	
Child Abuse Potential (CAPI)			X	X
Socioemotional adjustment				
YSR behavior problems	X			
YSR social competence	X			
Trust of mother			X	
Alienation from mother			X	
Communication w/mother			X	
Self-esteem				X
Anxiety				X
Depression				X
Life Stress				X
Social Support				
From Mom	X	X	X	X
From partner	X	X	X	X
From friends	X	X	X	X
Child care from grandma		X		
Child care from partner		X		
Child care from others		X		
Child care from self		X		
Child variables				
Gender		X		
Bayley – MDI and PDI		X	X	
Temperament			X	X
Stanford–Binet L–M				X
Adaptive Behavior				X
Internalizing problems				X
Externalizing problems				X
PPVT–R				X

Note. MCRS = Mother Child Relationship Scales, YSR = Youth Self-Report, PPVT–R = Peabody Picture Vocabulary Test – Revised.

TABLE 8.4
Stepwise Discriminant Analysis Model of Prenatal Predictors of Resiliency Status

Variable	Step	pr^2	F	p	RMRC	RMVC	VMRC	VMVC
Grade level	1	.131	6.15	.0006	11.1[a]	11.1[a]	10.2[b]	10.0[b]
Age	2	.135	6.32	.0005	16.6[a]	16.7[a]	17.1[ab]	17.3[b]
Cognitive readiness	3	.096	4.27	.0067	106.00[b]	97.93[b]	96.65[b]	93.68[b]
Support from partner	4	.071	3.02	.0324	15.49[b]	12.78[b]	16.00[a]	13.76[b]
Social competence	5	.074	3.16	.0273	12.57[ab]	13.78[a]	10.52[b]	11.88[b]

Note. $r^2 = .16$, $n = 126$.

[a]RMRC = Resilient mothers with resilient children; RMVC = Resilient mothers with vulnerable children; VMRC = Vulnerable mothers with resilient children; and VMVC = Vulnerable mothers with vulnerable children.

[b]Means reported are adjusted Least Squared Means controlling for the effects of variables in all prior steps; different letters indicate significant differences ($p < .05$) between the groups.

Least-squared analyses indicated that grade and age at the time of the pregnancy discriminated the two resilient mothers groups from the two vulnerable mother groups (see Table 8.4). At the time of their pregnancy, the average age of the resilient mothers was 17.25 ($SD = 1.26$, range = 14.5 – 19.6), and the majority (78%) were in the 11th or 12th grade. Resilient mothers tended to be at grade level for age, and therefore, within each grade level were younger than vulnerable mothers. Only 16% had ever repeated a grade. Vulnerable mothers tended to be younger ($M = 16.93$, $SD = 1.36$, range = 13.9–19.6) and to have completed less education at the time of childbirth. Sixteen percent of the vulnerable teens were in Grades 7 or 8, 36% were in 9th or 10th, and 49% were in 11th or 12th grades. Although, overall, these mothers were younger than mothers in the other groups, they were older than they should have been based on their current grade levels, with 41% repeating a grade. Social competence also emerged as an important buffer for the resilient adolescent mothers. Both groups of resilient mothers scored higher on social competence than the two groups of vulnerable mothers. Resilient mothers were more involved in school activities and clubs, had more hobbies, and reported engaging in more activities with their friends than vulnerable mothers.

In comparison to the other three groups, resilient mothers with resilient children were also more cognitively ready for their maternal roles. For example, they believed it was important to pay attention to their

TABLE 8.5
Stepwise Discriminant Analysis Model of 1-Year Predictors of Resiliency Status

Variable	Step	pr^2	F	p	RMRC	RMVC	VMRC	VMVC
MCRS - acceptance	1	.161	5.42	.0018	45.14[a]	40.90[b]	39.39[b]	38.83[b]
Child care by Grandmother	2	.124	3.97	.0107	33.55[b]	40.71[ab]	57.09[a]	28.56[b]
Grade level	3	.104	3.21	.0273	11.00[ab]	11.15[a]	10.27[b]	10.22[b]
Age	4	.101	3.08	.0320	16.78[a]	16.83[a]	17.26[ab]	17.37[b]

Note. r^2 = .15, n = 89.

MCRS = Mother Child Relationship Scales.

RMRC = Resilient mothers with resilient children; RMVC = Resilient mothers with vulnerable children; VMRC = Vulnerable mothers with resilient children; and VMVC = Vulnerable mothers with vulnerable children.

Means reported are adjusted Least Squared Means controlling for the effects of variables in all prior steps; different letters indicate significant differences (p < .05) between the groups.

children's feelings, to meet their basic needs, and to listen to their children's concerns. They believed in showing their affection with hugs and kisses. In addition, they held appropriate expectations about developmental milestones. The other three groups did not differ significantly on cognitive readiness, although the vulnerable mothers with vulnerable children group scored somewhat lower than the other two groups.

Finally, emotional support from the primary partner differentiated mothers of resilient children from those with vulnerable children. Mothers of resilient children reported stronger feelings of closeness with their primary partners, indicated their partners understood them, and expected that they would provide considerable emotional and material support. In contrast, resilient mothers of vulnerable children reported significantly less emotional support from the fathers of their babies.

Six-Month Predictors of Resiliency Classification. The five significant prenatal variables were carried forward and included in the analysis of 6-month predictors. This strategy enabled us to identify the extent to which early postpartum processes contributed to resiliency, over and above characteristics present before the baby's birth. None of the 6-month variables accounted for significant amount of variance beyond that explained by prenatal predictors.

One-Year Predictors of 5-Year Resiliency Classification. In order to ascertain the extent to which variables assessed at 1-year postpartum added to the variance explained by the prenatal predictors, the five significant prenatal variables were again carried forward, and included along with the 1-year predictors listed in Table 8.3. Discriminant analysis revealed that two 1-year variables (maternal acceptance of infant and grandmother care of infant) and two prenatal variables (grade and age at time of pregnancy) accounted for a significant amount of variance in 5-year outcomes (see Table 8.5). Forty-four percent of the young mothers were correctly classified into resiliency categories on the basis of these four variables [χ^2 (9) = 21.6, p < .01]. The smaller sample size at 1-year postpartum may explain the slight loss of predictive accuracy compared to the prenatal analysis.

Compared to other early childbearers, resilient mothers with resilient children were significantly more accepting of, and involved with, their children. Roth (1980) defined *acceptance* as "an expression of an adequate mother–child relationship in terms of the mother's sincerity of affect expression, interest in child's pleasures, activities, and development, and perception of the child as a good child" (p. 1). This attitude of maternal acceptance replaced cognitive readiness in the discriminant analysis, suggesting that young mothers who were more cognitively prepared prenatally were more accepting of their 1-year-old infants. Further analysis confirmed a relation between prenatal cognitive readiness and 1-year acceptance (r = .53).

The percentage of time infants spent with grandparents also emerged as a significant predictor of resiliency classification. Resilient children of vulnerable mothers spent a significantly greater amount of time with their grandparents than children in the other groups. Somewhat surprisingly, however, these vulnerable mothers reported lower levels of emotional support from their mothers. In other words, even though the infants' grandparents were providing extensive, and in some cases total, child-care, the mothers' perceptions of support were not uniformly positive.

Three-Year Predictors of 5-Year Resiliency Classification. The four significant predictor variables from the prior 1-year analysis (i.e., grade and age at the time of the pregnancy, maternal acceptance and grandmother care of infant at 1 year) were carried forward and included with the 3-year predictor variables (see Table 8.3). Many of the outcome measures that differentiated the four groups at 5 years postpartum emerged as predictors at 3 years postpartum. Thirty percent of the variance between the four groups was explained by seven variables: two maternal variables (current SES and self-esteem), three child variables (adaptive behavior, intelligence, and temperament) and two support variables (percent of time in grandparent care at 1 year and emotional support from primary partner at 3 years; see Table 8.6). The discriminant function based on the seven variables correctly classified 64% of the young mothers and children into an appropriate resiliency category [χ^2 (9) = 89.0, $p < .001$].

TABLE 8.6

Stepwise Discriminant Analysis Model of 3-Year Predictors of Resiliency Status

Variable	Step	pr^2	F	p	RMRC	RMVC	VMRC	VMVC
Current SES	1	.282	14.04	.0001	58.55[a]	61.00[a]	66.13[b]	66.00[b]
Adaptive vehavior	2	.175	7.47	.0001	96.76[a]	83.83[c]	91.53[ab]	89.92[b]
Child IQ	3	.141	5.75	.0011	83.44[ab]	81.17[b]	88.79[a]	76.99[b]
Maternal self-esteem	4	.145	5.87	.0010	80.76[a]	64.16[bc]	72.96[ab]	60.20[b]
Child care/								
grandmother	5	.093	3.53	.0175	37.50[ab]	41.20[ab]	52.41[a]	29.64[b]
Support from partner	6	.076	2.79	.0445	7.14[ab]	7.95[ab]	8.85[a]	6.25[b]
Child temperament	7	.076	2.75	.0465	16.27[a]	17.82[b]	17.44[b]	17.50[b]

Note. r^2 = .30, n = 111.

[a] RMRC = Resilient mothers with resilient children; RMVC = Resilient mothers with vulnerable children; VMRC = Vulnerable mothers with resilient children; and VMVC = Vulnerable mothers with vulnerable children.

[b] Means reported are adjusted Least Squared Means controlling for the effects of variables in all prior steps; different letters indicate significant differences ($p < .05$) between the groups.

Three years after the birth of their first child, both groups of resilient mothers continued to surpass vulnerable mothers in educational attainment and job status (i.e., SES). Once current SES was entered into the discriminant analyses, grade and age at the time of pregnancy dropped out as significant predictors. Resilient mothers with resilient children had significantly higher self-esteem at 3 years postpartum than mothers of vulnerable children. Vulnerable mothers with resilient children reported both more child-care support from grandparents, and more emotional support from their partners than vulnerable mothers with vulnerable children. In contrast, resilient mothers, with and without resilient children, did not differ significantly on these social support variables.

Resilient children of resilient mothers exhibited significantly higher levels of adaptive behavior and easier temperaments at 3 years of age than both groups of vulnerable children. These children also exhibited somewhat higher levels of adaptive behavior and somewhat easier temperaments than resilient children of vulnerable mothers. In contrast, resilient children of vulnerable mothers had higher intelligence scores than children in the other groups, whereas vulnerable children with vulnerable mothers had an average IQ of 77, significantly lower than both groups of resilient children.

Racial Considerations. In order to explore potentially different processes of resiliency associated with race, the discriminant analyses were rerun with only the African-American adolescent mothers. There were insufficient numbers of Euro-American or Hispanics for separate analyses of these groups. Differences in results of the prenatal analysis with the full sample were minor. Although the ordering or the magnitude of the predictors changed slightly, the variables themselves did not. At 6 months postpartum, parenting emerged as the most important predictor of resiliency classification among the African-American mothers. All three resiliency groups were observed to have more positive interactions with their 6-month-old infants than vulnerable mothers with vulnerable children. Prenatal cognitive readiness, social competence, and grade accounted for additional significant variance, with an average squared canonical correlation of .24, suggesting that the discriminant variables were somewhat more predictive for the African-American teens than those from other racial backgrounds.

The discriminant analysis of 3-year variables indicated that children's PPVT–R scores accounted for 27% of the variance, with all other predictors controlled. Resilient children, with and without resilient mothers, scored significantly higher on the PPVT–R than either group of vulnerable children. Current SES, child's adaptive behavior, maternal anxiety, grandmother care, social support from partner, life stress and child abuse potential all contributed significantly to the discrimination between the resiliency groups. Thirty-seven percent of the total variance was explained by these eight variables. Variables generally explained more variance when confined to African-American teens even though sample size was reduced.

Two specific differences are worth noting: the increased importance of quality of early parenting for resiliency in African-American children, and the differential predictiveness of the PPVT–R versus the Stanford-Binet. Early developing language skills were more strongly associated with later resilience in African-American children than was intelligence.

DEVELOPMENTAL INTERPRETATIONS
OF RESILIENCY OUTCOMES

The discriminant analyses reported in this chapter are generally consistent with findings presented earlier in chapters 5 and 7. Confirming the parenting model presented in chapter 2, prenatal cognitive readiness emerged as an important early predictor of resilience in both adolescent mothers and their children. By 1-year postpartum, cognitive readiness was replaced by a related measure that assessed the mothers' acceptance of their children.

An especially important predictor of maternal resiliency (as distinct from resiliency in children) was level of education. At each time period, adolescent mothers who had completed more schooling were more likely to show resilience. However, school success was also important. For example, a pregnant 10th grader who was in an age-appropriate grade was more likely to be resilient than a 12th grader who had been held back. It remains unclear whether the advantage conferred by educational success has to do with the knowledge learned in school or the teens' histories of academic success. Social competence also emerged as a predictor of maternal resilience. It may be that social competence provided resilient mothers necessary coping skills to relate to social services agencies, obtain other social supports, and to deal with socioemotional stressors.

Social support appeared to serve as an important factor in the lives of children of adolescent mothers. Children were more likely to be resilient if their fathers (or mothers' primary partner) provided the mothers with emotional support during the prenatal period. It may be that prenatal support was indicative of continued postpartum support. This supposition was partially confirmed by the reemergence of social support from partner as a significant discriminatory variable at 3 years postpartum. At this time, however, support appeared to interact with the resiliency status of the mother: If the mother was resilient, social support from the primary partner did not differentiate resilient from vulnerable children. It did, however, significantly predict the resiliency status of the children with vulnerable mothers.

Child-care support from the grandparents also appeared to be a protective factor that was more important for children of vulnerable than resilient mothers. This positive effect could be due to the development of a secure attachment relationship with a grandparent; the provision to the children of important material resources not available from mothers; or the stimulation of verbal and cognitive skills. In contrast to the positive influence of grandparent support on the lives of children of vulnerable mothers, use of child-care support by resilient mothers was associated with vulnerability in their children. The next section describes different pathways to resiliency and how these pathways manifested themselves in the lives of three dyads.

PATHWAYS TO RESILIENCY

Resilient Mothers and Resilient Children

Resilient mothers with resilient children exhibited a consistently adaptive pattern beginning in the prenatal period and continuing through 5 years postpartum. The mothers began their transition to motherhood with more resources than adolescents in the other classifications. They had completed more education at the time of the pregnancy and were, on average, at the appropriate grade level for their age. Resilient mothers were cognitively prepared for their maternal role, with adaptive parenting attitudes, adequate knowledge, and appropriate expectations regarding the development of their infants. They received considerable support from their primary partners and were generally socially competent. They were also involved in a variety of school and other social activities.

One year following the infants' births, most of the resilient mothers were the primary caregivers for their infants. They were accepting of their infants and indicated satisfaction with their maternal role. At 3 years postpartum, they generally had improved their SES. They had high self-esteem, and continued to report high levels of support from their primary partners. By 3 years of age, their children were already demonstrating the average levels of adaptive behavior and intelligence that were subsequently used to classify them as resilient at 5 years.

Despite common characteristics shared by resilient mothers with resilient children, there was variability among the 22 mothers and children in this classification. A more detailed consideration of a specific resilient mother and child dyad (Tonya and Kiesha) provides further insights that help explain the resilience of mothers and children in this category. Tonya was 18 and had finished high school on schedule at the time of Kiesha's birth. She had maintained an adequate GPA her senior year. Tonya never repeated a grade nor experienced serious problems in school. Her school success was somewhat surprising considering that she scored below average in intelligence (IQ = 79). It seems likely that Tonya's positive socioemotional adjustment contributed to both her and Kiesha's eventual resiliency. She participated in several sports and hobbies, and enjoyed spending time with her friends. In contrast to most resilient mothers with resilient children, Tonya received minimal support from Kiesha's father. At the time of Kiesha's birth, Tonya was no longer in contact with the biological father and did not expect him to provide emotional or financial assistance in the future.

When Kiesha was 6 months of age, Tonya reported experiencing stress related to her parenting role. However, she continued to express the same nonpunitive, empathetic attitude toward childrearing that she had espoused before Keisha was born. Tonya maintained a close, supportive relationship with her mother throughout her pregnancy and after Kiesha's birth. Her mother, however, provided little routine child-care for Kiesha. At the time of the 1-year interview, Tonya indicated that her mother understood and supported her and accepted her as she was. Tonya, in turn, expressed a similar type of acceptance of her daughter, Kiesha.

At 3 years postpartum, Tonya was engaged to be married for the first time. She and Kiesha were living with Tonya's fiancé. Tonya reported high self-esteem and relatively few life stressors. She had just begun a new job as a receptionist and reported some financial stress due to the purchase of a new car. At this point, Kiesha had an IQ of 86, an above average adaptive behavior composite and no serious signs of internalizing and externalizing problems. At the time of the 5-year interview, Tonya, now 23, had been working full time for 3 years as a receptionist in a local factory. She had a moderate income without reliance on welfare. Although Tonya had grown up in a part of town known for its poverty and high drug-related crime rate, she had moved and was currently living in a nice apartment with her daughter and current fiancé. She was pregnant with her second child. Tonya reported high self-esteem, with no signs of depression or anxiety. Kiesha, who had been in preschool since age 3, had an IQ of 94, an adaptive behavior score of 90, and a T score of 53 on CBCL, development appropriate for her age. Both mother and child seemed to be increasing in resiliency over time.

Resilient Mothers and Vulnerable Children

Resilient mothers with vulnerable children possessed some of the same critical prenatal resources as resilient mothers with resilient children. Both groups were similar in terms of grade level and age at the time of the pregnancy. In addition, both groups of resilient mothers had higher levels of social competence. However, resilient mothers with vulnerable children were less cognitively prepared for their transition to motherhood, and felt less emotional support from their partners than did mothers of resilient children. During the postpartum period, differences between resilient mothers with vulnerable children and those with resilient children appeared to be quantitative rather than qualitative. Mothers of vulnerable children were somewhat less accepting of their maternal role at 1 year, had somewhat lower self-esteem at 3 years, and felt less emotional support from their primary partner. Although their vulnerable children scored slightly lower than resilient children on both the 6-month and 1-year Bayley, the difference in intelligence only reached significance at 3 years of age. Differences between the two groups of children on adaptive behavior at this point was even more striking than the intellectual differences. In general, resilient mothers had sufficient resources to enable them to overcome the challenges of early motherhood, but without adequate cognitive preparation for their new maternal role, or the additional supports of a partner, they seemed less able or willing, to provide their children with appropriate developmental experiences.

Dawn and Jessica are an example of a resilient mother–vulnerable child dyad. Many of the cognitive, socioemotional, and social support factors that characterized Tonya as a resilient mother were also present in Dawn's life. Dawn was 18 and in the 12th grade when she became pregnant with Jessica. Dawn had done fairly well in school, although she had failed English during her final semester. She was taking mostly technical courses including office supervision, management, and accounting. She graduated on time for her age, and reported a high level of social competence. She liked to play baseball, basketball and swim, and considered herself better than average on cross-stitching and making doll clothes. She was actively involved in her youth group at church, as were several of her closest friends. Although she identified Shannon as her best friend, she indicated she had four or more friends with whom she was close and did things with several times a week. She babysat to earn extra money.

Even before Jessica was born, however, factors were missing from Dawn's life that would have improved Jessica's chances for more satisfactory developmental outcomes. Dawn described Curt (Jessica's father) as immature and unsupportive. She did not think that he would provide financially for the baby and that he was a "no-good" type of guy. Dawn's perception of Curt's lack of support is similar to that of other resilient mothers with vulnerable children.

At 1-year postpartum, Dawn's social competence seemed to compensate for familial problems in her life. She reported that she was extremely close to her girlfriends and that they provided considerable emotional support. She had separated from Jessica's father who was becoming alcoholic and abusive, and moved back home with her parents and younger brother. Dawn felt her mother expected too much of her and didn't understand what she was going through. Although her mother helped out with child-care, the percentage of time was less than for other young mothers in this group. Jessica's vulnerability at age 5 was foreshadowed by her low score of 84 on the Bayley Mental Development Index at age 1.

At the time of the 3-year interview, Dawn was still struggling with her relationship with Jessica's father, Curt. They had reconciled for several months and separated again. Dawn admitted Curt still had serious problems with alcohol and other drugs and continued to be abusive to her and Jessica, likely contributing to her low self-esteem. For the previous year, Dawn had worked full time as a loan processor. Jessica was in day-care for about 10 hours a day while her mother worked; both mother and daughter had had several bad colds and upper respiratory infections.

Jessica was showing clear signs of developmental problems at age 3. Her intelligence score was 83 with an adaptive behavior composite of 90. Jessica's scores on both internalizing and externalizing problems were in the clinical range. From the age of 3 to 5, Jessica's development was unstable. Jessica had attended both 3- and 4-year-old kindergarten, and stayed with an aunt while Dawn worked. Her intelligence score improved to within a normal range, and her behavior problems had decreased to normal levels. However, her adaptive behavior, which had been appropriate at age 3, had not kept pace with her development in other areas, and, at age 5, was lagging behind what is typically expected of 5-year-old children. Jessica did not know her phone number, address, or birthday and was not even reading common signs. She had few children in the neighborhood to play with, except for one cousin. Her activities were unstructured and consisted mostly of playing outside with the dog or watching television.

During this period, Dawn received several promotions in her job as a loan processor. She made enough money to support herself and Jessica without additional governmental aid. At the time of the 5-year interview, Dawn was in the process of purchasing the comfortable trailer she and Jessica were living in outside the city. She was not currently involved in an intimate relationship. Although Dawn reported high self-esteem and low depression and anxiety, she also indicated that she had not been completely satisfied with her life the past year. This story represents a resilient mother and vulnerable child.

Vulnerable Mothers With Resilient Children

The pathway to resiliency for the 17 resilient children with vulnerable mothers was distinctly different from that of resilient children with resilient mothers. The vulnerable mothers of resilient children tended to have less education at the time of childbirth, and although they were younger overall, they were older than they should have been based on

grade level. In addition, these vulnerable mothers were relatively unin-
volved in any school or social activities, and were less cognitively prepared for their maternal role than resilient mothers. The only positive
prenatal resource appeared to be an emotionally supportive partner. By
1-year postpartum, many of the vulnerable mothers were less accepting
of their infants and appeared to have rejected their maternal role. The
infants' grandmothers appeared to be a source of conflict and tension for
the mother. Although many parents of vulnerable mothers had assumed
primary responsibility for caring for the infants, the adolescent mothers
reported receiving little emotional support from their mothers. By 3 years
postpartum, maternal and child outcomes had diverged. Although
mothers had moderate self-esteem and continued to feel emotionally
supported by their partners, most had experienced little educational or
job success. In contrast, their children were, for the most part, indistin-
guishable from resilient children of resilient mothers. They had average
intelligence and adaptive behavior scores.

The experiences of Juanita and Jolene are similar to most of the other
vulnerable mothers with resilient children. Jolene was born the summer
following Juanita's junior year in high school. Juanita had missed so
much school during her pregnancy that she believed she would have to
repeat 11th grade. Juanita's vulnerability was also foreshadowed by her
low social competence. She was not involved in sports, had only one
hobby and had no close friends. Juanita's socioemotional problems may
have been related to a history of sexual abuse and to her father's alco-
holism. She spent the early part of her adolescence in several foster
homes because of the physical and sexual abuse she suffered from her
parents. Nevertheless, she was living at home with both parents at the
time of her pregnancy.

Despite the many factors that appeared to work against a positive
outcome for Juanita and Jolene, the strong support from Jolene's father,
Manuel who was 19 years old, likely served as a compensatory factor
that assisted Jolene on a path toward resilience. Juanita indicated she felt
almost total support from Manuel. She reported that Manuel was happy
about the pregnancy, that they were in love, and that he was "very protective" of her. She believed he would provide emotional and financial
support as well as assist with child care.

At 6 months postpartum Juanita moved out of her parents' home to
live with Manuel. She enrolled in the high school's program for pregnant
and parenting teens, and was able to make up the credits she had missed
earlier. However, she felt the program limited her both academically and
socially and soon transferred back to the regular curriculum. Because she
lived in tenement housing outside the bus route and had no transportation of her own, she faced a serious challenge getting to school. In addi-

tion, there was no one to provide child care for Jolene. Fortunately, the school provided assistance. For several months during her senior year, the school provided a taxi to pick up both Juanita and Jolene. Jolene attended the high school day-care center while Juanita was in classes.

Despite her academic progress, Juanita was experiencing clinical levels of parenting stress, perhaps in part because she lacked knowledge about normal child development and was not strongly child-centered. To her credit, however, she did not believe in using physical punishment. Although Juanita and her mother had never been close, the relationship became even more strained after Jolene was born. Juanita stated that her mother did not provide much emotional support. Nevertheless, her mother served as the only substitute caregiver for Jolene, often taking Jolene overnight and on weekends. Juanita felt that the few friends she had were excluding her because of Jolene.

At the time of the 3-year interview Juanita and Manuel were still together and had a second child. Juanita had finished high school, but was not working. She reported moderate self-esteem. At this same point, Jolene was assessed as having an IQ score of 84. She exhibited few internalizing or externalizing problems. Both Juanita and Jolene showed similar functioning between the 3- and 5-year interviews, although Jolene's intelligence and adaptive behavior scores had improved somewhat. In addition, Juanita had gotten and retained a job in a grocery store soon after Jolene turned 3. During this period she reported, however, having a high level of anxiety and concerns about the future. Her high level of anxiety combined with no work experience for the first 3 years following Jolene's birth kept her from meeting the criteria for resilience. The story of Juanita and Jolene illustrate the case of a vulnerable mother with a resilient child.

IMPLICATIONS FOR INTERVENTION

Several implications for intervention may be gleaned from the statistical analyses and case histories presented in this chapter. First, children were more than twice as likely to be resilient if their mothers were resilient. Therefore, efforts to enhance the resilience of adolescent mothers would appear to confer benefits on their children as well. Our results suggest that interventions to maximize the developmental outcomes of young mothers need to begin early—even during the prenatal period—and continue through early childhood. Enhancing maternal cognitive preparedness for parenting responsibilities appears to be the most promising approach for promoting resiliency in both adolescent mothers and their children. Because adolescent mothers with successful learning experiences and social competence were more likely to be resilient, interventions may need to focus on these domains. Because many vulnerable mothers lacked social competence and experienced a series of problematic relationships, they likely had difficulty asking for, or receiving, emotional and instrumental supports. For these mothers, additional educational and clinical services from sources outside the immediate family would likely be of benefit.

Second, some protective factors contributed to the resilience of children but not mothers. Social support, especially from the child's father and grandmother, appeared especially important for children if their mothers were not resilient. To the extent that involvement of grandparents promotes independence and competence in teen mothers, this support should positively contribute to the development of both mother and child. However, grandmothers may sometimes be perceived as interfering thus leading to increased conflict and stress for adolescent mothers. Programs for grandmothers and mothers need to assist families in establishing the adolescent mother in her role as primary caregiver, but for those mothers who have more difficulty with this role, provide more direct intervention with the children, and perhaps with the family. In chapter 10, the implications of our results on resiliency for social policy and community services are explored in greater depth. Before this discussion, however, we take a closer look at the life stories of four mothers and their families. Our aim is to show how unique, idiosyncratic factors sometimes produce resiliency in the lives of adolescent mothers.

9

Life Stories of
Adolescent Mothers

---

with Sebrina Tingley

In the preceding chapters we examined, from a quantitative perspective, the lives of adolescent mothers and their children, as well as how mothers influence their children's development. The data revealed problematic development, especially among the children, but considerable variability as well. Whereas some adolescent mothers were resilient and able to meet the challenges presented to them, others continued to have difficulties during the first 8 years of parenthood, depending greatly on the assistance of others to meet their day-to-day needs. Some children were greatly affected by the turmoil in their mother's lives, whereas others appeared less impacted. In this chapter, we use a qualitative approach to examine more closely the lives of selected mother–child dyads. The reason for this qualitatively driven search is that the quantitative approach is limited by the scope of our measurement scheme, especially by the type of assessments employed and the timing of those assessments, both of which restrict the set of questions that can be asked.

In this chapter, we take a closer look at the life circumstances of four mother–child dyads, chosen because they reflect a range of outcomes. Our intent is to use interview data to search for major life themes looking beyond the objective measurement scheme. We focus on variations in these themes, observing for example how families dealt with early pregnancies, how young mothers met the challenges inherent in adolescent development, and how they assumed the difficult task of rearing a young child while simultaneously progressing toward adulthood. The narratives in this chapter provide the readers insights into the reasons for the diverse developmental trajectories of mothers and their children— paths that are only partially explained by our formal measurement scheme. Each story is unique, as is each dyad's in our entire sample.

The chapter is structured so as to provide the reader with a brief, initial glimpse of each dyad, as revealed by objective evaluations. Next, each mother's personal story is told and interpreted. The stories include, whenever possible, the mother's own words.

GLORIA AND EDDIE: THE IMPORTANCE OF FAMILY

Databased Description:
Maternal Depression and Academic Difficulties

Gloria was typical of many of our adolescent mothers; she was 16 when she became pregnant. Our formal assessments indicated that she had low to average cognitive ability (with a particular deficiency in verbal reasoning skills), limitations in her cognitive readiness to parent, and poor social competence. She differed from most mothers in our sample in that she married the father of her baby. Gloria dropped out of school having completed the 10th grade. Although she planned to return to school following Eddie's birth, she never did. Five years after Eddie was born, at age 21, Gloria reported significant life stress, high state and trait anxiety, and mild depression. Three years later, the state anxiety had lessened but the depression had increased.

Eddie was born full-term, a healthy 9-pound, 9-ounce baby. Gloria's perception of Eddie was that of a difficult child, irregular in his biorythms and slow to adapt. Scores on the CBCL indicated behavioral problems that fell within the clinical range at 3 and 5 years. It was also apparent early on that Eddie was not developing appropriate cognitive skills. The SBIS (Form L–M) and the PPVT–R results at both 3 and 5 years suggested mild developmental delays, with scores below 70. Adaptive skills were rated only slightly higher, with some strength in daily living skills. Academic concerns were noted initially in math readiness at 5 years. By 8 years of age, Eddie had an estimated IQ of 68, and standard scores of 67 and 68 in math and reading, respectively. Clearly he was experiencing academic difficulties.

The Life Story: Gloria's Focus on Family

Although the quantitative data suggest that both Gloria and Eddie were experiencing developmental problems, Gloria's personal narrative reveals a different side of their life story. Gloria has lived in Indiana since the age of 12 after her family moved there from Texas. She grew up in a two-parent family surrounded by seven siblings. At 16, while she and her family worked in the cornfields to supplement their meager income, she met a 21-year-old migrant worker who had left Mexico 5 years earlier. The following February they were married, with their first child arriving in June. During the following 5 years, they had three more children. Gloria stayed home to care for their children as well as a niece, while her husband worked a steady, full-time job in a paper factory. They currently live in a four-bedroom, two-story home in a downtown area, near two homeless centers, several bars, a pornography shop, and a storefront church.

Gloria's four children have a variety of needs. Her first born, Eddie, is currently in the fifth grade, receiving supplemental speech services. In the fourth grade, he was referred for evaluation due to academic problems but the school did not find him eligible for special education services. Gloria's third son has mild cerebral palsy and receives special education services. Her youngest child, a daughter, currently attends Head Start. At this time, her greatest challenge is her second son, David, who has speech and reading problems along with serious behavior problems that have surfaced at school. Because David wasn't receiving speech therapy, contrary to what special education teachers had told her, Gloria protested until David received the recommended therapy. David's behavior problems became so severe that the school was calling home, often daily, requiring Gloria's husband to take time off work to pick up David. Gloria's husband was on the verge of losing his job when the school expelled David. According to Gloria, the problem was a combination of David being teased because of his disabilities and his own uncontrollable temper. It is important to note that Gloria does not see this disruptive behavior at home. Through the assistance of a local center, David, Gloria and her husband received counseling. The point at which David was able to resume his education was a moment of triumph for the family. Gloria acknowledged that in the years ahead, her greatest challenge will be keeping David in school.

Gloria's normal day begins at 5 a.m. in order to prepare her husband's breakfast, with her niece arriving 30 minutes later. When her husband leaves for work she helps her children and niece prepare for school, sending them off only after a good breakfast. After school she supervises their homework, play time, and baths. The children help set the table for dinner so that by the time Dad arrives home they are ready to enjoy supper. Evenings are spent reading, talking, playing games, and occasionally watching television.

Through their financial savings plan and penny pinching, Gloria and her husband have paid off their mortgage, 5 years after the purchase of their home. To do this, they often went without material things such as furniture, beds, extra clothing and toys, and did not spend money on entertainment. Even the eldest child, Eddie, contributed to the mortgage fund from his paper route. The month after they paid off their mortgage, they purchased a van. Subsequently, they took the children on a promised family trip to Florida, which included Disney World. Gloria stated they were able to take the trip because they all saved and had family in Florida with whom they stayed.

The most important part of Gloria's world is her family, especially the children. She is very child-centered, living her life through her children. She has strived to create a close-knit family and in so doing has tried to choose carefully what family rituals and patterns to maintain. Gloria is Catholic. She recalled fondly when as a young girl she and her sister would enact a drama of the massacre of the Lady of Guadeloupe. Gloria says of her faith:

> We believe a lot in the Catholic religion. Some people don't, and some people do...yeah, we grew up like that, you know, and so that's how we raise the kids too.

Gloria and her husband reject the negative childrearing practices passed on by their parents. Despite her parents' preference for punitive discipline, Gloria refuses to paddle her children or to rely on other negative disciplinary techniques, rather she tries to consistently use a positive approach. Gloria states:

> We're not a perfect family but we're not abusing them or nothing. Because, you know, my husband, he was beaten up a lot from his daddy, and he said, "I'm not going to do the things that my dad did."... he said, "No, I don't want that for my kids. I don't want them to go through what we did."

Gloria's husband is receptive to Gloria's innovative and creative ways in dealing with the children. They are willing to try new methods such as to reducing television watching and rewarding the children's good behavior with a "movie ticket." Gloria and her husband also limit their own television viewing time. As a family, they enjoy bike rides, playing basketball and touch football, and visiting local parks during the weekends. During the interview Gloria related the following family incident:

> Yesterday, they were planting little shrubs so they got all muddy, and he got the video camera and got all the kids all muddy; then they ended up fighting with the mud, playing around, throwing it at each other. It was nice when we saw it in

the videotape; we do mostly everything together. Yeah, they're very close with their dad.

Besides the children's academic needs, health problems and other family concerns have impacted their daily lives. When they were first married, Gloria's husband was an alcoholic and continued his drinking until she gave him an ultimatum while pregnant with their third child. She had decided she could no longer live with his heavy drinking. Two months before the birth of their third child, he came to the conclusion that his family was more important than alcohol and quit drinking. The only time they have left their children with another adult was to attend an Alcoholics Anonymous meeting where her husband was the guest speaker. More recently, her husband was diagnosed with diabetes. Because Gloria's mother has diabetes and a cousin died of this disease, she takes this illness very seriously. Much of her life revolves around her husband's diet and keeping him healthy. She has no doubt they can control his diabetes.

The reason behind their Florida trip was a feeling that time was running out, or in Gloria's own words, "We just had to get out before anything happened." This feeling was related to the fact that a number of suicides have occurred on both sides of the family. She and her husband have lost aunts, uncles, cousins and siblings. Gloria also suffered serious depression after the birth of her second son, depression serious enough to require medical care. Her husband teases her about the time when she didn't want their second son, but she now understands her feelings resulted from depression.

When asked, "Is there anything you would do differently?" Gloria's response was, "Finish school." However, it is more important to Gloria that each of her children graduate from high school. Gloria reports that her husband, who has a sixth-grade education, is trying to learn to read and write enough English to apply for U.S. citizenship. Gloria, having a 10th-grade education, would like to earn a GED, but has been unable to pursue it. Gloria's attempt at employment was short-lived as David's school problems interfered. She was invited to be a teacher's aide in her youngest child's Head Start class. As part of the job application process, Gloria passed what she felt to be a difficult test. But after a couple days in her new job, David's school began calling her daily concerning his behavioral problems and she quit. Gloria believes that it is more important to be home for her son than to work.

Gloria knows David is slow and falling well behind his classmates. Because of his disability she believes the school system is determined to expel him; Gloria knows she will need to continue to be his advocate. She knows that she and her husband are the only ones who can make sure their children receive the education they need in order to succeed. Gloria hopes her children "get better at school." And for herself, she hopes to return to school so she can eventually get a job. She dreams of being a teacher's aide.

Not for a moment does Gloria regret having children. Neither does she regret getting married. Her life revolves around her children and husband and she considers herself lucky. When asked about advice she would give to a teenage girl thinking about getting pregnant, Gloria emphasized the importance of marriage and father involvement: Gloria feels that although her marriage is not perfect she is in a far better position than friends who are raising their children alone. She advises adolescents to consider the possibility that the father might not be there to support her and their child.

Final Thoughts

In many ways, this is one of the more positive family stories among our sample of teen mothers, despite the vulnerability of both mother and child. Two characteristics distinguish Gloria and her family. One is the support that the family provides each other and derives from their religious beliefs. The other is Gloria's child-centered orientation, which includes her and her husband's commitment to avoiding the use of physical punishments as a parenting technique. Gloria functions as the heart and soul of this family. She has a very strong sense of family, often putting her family's needs ahead of her own. Religion plays a supportive role in family cohesion. Despite limited resources and unlimited family needs, Gloria, her husband, and the children have worked together to pursue family goals, actively struggling with medical, educational, emotional, and economic difficulties. Nonetheless, Eddie is considerably behind in school, and despite repeated attempts for additional support, special services have been denied. His prospects for fulfilling his mother's dream—graduating from high school—are not good.

DIANE AND DARLENE:
THE IMPORTANCE OF COMMUNICATION AND RELIGION

Databased Description: An Emerging Learning Difficulty

Diane, pregnant at age 16, delivered a few weeks before her 17th birthday. Educationally and intellectually, she was similar to most of our participants; she was a junior in high school and had a low to average intelligence. Her cognitive readiness to parent score was also similar to other adolescent participants but below that of typical adult parents. However, Diane differed from the rest of her cohorts in the area of social competence: In high school, she was more socially involved in activities. She participated in sports, hobbies such as sewing and singing, and clubs such as the multicultural and spirit clubs. However, family closeness was elusive. Diane's ratings of her attachment to her mother indicated alienation and poor communication. Eighteen months after delivering Darlene, Diane had graduated from high school. She worked as a nursing assistant, remained single, and lived with her parents.

Although physically healthy at birth, her daughter Darlene required bilateral leg braces during infancy because her legs turned in. At 6 months, Bayley scores suggested normal development. One-year Bayley scores were lower, but the examiner felt this may have been due to the fact that Darlene was tired and refused to participate in some tasks. At 3 years, however, the picture began to change. Although her cognitive development, measured by the SBIS (Form L–M), still appeared normal (IQ = 94), Darlene's performance on the PPVT-R, a standard score of 76, suggested significantly weaker receptive language skills. This same pattern existed at 5 years. Although early measures of academic achievement at age 5 did not reveal a problem, academic difficulties were clearly evident by the time of the 8-year assessment (e.g., standard scores of 74 in mathematics and 66 in reading on PIAT–R). Although the overall intelligence score continued to be within the normal range, verbal-performance discrepancy was found (estimated Verbal IQ of 65 vs. Performance IQ of 105). At age 8, a significant discrepancy between expected achievement, based on her cognitive ability and her actual academic achievement, suggested a learning disability. Similar discrepancy scores were obtained when Darlene was 10 years old. Despite her achievement difficulties, Darlene remained in a regular classroom. Her teachers often praised Darlene to her mother, possibly referring more to her positive attitude and personality than her skills and achievement.

Life Story: Achieving Happiness But Missing a Learning Problem

Diane, along with her four sisters and a brother, grew up in South Bend under the care of loving and hard working parents. Her father was, and still is, a minister while her mother is a homemaker. Diane's childhood revolved around church, which the family attended on an almost daily basis. When she reflected on her childhood she saw herself in a car going to and from church or sitting in the pews during a sermon given by her father, the pastor. Although Diane reported that her parents were "wonderful," she also stated that the family was not close. At home, her father rarely talked and her mother always seemed to be at the stove.

At age 16, after 2 years of dating her boyfriend, Diane learned of her pregnancy. She anticipated considerable support from her boyfriend, and that her parents would assist when needed. However, when she was 6 months pregnant, reality "kicked in." Her boyfriend dropped from the scene. Diane found herself removed from her previous routine. She enrolled in a special high school program for pregnant teens. Soon she was concerned more about whether she could afford diapers for her upcoming baby than about whether or not her boyfriend called every night. Just before her 17th birthday, she delivered a healthy daughter. The baby's father was never able to help out, and about five years later died in an automobile accident.

Diane heavily depended on her parents for help with her daughter, as well as a son born 4 years later. With their assistance, she was able to complete high school and attend a local college full time for 1 year. At age 22, Diane married a man, who like her father, was a pastor. They immediately had two more sons in successive years. Before the second child was born, her husband became involved in drugs and abandoned both Diane and the children. During this difficult time, Diane reexamined the role of church, God, and family. She came to understand the difference between her infatuation with men and the love she sought. She "gave her life to the Lord," although recognizing the limited role religion played in meeting the needs of her family.

At the time of the last interview, Diane had been happily married for 2 years to a "most wonderful husband." She reported that her four children, ages 4 to 12, were doing well. She acknowledged, however, that her current marriage was a challenge, as she, her husband, and the children learned about each other's good and bad traits. She felt blessed with the large measure of love she experienced in her home, in sharp contrast to her family experiences as a child.

At this point, Diane is employed as a counselor at a women's care center, a job she thoroughly enjoys. Diane's job includes running pregnancy tests and counseling young pregnant women who find themselves in the same position she was in 12 years earlier. For her, this is a challenging and rewarding job. Diane is able to bring her own experience of being "a frightened, pregnant teenager" into her work with young teens. Diane has repeatedly turned down full-time positions in favor of this part-time position in order to be home with her children when they return from school.

As in her youth, the church has been central for Diane and her family. Her current husband is a minister, like her first husband and her father. Although her parents "gave the church" the responsibility of communicating values, morals, and ethics to Diane and her siblings, Diane does not look to the church to play that same role in the lives of her children. Even though her husband is a pastor, she refuses to allow the church to absorb her life. She and her family attend church regularly, but no more than twice a week. As she watches her daughter draw pictures during the service, she knows her daughter isn't listening to the sermon any more than Diane did at her age. She strives to open and maintain lines of communication with her children. Diane stated: "I not only take her to church, but I talk to her about church. I talk to her when we are not at church. I don't look to the church to do everything and I think that's kind of where my parents looked to the church to do everything." Laughingly she continued "but I don't know why they thought we would listen! I just don't know why they thought we were in tune to all that."

For Diane, the importance of listening and nurturing communication between herself and her children is extremely important. She talks to her children about their day at school, about what they are watching on TV, and encourages them to talk to one another. And when her daughter is reluctant to talk, Diane sees it as her mothering role to "dig" because that is the most important time for communication. She feels she has found a balance between the church's message of hope and personal communication about life's struggles.

Diane's emphasis on communication comes from her own childhood in which her parents seemed clueless about what she was doing and feeling. She related her story about dating the same boy for 2 years, spending time every night on the phone, and ultimately becoming pregnant. When she was 3 months pregnant, she decided to share her condition with her mother. She went into the kitchen where her mother was cooking at the stove. Before Diane said a word, her mother asked, "Diane, don't you think you're seeing a little bit too much of him? I think you all are getting a little too close." It was another month before Diane could tell her mother that she had indeed gotten "a little too close." Diane felt that her parents were there for all the children, and that they loved each of them deeply; but at the same time she also observed that they didn't talk to one another and they were individuals living in a house rather than a family.

Diane is proud of her endurance, her ability to hang in there for herself and her children. She is optimistic about her own and her family's future. Unlike many of her friends, she indicated that she never once abandoned the care of her children to her mother or relied on drugs to relieve her pressures. She wants her daughter, Darlene, to have fulfillment in life, a wonderful husband, a relationship with the Lord and to know that Diane, her mother, will always be there for her.

Whether a woman is married or not, Diane feels all babies are gifts from God. How the baby has been conceived may be "wrong," but the baby is still a life growing inside of the woman. And although most of her clients at work look at their babies as "problems," she believes the "real problems" are what is happening in the teen's life or in their relationships with boyfriends. In looking back over her own life the one thing that Diane would change would be the dating process. For one, she would not have started "talking to guys so early in life"; she hopes her own daughter does not start dating until she is in her very late teens, or better yet, her early 20s. During her own teen years, young men consumed her life; Diane wishes she had not thought them to be so important. She reflects:

> You're trying to please so many people during your adolescent years. You know, you just want people to like you and you want to be accepted so much, so that it consumes you. I would have changed that.

The frustration Diane feels in her inability to have an impact on so many of the teen girls she counsels is evident. The paradox for Diane is knowing how different her own life would have been if she had not been like that thirteen old girl who left her office, having apparently not absorbed words of the wisdom Diane tried to impart. Diane wishes she could give all teen girls the following advice:

> Be very careful who you let into your life because your life is so precious. You only get one life and don't ever settle, never, ever settle. I settled, you know, in so many instances and so many areas of my life, I settled for less, but now, I realize I don't ever have to settle. I don't want whoever listens to wait till they get 28 to realize that. Okay?

Final Thoughts

In many ways, Diane is an admirable and resilient person. She appears family- and child-centered and has a well-developed value system. She has a job she likes and is hard-working, maintaining a reasonable balance between work and home. She seems oblivious, however, to her daughter's academic problems. In the interview she talked mostly about herself, seldom mentioning her daughter. Although Diane emphasizes the importance of maintaining good communication with her daughter, she also seems to have some of the same self-centeredness that she reports in her parents.

Unfortunately, Darlene is experiencing learning problems and will likely require extra support from the school and home in order to achieve at grade level. Although teachers have consistently reported on standardized forms that Darlene is below average in most academic areas; they have not felt this problem was significant enough to warrant further evaluation or special educational intervention. It is surprising that Diane has not recognized Darlene's school-related problems, given her regular attendance at parent–teacher conferences. Darlene seems to have good social skills like her mother; her ability to get along with others is often noted by her teachers. It is likely that Darlene's teachers have focused on her good behavior—reporting this to Diane during parent–teacher conferences—rather than her test scores. Good conduct seems, however, to be masking the emergence of Darlene's learning disability.

SHARON AND SHANEQUA: ESCAPING POVERTY

Databased Description: Multiple Problems in Mother and Child

Sharon was an older adolescent, age 18, when she had Shanequa. Sharon's ability level was below average, with an estimated IQ of 73. Her knowledge of child development was also lower than most teen mothers; although her parenting style and attitudes about children were similar. Her internalizing behavior score on the YSR was slightly elevated. After entering the second semester of her senior year, she dropped out of school. Many years later she completed work for a high school diploma. Five years after the birth of Shanequa, Sharon reported high state and trait anxiety, moreover, her self-esteem was low and her potential for child abuse elevated. Three years later, she was depressed. According to our criteria, Sharon is considered a vulnerable mother because of her inconsistent employment record, dependence on public assistance, and socioemotional difficulties.

Sharon's daughter, Shanequa, appeared to be developing normally early, with 6-month and 1-year Bayley scores of 102 and 103. By 3 years, however, developmental delays were noted: Shanequa had an IQ of 73 on the SBIS (Form L–M) and a standard score of 59 on the PPVT–R. Shanequa was evaluated as slow-to-warm-up in temperament, with both arrhythmic and withdrawn scale scores elevated. On the CBCL, her anxiety/depression subscale score was in the borderline range. A similar pattern of scores on these measures was observed at 5 years. At 8 years, Shanequa's estimated IQ was 70, visual organization was a strength relative to verbal reasoning. Receptive language was assessed at 76. Academic achievement was poor, with standard scores of 65 and 63 in reading and math on the PIAT–R at age 8. Socioemotional difficulties were also evident on the TRF of the CBCL (i.e., internalizing behaviors were in the clinical range); maternal ratings on the CBCL were not as negative as the teacher's. Shanequa's responses on the Children's Depression Inventory indicated severe depression. Her assessed intelligence and academic progress suggested the need for intensive intervention, tutoring, and educational programming in order to succeed in school. Her emotional difficulties also likely warrant professional assessment and perhaps intervention.

Life Story: The Need for Support Systems

Sharon shared her childhood with her "sister-cousin," a cousin close in age who her mother raised as her own and as Sharon's sister. When Sharon was 7, her mother had a son followed by another daughter; Sharon helped to raise both her younger siblings. She and her sister-cousin shared many adventures during their teens, including sneaking out of the house, dating boys, and attending parties late into the night. From age 15, until she found herself pregnant at 18 years of age, Sharon dated Tom. They planned on marrying sometime in the future, and both were happy about her pregnancy.

Sharon's first child, Shanequa, was born in the spring of her senior year in high school. Although Sharon was very close to graduation, she dropped out of high school. Within a 18 months, Sharon and Tom had a second daughter, Toni. During this time Sharon was employed at fast food restaurants, nursing homes, and as an attendant at gas stations, each for short duration of time. Unable to depend on either Tom or her part-time jobs for financial support, Sharon began to rely on government benefits and her mother for support. Sharon and the girls lived with her mother until Shanequa was 4 years old. At this time Sharon and the girls moved in with a new boyfriend, Don.

While living with Don, Sharon remained in poverty. She was deeply in debt and unable to pay her basic bills, always waiting anxiously for her monthly government check. After earning her GED, she was able to obtain a job at a local health care facility. Although not practicing birth control, Sharon says she was surprised to find herself pregnant again when her eldest daughter was almost 8. During this pregnancy, Sharon suffered high blood pressure and other medical problems, resulting in a lengthy hospitalization. Nevertheless, Sharon delivered a healthy baby boy, Jerome. Don was supportive, both emotionally and financially. In contrast, during this time, her first boyfriend, Tom, who was in prison or unemployed, was unable to assist Shanequa financially. During most of Sharon's relationship with Don, Shanequa lived with her grandmother. She eventually moved in with her mother and Don after her grandmother married.

Sharon reported she may have partied too much over the years, sometimes ignoring her children. Recently, after barely missing being a part of a shooting incident at a local bar, Sharon became convinced that her "nights out" should end. Sharon is trying now to be a "good mother," by being at home more for her children after school and during the evenings. She plans to pursue more activities and outings with the children, especially her eldest daughter, Shanequa.

Sharon's story is one of poverty and interpersonal turmoil. Poverty is a condition that Shanequa accepts but the second daughter complains about. Sharon has tried to teach the children to be grateful for what they have. For instance, when her children put an abundance of sugar on their rice and then didn't eat all of it, Sharon expresses concern: "Look," she told her children, "there are kids who wish they had that rice." She emphasized that it's getting harder to be a parent as her daughters get older because they want nice clothes and shoes. She "does what she can" and has faith that one day they will have what they need. Although Sharon doesn't attend church, she believes in God: "For but the grace of God, I didn't know where my food was coming from, but we ate." She prays to God for a better way of life.

Her desire to party and drink have made it difficult for her to maintain a full-time job. Yet, Sharon believes that education is the key to success. She advises her little sister to finish school before she has children, and suggests that if a man loves you he will wait. Sharon tried four times to finish school but each time the needs of her children and her interpersonal situations held her back. It took her almost 10 years to earn her GED even though she had been just a couple months from graduating from high school. Once Sharon finished her GED, she entered a local technical school only to drop out. Sharon does not believe in quitting: She intends to begin technical school again this fall, with hopes of finishing a 1-year degree program that will enable her to secure a better paying, full-time position. A lack of education has kept Sharon from gaining a higher paying job, with a benefits package.

Sharon hopes that her daughters, Shanequa and Toni, will graduate from high school and wait to have their own children. She appears deeply concerned for their welfare, especially her eldest daughter. Shanequa who will soon be 12, is shy, depressed, "cries at every little thing," and does not like being around men. Shanequa dislikes her step-grandfather so much that she now refuses to go to her grandmother's house. Neither Shanequa's father or his family have been able or willing to participate in her life. Sharon does not know what her eldest daughter is thinking or feeling. Sharon feels guilt over Shanequa's current emotional state. Sharon says she herself is going through a rough time and is unable to meet Shanequa's needs or reach her at all. Sharon feels that her children do not respect her and hopes by being home more that her children will learn to respect her more, as she respects her own mother. Although Sharon has been advised to take Shanequa to a local mental health center, Sharon insists that if she can only spend time alone with her daughter "she'll open up and talk to her." So far this has not happened.

When Don buys clothes and shoes for their son Jerome, he purchases expensive, name-brand items. He takes his son out with him everywhere he goes, and Don's parents have Jerome over every chance they get. Don helps out with the girls but the discrepancy between what the two sisters receive compared to their brother is large. The two girls wear second-hand shoes, Jerome, at age 3, wears expensive new shoes. In explaining this difference to her daughters, Sharon states it is because they have different fathers. Sharon tries to make up some of the difference in material goods in order to create a balance in what the three children receive.

Final Thoughts

Overall, the developmental trajectories of Sharon and Shanequa appear somewhat divergent. Sharon is excited about the prospect of entering technical school again, feeling that this time she'll make it through to graduation. She advises other young women to wait to have children because of the demands associated with combining schoolwork and family life, but currently does not practice any form of birth control. She believes that if she had another child, it would be a gift from God. Although struggling with poverty, medical problems, and with Shanequa's emotional difficulties, Sharon would like to have another child. Sharon is happy about the house they are living in, acquired with help from a housing subsidy. For the first time her daughters share one room, while her son has his own room. Sharon is trying hard to change her life and is optimistic about her own and her family's future. In contrast, Shanequa is depressed and experiencing academic difficulty. Sharon appears superficially concerned, seemingly unaware of the extent of Shanequa's emotional problems, focusing instead on trying to give her more clothes so that she won't compare herself to Jerome.

ROCHELLE AND MARCUS: SUPPORTIVE MOTHERS-IN-LAW

Databased Description: Predictors of Success

Rochelle was 16 and a sophomore in high school when she learned of her pregnancy. She differs from most of the other mothers in our project in that her intellectual abilities fell within the superior range. She appeared, based on her cognitive readiness scores, more prepared to parent than her peers, in terms of her knowledge of child development and parenting style preferences. Her responses indicated that she would be a more responsive and less punitive parent than most adolescent mothers. By our definition, Rochelle is considered resilient in that she continued her education beyond high school, has a profession, and exhibits no significant socioemotional difficulties.

Marcus was born full-term, weighing 7 pounds, 6 ounces. He has consistently scored in the average to above average range on measures of intelligence, language development, and academic achievement. Rochelle's ratings on socioemotional measures have consistently indicated that Marcus is an "easy" child who has demonstrated no behavioral difficulties. Marcus is excelling at school and is involved in many extracurricular activities, including student council and school sports.

A Successful Life Story

Rochelle grew up with two sisters and two brothers. Her parents divorced when she was 14. Although her father maintained weekly contact with the children, Rochelle views her father as "crazy" and does not like to discuss him. Rochelle started dating Joe when she was 15, becoming pregnant less than 1 year later. Although she gets along well enough with her mother, she chose 7 months into her pregnancy to move in with Joe's family where she stayed until her son, Marcus, was 18 months old. During this time, she finished high school and enrolled at a local college.

Rochelle knew from the time she was first pregnant with Marcus that she wanted a family, including a father for her son. Rochelle felt Joe would be a good father and her "in-laws" a good family. However, from the time she moved into Joe's home until her baby was born, no one spoke to her. Once the baby arrived, the family dynamics changed; she and the baby became the center of attention. She expected this change because she viewed the family as really good people who "were just very disappointed in both of us." Rochelle recalls watching her "mother-in-law" take care of her infant son and then emulating her actions.

After Marcus was born, Rochelle attended school and took care of her son. Her boyfriend worked nightly and weekends to buy the things they needed for their baby. Rochelle cut corners by using cloth diapers at a time when no one else around her did. Although she did the bulk of child-care, Joe also took care of their son, getting up in the middle of the night as often as she did. When her son was 18 months old, Rochelle discovered that Joe was seeing someone else. At age 19, she moved out to live on her own; enmeshed in bitterness.

Nevertheless, she finished her associate's degree, held several part-time jobs, and was hired full time as a case worker—a job she still holds. At 25, Rochelle has married and has had a second child. Currently, she, her husband, and the two children live in a large home that they are buying from his parents while his parents continue to live in the upper level.

While Rochelle and her husband are at work, the grandparents of her first child (Joe's parents) take care of her new son. It is not also unusual for Rochelle and her husband to take care of Joe and his wife's children. Marcus spends half the week with his dad (Joe) and half with Rochelle; he often chooses the better deal depending on what each set of parents is doing. Marcus is completely integrated into both his mother's and his father's families. For special events, Marcus' little brother is also included with Joe's family. It is not unusual for Rochelle, her husband, Joe's parents, Joe and his wife and all the children to spend the holidays together. Rochelle considers them to be her family.

When asked what she hopes for in the future, she replied: "I hope that things stay the way they are because everything's really good right now." She finds her job as a senior case worker in child services challenging and rewarding. In addition to the home they are purchasing from her in-laws, she and her husband own three cars, a van, and take family vacations. She cannot think of anything right now that is not going well and hopes it will remain that way.

Rochelle feels, however, that if she had waited to have a child, she could have done more with her life. Reflecting on her teen years before she became pregnant, Rochelle recalls that she and Marcus' dad had begun to regularly skip classes and engage in sexual behaviors. Although she was able to get good grades, even with skipping and not doing homework, she feels she could have obtained straight As if she had studied more. Nevertheless, having the baby forced both she and her boyfriend to think differently about the future: "When you have a purpose, you have someone else to live for or someone else to get these grades for, it kind of straightens you out." Thus, although she regrets not having done more with her life, she recognizes that the birth of Marcus dramatically changed for the better the direction of her life.

Rochelle's son, Marcus, is doing extremely well, and she is very proud of him. Rochelle had looked forward to participating in her follow-up interview with the Notre Dame Parenting Project because she wanted to describe how well Marcus was doing. She brought certificates and pictures to the interview to demonstrate his many successes. For example, Marcus has received awards for attendance, honor roll, and participation in the quiz bowl. He was on the Student Council and participated in school sports. Marcus has transitioned from an easy infant to an easy-going adolescent. Except for a messy bedroom, Marcus completes his chores and abides by house rules. He moves easily from one household to the other. If there is one thing Rochelle hopes to offer in her role as mother, it is to raise "a good man." For Rochelle, a good man takes care of his children and is an equal partner, even doing the laundry and cooking.

> I hope that I'm making a good man because there's so many bad men out there. You know, I see, because of where I work, there's so many not so good men who don't really care about things and I hope that I'm making my future daughter-in-law a good man. My mother-in-law made a good man for me.

Despite Marcus' success, Rochelle has many worries. As a mother of an emerging adolescent, she is concerned about the cycle of teen parenting and hopes she is doing enough for her son to break the cycle. She fears that her son, even though he is doing so well, will consider having a baby as a teenager because it is "normal." As good as things are, Rochelle knows she could have done even more with her life, and wants her son to fulfill his potential. As with many of the mothers in our study, Rochelle also worries about her son "falling off the edge," something that can happen to a lot of different kids no matter what their background or intelligence level. For Rochelle, having a baby as a teen helped her pull her life together and, being a teen mom required many sacrifices, but produced great joy. However, when asked to talk to teens she avoids mentioning the joys of parenting and relates only the sacrifices. The message is: "I've made the best of my situation, but I don't recommend it for you."

Final Thoughts

The developmental trajectories of both Marcus and Rochelle are optimal, unequalled by any other dyad in our project. Particularly unique in their story is the consistency of the instrumental and emotional support provided by the in-laws. Finally, their success is, in no small part, due to Rochelle's many positive qualities, including intelligence, personal adjustment, and parenting skills.

SUMMARY

As these stories illustrate, the lives of adolescent mothers and their children are extremely diverse. Empirical data cannot fully depict the durability of the human spirit or the uniqueness in each mother–child story. By listening to each mother tell her own story, we begin to see the differing ways in which our data set weaves into the total picture of mother–child development.

Although none of the mothers stated that she regretted having her children, a common theme was that they all wished they would had waited longer. Many believed they could have done more with their lives if they had delayed their first child, and some felt a sense of lost potential. A possible reason for the feeling of loss may be related to the fact that adolescence is a time of identity formation and exploration. Some mothers adopted an identity "as mother" rather than searching out other potential alternatives. To the extent this identity met the young mother's needs for self-esteem and intimacy, the alternatives not pursued may not have been more fulfilling. For instance, Rochelle attributed much of her motivation to get her life together to the birth of her son, and received both recognition and reinforcement from her maternal role. Gloria, on the other hand, had to adjust her expectations based on the problems her children were experiencing. Rather than receiving major gratification from the achievements of her children, her validity as a mother came from fighting for educational services for her children. In the absence of external validation for her efforts, Gloria experienced both anxiety and depression. In contrast, Diane's need to be perceived as a good mother blocked her willingness to acknowledge Darlene's learning difficulties— an acknowledgment that might have helped Darlene as well as enhanced her own self-esteem. Finally, unlike Diane, Gloria, and Rochelle—who adopted motherhood as central to their personal development—Sharon appeared unable to integrate motherhood into her adolescent identity in any meaningful way, and yet was unable to establish an alternative identity.

Intimacy issues also surfaced in all four stories. Although the mothers were currently involved in relatively stable relationships with men, they experienced considerable turmoil as in their attempts to establish these relationships. Neither Darlene nor Shanequa had contact with their biological father. Rochelle, on the other hand, was able to achieve an unconventional, but functional arrangement between Marcus' father and stepfather. Only Gloria was able to maintained a long-term, satisfying relationship with her husband, Eddie's father. All agreed that they became involved with relationships too early in their lives.

All four mothers were also concerned about the kinds of decisions their children will make as they proceed into their adolescent years. They worried often that their children would make the same mistakes they had made. All stated that they would advise other young women to postpone becoming pregnant. Interestingly, two of the women interviewed had jobs that involved them daily with young girls, a number of whom were also facing the challenges of teen parenting.

The four stories dramatically illustrate the limitations of an exclusive quantitative approach to understanding the complexities of the lives of adolescent mothers. Whereas Gloria relied little on her parents for support, Diane would have been unable to finish school, or to get a satisfying job, without the financial and material support of her parents. Sharon's mother appeared to provide support, serving as primary caregiver for Shanequa for a time. However, Sharon was unable to convert this support into opportunities for either herself or for Shanequa. Finally, Rochelle received support from the family of her baby's father rather than her own, but only after Marcus was born.

One common theme was the lack of support the children and their parents received from the educational system. Many children had unmet educational needs. If the child wasn't disruptive, as in the cases of Darlene and Shanequa, learning impairments were usually ignored. Neither Darlene's learning disability, nor Shanequa's mental health problems, were addressed by the school system. For those children whose developmental problems caused disruption in the classrooms (e.g., Alex), the schools appeared unable to work with the families toward a realistic and effective solution. The mental health needs of both the adolescent mothers and their children often went unacknowledged and unattended. Although schools should have been in a position to work with these children, they often relegated all responsibilities to the parents. When parents are young, uneducated, and struggling to meet their families' basic life needs, this strategy is clearly insufficient.

In contrast to the limited support provided by schools and mental health professionals, the mothers often found support and encouragement through their churches and faith. Their faith sustained them as they struggled to achieve a better future for themselves and their children whereas their church provided emotional, and in some cases, material supports. It is interesting to note the perceived positive impact that the Notre Dame Parenting Project had on the mothers, even though there was no "intended intervention." Some mothers commented that merely reading and responding to the questionnaires made them think and re-evaluate whether their parenting practices were adequate. Rochelle stated: "What is the right answer? ... There's gotta be a right answer and you have to be doing the right thing. You have to, and if you're not, then you better change it. And so, I wanted to know what the right answer was and do it that way."

Diane also indicated that questions about children's development made her pay more attention to her own daughter's development. Rochelle recalled that getting birthday and Christmas cards made an impact on her life, noting that "just a card can be important at certain times in your life." These reactions show the importance of having a reliable support system—perhaps even an unintended one—as the teen mother becomes an adult parent and, from a measurement perspective, "hints at" the potentially confounding effects of repeated measurement in longitudinal research.

These comments attest to the constructive impact of consistent, nonjudgmental involvement of others in the lives of adolescent mothers and their children. Most of the adolescent mothers in our project had the desire to be good mothers and good role models for their children. Many, however, had competing needs and limited resources that stood in the way of achieving those goals. From an intervention perspective the challenge is to provide those families with the needed assistance—including mental health, legal, educational, and occupational resources—a topic to which we now turn to in the next and final chapter.

10

Implications for Social Policy

Because the birth rates among most adolescents in the United States, except those under 15, have steadily declined in the past decade, there may be a tendency for policymakers to minimize the extent of teen parenthood as a serious social problem. The trend in birth rates are, however, misleading. Despite a reduction in birth rates since the early 1990s, the number of children born to adolescent mothers remains extremely high, more than 400,000 per year. The birth rates among mothers in the United States also stand in striking contrast to much lower birth rates to adolescents in most other industrialized nations (Coley & Chase-Lansdale, 1998). These demographic data are particularly troubling because U.S. adolescent mothers and their children are at significant risk for developmental problems. In the majority of the adolescent mother–child dyads (82%) in the Notre Dame Parenting Project, one (33%) or both (49%) members showed signs of maladjustment during the early stages of parenthood and/or childhood. Only 18% of the dyads had mothers and children both of whom were functioning reasonably well when the child was five years of age. Based on the overall pattern of developmental data presented in this book, it should be apparent that intervention programs for adolescent parents and their children need to be a high priority for local community, state, and federal policymakers.

The Notre Dame Parenting Project, together with the Baltimore (Furstenberg et al., 1987) and the San Diego (East & Felice, 1996) projects, are among a handful of prospective, longitudinal studies of adolescent parents and their children. In all of these studies, delays in development were either observed either early in life (e.g., the San Diego project and this project) or later in the life cycle (the Baltimore project). In contrast to these other longitudinal studies, which have been either more sociological or medical in orientation, the Notre Dame Parenting Project has emphasized the measurement of psychological characteristics in its evaluation schema.

We focused on maternal variables (such as socioemotional adjustment, cognitive readiness, intelligence, perceptions of social supports,

219

and parenting behavior) and life course achievements (such as education, work, and family growth) as well as child development in multiple domains (cognitive, socioemotional, adaptive behavior, and academic). Our methodology and analytic scheme allowed us to evaluate the early precursors of later maternal and child outcomes, to examine the concurrent interrelationships between maternal and child functioning across multiple domains, and most importantly to isolate process variables that might become appropriate prevention or intervention targets. In general, our results suggest that teen mothers and their children experience a multitude of several problems that demand serious attention and warrant comprehensive intervention.

The social policy recommendations we make in this chapter are based on the major findings from our project as well as on past research and theory. One of the most striking themes that emerged in the life stories presented in the last chapter is the sense of "unmet potential." For many adolescents, their vision of what they might have done with their lives was constrained by the responsibilities of motherhood, poverty, and nonsupportive intimate relationships. Although the young mothers' visions for their children's futures were generally optimistic, their fears that their children's opportunities would be limited—much like their own—often proved to be a reality. This chapter outlines a set of policy-related recommendations designed to optimize long-term developmental outcomes in adolescent mothers and their children and to forestall the delays observed in the Notre Dame Parenting Project.

GENERAL INTERVENTION RECOMMENDATIONS

In this section we make six recommendations about the design of intervention programs that we believe will significantly improve the lives of adolescent mothers and their children. These recommendations, based on our findings as well as previous research, emphasize the need for interventions that

- recognize the diverse needs and characteristics of mothers;
- are child-centered as well as parent-centered;
- begin prenatally and continue services to children through the early school years;
- are developmentally based, focusing on both the changing needs of the adolescent mothers and children as they mature;
- empower adolescent mothers in their maternal roles; and
- are culturally relevant and involve a needs-based assessment approach.

Our recommendations attempt to address the unmet potential of adolescents as a result of their premature entry into motherhood, while acknowledging that adverse outcomes in this population are due not only to their early status as mothers but also to poverty, low education, and socioemotional difficulties. The recommendations take into consideration all these realities in an effort to provide opportunities for growth and development for the adolescent mothers and their children.

A Multidimensional Maternal Focus

Our analysis of child resiliency indicated that few children were able to thrive when their mothers manifested deficiencies in their social supports, socioemotional adjustment, social competence, cognitive readiness for parenting, and parenting skills. These early maternal deficiencies were associated with a variety of later adverse outcomes for the mothers as well as their children. In this section we describe databased, as well as theoretically derived, rationales for implementing multidimensional interventions with adolescent mothers and their children.

Cognitive Readiness. Our analyses indicated that adolescent mothers were significantly less cognitively prepared for parenting than adult mothers, especially in parenting attitudes, styles, and knowledge. For example, teen mothers—before and shortly after delivery—were more likely to believe that children should be expected to fulfill the mothers' needs, were more authoritarian in their parenting orientation, and were less informed about child development and less realistic in their expectations about what children should be able to achieve developmentally at various ages.

The data also indicated that maternal cognitive readiness for parenting was overall the best early predictor of later maternal and child functioning. Results by O'Callaghan et al. (1999) point out the central role that prenatal cognitive readiness of the mother played in parenting. Not only did cognitive readiness have a direct influence on parenting but also mediated the influence of maternal socioemotional and intellectual functioning on this important outcome. Prenatal cognitive readiness not only correlated with later cognitive aspects of parenting, but also with its behavioral and affective components. Moreover, it was the best predictor of maternal child abuse potential as well as one of the best predictors of maternal socioemotional adjustment 5 years into parenthood. In addition to predicting maternal functioning, maternal cognitive readiness, along with maternal IQ, was the best overall predictor of early child functioning, including children's intellectual, language, adaptive and academic skills as well as socioemotional adjustment. Thus, deficiencies in cognitive readiness were associated with adverse maternal and child cognitive, behavioral, and socioemotional outcomes.

These results underline the importance of preparing mothers cognitively for the transition into their parenting roles. The data suggest that by assisting mothers in their preparation for parenting, they will not only become more effective parents, but also improve their self-esteem and self-efficacy. Although our analyses were not able to trace the exact paths of influence of cognitive readiness to child outcomes, it seems likely that cognitive readiness exerts its impact on child development through its influence on maternal parenting behaviors and socioemotional adjustment. Based on our research and observation, we believe interventions designed to improve cognitive readiness should focus on teaching young mothers about the following aspects of child development and parenting:

- What constitutes normal development?
- When is a child's functioning atypical?
- What do children need most from parents?
- How do children signal what they need and how are these needs best satisfied?
- Why do children become upset and misbehave?
- How should child misbehavior be dealt with and, most importantly, how should mothers meet their children's needs when they themselves are upset and having difficulty coping with stress?

Socioemotional Adjustment. Our analyses also emphasized the appropriateness of maternal socioemotional adjustment as a target for intervention. Compared to adult mothers, adolescent mothers were more likely to manifest externalizing and internalizing behavioral problems during pregnancy and parenting stress 6 months following delivery. Three and 5 years later, they frequently displayed feelings of anxiety, depression, and low self-esteem. The prenatal measures of socioemotional adjustment not only predicted later parenting stress, child abuse potential and maternal socioemotional functioning but also was the best predictor of children's socioemotional adjustment. Early maternal socioemotional adjustment was also significantly related to later child language functioning and achievement. Finally, the results of the O'Callaghan et al. (1999) study suggested that a mother's cognitive readiness to parent was directly influenced by her socioemotional adjustment.

The rationale for developing interventions to help mothers cope with their early socioemotional problems are based on three assumptions: First, interventions will reduce the probability of later maternal anxiety and depression problems as well as improve maternal self-esteem. Second, interventions increase the likelihood that young mothers will benefit from and utilize other interventions and social supports, such as those directed at enhancing their cognitive preparation for parenting. Finally, inverventions will reduce stress associated with the parenting role, thus allowing mothers to focus less on themselves and more on meeting their children's needs.

Although the results of our research suggest the critical role of maternal socioemotional adjustment in successful maternal and child outcomes, few intervention studies with adolescent mothers have made maternal mental health a high priority. Cognitively preparing adolescents to be competent mothers without addressing their socioemotional needs ignores the influence that socioemotional factors have on parenting effectiveness. Interventions that focus on reducing maternal anxiety and depression, and enhancing maternal self-esteem, can be time intensive and costly. However, the lasting effects of parenting interventions are likely dependent on addressing the full range of maternal socioemotional problems.

Therapeutically oriented interventions should also help mothers to identify major stressors in their lives and to develop and implement problem-solving strategies for addressing these life stressors. As emphasized by Musick and Barbera-Stein (1988), interventions with adolescent mothers need to address silent topics, particularly sexual abuse because a high percentage of young mothers may have been, or still are, victims of such abuse.

Relatedly, social competence deficiencies emerged as an important characteristic of adolescent mothers. Although few interventions with adolescent mothers have targeted social competence, our data suggest that many young mothers are deficient in their social interaction skills. Involvement in structured, group support activities may provide an important source of social support and self-esteem, as well as learning opportunities for adolescent mothers with limited success in past social relationships. One of the young mothers in our sample was worried about her 12-year-old daughter who only wanted to sit in the house and watch television all day. She reflected, "I wonder if she is getting that from me because I don't go to many places outside of work, shopping, and basically, I don't hang out with a 'lotta [sic] friends." As our findings suggest, the cognitive, adaptive, and socioemotional outcomes of children are interwoven with the successful social adaptation of their adolescent mothers. Few children thrive when their mothers are struggling with their own socioemotional troubles.

Social Support. Although social supports for teen mothers are vitally important, they differ in a variety of ways from the social supports typically utilized by adult mothers. Adolescent mothers are less likely to be married, less likely to get married, more likely to be divorced if they do get married, and less likely to be involved in a stable intimate relationship. The absence of a spouse or significant life partner in the lives of adolescent mothers means they are denied an important source of emotional, instrumental, and financial assistance. As a consequence, teen mothers are often forced to rely on their family of origin for support, particularly their own mother, as well as social agencies. Although the presence of family support for the adolescent mother is encouraged by new welfare reform legislation, specifically the Personal Responsibility and Work Reconstruction Act of 1996, the provision of this type of social support may be associated with adverse consequences for the adolescent mother, her child, and the child's grandmother. Family support could be detrimental especially if the daughter–mother relationship is conflicted, the grandmothers' parenting skills are limited, an overdependent relationship by the adolescent mother on her mother is established, or if the physical or financial resources of the extended household are restricted. There is growing evidence that older teen mothers and their children function best when living independently (East & Felice, 1996; Spieker & Bensley, 1994).

Although our analyses revealed fewer correlations between social supports and mother–child outcomes than for other constructs (e.g., cognitive readiness and socioemotional adjustment) in our parenting model, discriminant function analyses suggested that social support was an important compensatory factor in the lives of children of adolescent mothers: For example, children were more likely to be resilient if their mothers received emotional support from their fathers, with such support being particularly important for mothers who were already vulnerable. Similarly, child-care support from grandparents appeared to be a protective factor for children, but again only for vulnerable mothers.

In summary, although social supports from the teen's immediate family, other relatives, partner, and friends seem critical given the many needs of adolescent mothers, these supports are often either absent or conflicted. Perhaps because of their limitations in social competency, many teenage mothers are unable to develop or maintain such supports. Based on our findings, along with those from previous research, helping adolescent mothers create and sustain a variety of social supports could serve a number of functions, including the provision of shelter, financial aid, emotional support, and child-care assistance. It is expected that these types of social supports should have both direct influences on child functioning and indirect effects on the children by improving maternal socioemotional adjustment, cognitive preparation for parenting, and actual parenting behaviors.

Parent Training. Parenting involves cognitive, affective, and behavioral components. As discussed earlier, teen parents in our sample often possessed less accurate knowledge about parenting and child development and were more stressed in their parenting role. Compared to adult mothers, they also interacted less with their children, paid less attention to their children's activities, were less flexible and more authoritarian, less verbal, less positive and encouraging, less in tune with their children's emotions, and less skillful in their instructions.

Our data further suggest that maternal parenting attitudes, stress, and behavior influence one another in a reciprocal fashion. If this is the case, it is likely that previously discussed interventions—directed at increasing maternal cognitive readiness for parenting and improving maternal adjustment—will have a positive impact on actual parenting behavior. Although such interventions are likely very useful, they are unlikely to be sufficient given the complex skills required for effective parenting. Our results suggest that a behaviorally oriented parenting intervention could have additional positive consequences including reducing parenting stress, improving parenting attitudes, reducing mother's potential for child abuse, and improving a variety of child outcomes, including language skills and school achievement.

Education and Job Training. Thus far, our focus has been on the discussion of mother-centered programs designed to affect specific maternal characteristics, including cognitive readiness for parenting, socioemotional adjustment, social competence, and parenting behavior. In addition to these programs, Brooks-Gunn (1995) discussed the benefits associated with mother-centered programs that focus on education and job training.

The passage of the Health Services and Centers Amendments of 1978 helped to promote a number of school-based interventions with adolescent mothers, targeting both prevention of future adolescent pregnancies and the support of adolescent parents. Both educational and parenting goals have been promoted as part of such interventions (Bennett & Bardon, 1977; Klerman, 1981; Roosa, 1984; Roosa & Vaughn, 1983). Although school-based programs vary considerably in how they are implemented, most provide some sort of alternative curriculum consisting of the required general education courses as well as courses in child development and parenting. Most programs enable the young mother to bring her child to school with her, which helps to solve the mothers' child-care problems, as well as provides mothers an opportunity to learn parenting skills while interacting with their infants.

Many of the adolescent mothers in the Notre Dame Parenting Project had a history of school failure, and an active dislike of learning, in part because of the way alternative school programs for young parents were structured. Rather than providing supports for learning, some programs appeared to make minimal demands and have low expectations. One of the adolescent mothers in our sample confided that she had returned to a regular classroom program after spending several weeks in the school-aged mothers program. She felt that the alternative program was geared merely toward getting the mothers through school, rather than providing a useful education that would help her get a job.

In addition to ensuring that mothers receive a well-rounded and skill-based education, job training is obviously critical for mothers. However, juggling the demands of work and family creates stress in even the most prepared parents. Stable employment is particularly challenging for adolescent mothers who have young children and limited support from partners or extended families. For such mothers, just addressing the routine needs of their children (e.g., child care, parent–teacher conferences, medical checkups) often seems, at least in the short term, to preclude working.

The promotion of economic self-sufficiency of adolescent mothers has been a primary goal of some intervention programs. For example, the Teenage Parent Welfare Demonstration program, sponsored by the U.S. Department of Health and Human Service, focused on providing an alternative to traditional welfare services for adolescent mothers and children (Zaslow et al., 1998). All primiparous pregnant teens or adolescent mothers who applied for AFDC at three sites (Chicago and two New Jersey cities) during the program's 2 years were randomly assigned to a control group that received traditional welfare services or to an intervention program. Young mothers in the intervention condition received enhanced services that required them to develop and follow through with a plan to be either in school, job training or employed. In addition they had to cooperate with case management services and participate in life skills classes. Failure to comply with the program's requirements resulted in reductions in the amount of their monthly welfare benefit. Results indicated that the intervention was effective in increasing the mothers' involvement in school, job training, and employment. However, although their monthly earnings increased, the subsequent decline in welfare benefits resulted in no difference in overall income or in the rate of repeat pregnancies. From a social policy perspective, it appears that job training and employment requirements for adolescent mothers will help foster family autonomy from welfare and poverty, only if a just and adequate minimum wage standard and supports for working mothers, like transportation and child care, are in place.

As part of a total intervention package, we think it is especially critical that a job training component be introduced in a way so as not to conflict with the provision of adequate child care. Job training programs need to insure that the needs of the children are provided while mothers are in training, and also later when mothers enter into the work force. Ideally, job sites need to incorporate child care into their program, perhaps with government assistance. Whenever possible, job training should be given only after parents have obtained their high school degree or a vocational equivalent.

Interventions and Low IQ Adolescent Mothers. The majority of adolescent mothers in our project were operating in the low average, borderline, or mentally retarded range of intelligence. What are the implications of this fact for the design of intervention programs? The O'Callaghan et al. (1999) study found that although prenatal maternal IQ predicted 6-month parenting outcomes—with higher IQ parents showing better outcomes—the effect of IQ on parenting was mediated through cognitive readiness. This finding suggests that lower IQ mothers are less cognitively ready for parenting and that these mothers in particular would likely to benefit from a parent training program. Lower maternal IQ may also have special implications for the manner in which a parenting intervention program is delivered. Because low IQ is a predictor of learning problems in traditional educational settings, it seems likely that brief, intensive, didactic parenting interventions are doomed to failure. In contrast, intervention programs that are more hands on, concrete, interactive, personalized, and long-term are more likely to motivate participation and increase the probability that such programs will be effective.

Summary. In this section, we argued that an effective intervention program with adolescent mothers should include cognitive readiness, mental health, social competence, parenting training, and educational and vocational components. Programs also need to expand the sources of social supports available to these mothers. The components of a successful intervention should, however, be tailored to the specific needs of the mother. For example, well-adjusted, socially competent adolescents with good social supports who become mothers may only need specific interventions to prepare them for parenting, and to help them complete their education and to enter into the job market. As such intervention programs are developed, they need to take into account the cognitive abilities of the adolescent mothers.

Child-Focused Programs

Coley and Chase-Lansdale (1998) suggested that "today's children of teenage mothers, faced with differing educational and employment demands of a changing global market, may fare worse, in fact, than longitudinal studies of previous cohorts of young mothers might imply" (p. 159). Because of such demands it is likely that mother-centered intervention programs will not be sufficient to satisfy the needs of the children. Although there is ample evidence that mother-centered programs help adolescent mothers, there is less evidence that benefits filter down to their children. For these reasons, we think it is imperative that mother-centered programs be supplemented by a strong child-focused educational program, which begins early and provides more than day care.

Child-focused programs would seem particularly important for children of adolescent parents who have marked educational deficiencies, parenting deficiencies, and socioemotional problems. Our research suggests that mothers with poor language skills, depression, low self-esteem and/or authoritarian approaches to parenting were less able to foster their children's development. Child-centered programs need to be directed at facilitating children's cognitive and language development, as well as enhancing their social competence and socioemotional adjustment. Although the success of cognitively oriented, education programs for children have been well documented (Ramey & Suarez, 1984), social competence training programs have neither been emphasized nor frequently evaluated (St. Pierre & Layzen, 1998). The results of our project suggest both types of programs are needed because child development in the cognitive and socioemotional domains is intimately intertwined.

Beginning Early

The rationale for early intervention is both mother- and infant-based. Because the characteristics of adolescent mothers, even before their babies are born, predict both later maternal and child outcomes, these factors can be used to identify at risk, pregnant adolescents to ensure that each is prepared physically, cognitively, and socioemotionally for child-rearing. Because engrained habits are resistant to change, it is important that good parenting habits be developed as soon as possible. Interventions that focus on breaking bad parenting habits are likely to be more difficult to implement, more lengthy, and at greater risk for being unsuccessful. Early interventions help establish a positive parenting trajectory by helping adolescent parents achieve early successes and personal satisfaction with their parenting role.

From a child perspective, the importance of early interventions for later development is well established. Greenough, Black, and Wallace (1987) distinguished between *experience-expectant* and *experience-dependent* environments. All but the most severely deprived environments provide the experience-expectant stimulation (e.g., variations in light and sound) needed for infants' brains to develop and basic sensorimotor processes to function. However, brain growth beyond this basic level is dependent on the quality of the stimulation provided. Although a wide range of environments may allow infants to extract the experience-expectant stimulation, it seems likely, based on our data, that the social environments provided by many adolescent mothers may not meet the minimal experience-dependent requirements of young children, particularly if these environments are characterized by neglect and abuse. Early interventions with adolescent mothers and their children need to focus on providing adolescent mothers and their children the opportunity to achieve mutually reinforcing and growth-enhancing interactions.

It should be mentioned, however, that there is debate concerning the importance of early stimulation programs for early and later child development. Some investigators, misinterpreting behavioral genetic studies of adopted twins and siblings, claim that cognitive and psychosocial differences among children are due mainly to genetic factors (Scarr & McCartney, 1983). They imply that early intervention efforts may be misguided or ineffective because children's eventual cognitive outcomes are constrained by their genetic potential. With the advent of more comprehensive and sophisticated psychobiological models of development, simplistic conceptions—that emphasize either nature or nurture to the exclusion of the other—have increasingly fallen into disfavor (Horwitz, 1999).

Elman and his colleagues (1996) disputed the notion of genes as blueprints or even as computer programs, instead espousing the position of genes as catalysts, active in concert with appropriately timed experiences. The establishment of neuronal connections among cortical regions between 8 and 10 months of age, and synaptic acceleration up to age 2 are examples of brain processes that are environmentally influenced. Exposure to language and social opportunities at these times facilitates the development of these processes. If the sensitive period for such a growth process (when long-range neuronal connections are created and synaptogenesis is occurring) passes in the absence of the expected environmental input, problems may arise. Alternative processes may emerge, limiting not only the initial development of preferred processes, but also the subsequent development of more complex processes. From this perspective, early intervention programs influence underlying biological structures while at the same time promoting learning. Although congenital biologically based problems can constrain early learning, the absence of stimulating environments can also restrict the early development of brain processes (Greenough et al., 1987).

Developmentally Appropriate Interventions

In addition to beginning interventions early in life, it is important that interventions be dynamically structured so as to accommodate the changing needs of both teen parents and their children. Parenting is a collection of related behaviors and competencies that emerge as parents and children develop. From a motivational perspective, skills are often best learned when they are needed. Interventions initiated during the prenatal period need to address, for example, maternal physical health and diet care issues. Parents' needs change dramatically in the early postpartum period. Once their infants are born, teen mothers need to be taught how to physically care for their infant. As infants' become ready to develop new skills (e.g., walking, talking), appropriate physical and cognitive techniques for stimulating children must be discussed with parents in order to ensure a solid foundation for development. Maternal self-esteem may need enhancing as young mothers compare themselves to their cohort without children or adult mothers. Supports may also be needed to assist young mothers in meeting normal challenges as they separate from their families of origin and establish their own households.

As young infants grow and try their mothers' patience, interventions need to focus on helping mothers interpret and cope with their children's behavior. The tendency of many adolescent mothers in our sample was to become more punitive when they perceived their child as misbehaving. Many commented on how badly their 6-month-old infants were behaving or on how they believed their infants didn't like them. One mother related how she had begun to slap the hand of her 5-month-old son when he did not share his toys. Other young mothers reported how they commonly reacted to irritating or frustrating infant behavior by yelling at their child. Early interventions need to replace these punitive, maladaptive parenting scripts—often learned from the mothers' own experiences during childhood—with adaptive, nurturing scripts. At this point, teen mothers may also need to address emotionally-laden parenting issues and myths originating from the adolescents' interactions with their own parents.

Many young mothers believe that parental practices that were "good enough for me" will be good enough for their own infants. They often feel comfortable with parenting skills and practices that are less than ideal. Interventions need to focus on preparing young mothers to cope with infants who are more active, more demanding, and less adaptable than expected. The goal is not only to teach mothers how to socialize infant behavior so that it becomes acceptable, but also to help young mothers understand that infant behaviors often reflect the child's individuality and search for independence. Interventions need to be directed at helping mothers interpret and respond to their infants' signals and that infant "misbehaviors" are not intentional actions designed to provoke the mother. Feelings of self-confidence and self-esteem may decline at first as the adolescent mothers come to realize the negative effects of their "preferred" parenting practices. The act of replacing a maladaptive parenting practice learned from one's own parents is not easy, nor can it be accomplished without provoking some distress. For this reason, the rebuilding of their personal self-efficacy needs to be a part of the intervention package.

In summary, services should be relevant and appropriate to the developmental level of the adolescent mother as well as her growing child. Teenage mothers are at special risk because they have to confront adolescent developmental tasks (such as developing their own identity, becoming independent, and forming intimate relationships with peers, including members of the opposite sex) at the same time they are coping with their parenting role. Because adolescent mothers present a curious blend of sophistication and vulnerability, interventions need to be sensitive to their maturational needs, acknowledging the special demands placed on the adolescent mothers while helping them cope with the often conflicting demands imposed on them as a developing adolescents. Interventions need to be sensitive to the perceived needs of both the expectant mother and the father, or other primary partner, as well as to the teens' parents. Potential conflicts arising from their differing needs and perceptions should be used as an occasion for teaching social problem-solving and conflict resolution skills, thereby enhancing the teen parents' social competence. Thus, in short, intervention programs need to prepare adolescent mothers for the unique challenges they will face and help them to coordinate and reconcile the many roles and tasks confronting them.

Empowering Mothers

While dealing with adolescent issues of identity formation and intimacy, teen mothers must also achieve emotional and financial autonomy. They must move from a position of dependence on their parents to one of self-sufficiency. Intervention programs targeting self-sufficiency often do not consider the complexity of this developmental transition and may limit their services to job training. As young mothers enter into intervention programs and are encouraged to apply the skills they acquire, care must be taken to avoid fostering dependency on others, but rather to facilitate maternal autonomy. One approach to instilling this autonomy is contained in the philosophy of empowerment. Within this philosophy, the professional's role becomes one of supporting the parent by helping her remove obstacles that hinder personal competence, growth, and independent functioning. Sociopolitical themes emphasizing family responsibility and parent participation in child development programs are consistent with this philosophy.

One interesting strategy for empowering parents involves the use of paraprofessionals as service providers in place of "experts." In a review of the literature on paraprofessional interventions, Musick and Stott (1990) emphasized the importance of the initial selection process, adequate training, and supervision. Paraprofessionals who come from the same cultural and socioeconomic backgrounds as the parents can serve as "believable" role models. Such paraprofessionals are thought to be more appreciative of the needs of disadvantaged mothers as well as more readily accepted by them. Empowerment is encouraged by a "since I made it, you can too" attitude. Using paraprofessionals has the added advantage of being a cost-effective strategy. Several intervention programs for adolescent mothers have employed paraprofessionals who themselves were teen moms (Halpern & Larner, 1988; Weed, 1997). These type of programs may benefit the paraprofessionals as much as the parents they serve, although the benefits have rarely been evaluated or even factored into cost–benefit analyses (Musick & Stott, 1990).

Culturally Relevant and Need-Based Interventions

A variety of factors can facilitate the effectiveness of intervention services. Unger and Wandersman (1988) evaluated adolescent mothers who benefited most from the Resource Mothers Program in South Carolina. The resource mothers were paraprofessionals, who were already acquainted with the culture and background of the adolescent mothers and became more familiar through regular structured contact with the pregnant and parenting teens in their homes. The paraprofessionals attempted to enhance the teen's social network by building family and community supports. Unger and Wandersman (1988), examining factors that influenced the participation of the pregnant and parenting teens in the program, found that the presence of supportive adults (usually the teens' parents) was helpful in promoting active and sustained program involvement by the teen, whereas competing maternal needs and priorities (e.g., health problems and peer pressures) inhibited program participation.

From our perspective, a need-based assessment should be a critical component of intervention programs for adolescent parents. Results of research by Dunst and Trivette (1988) with adolescent mothers and parents of handicapped children indicated that the greater the number of unmet parent needs, the lower the probability that parents would commit time or energy to intervention programs. Dunst and Trivette stressed that "efforts to meet more basic family needs must be made in order for parents to have the time, energy, and personal investment to work with their own children in an educational or therapeutic capacity" (p. 166). They further emphasized that "help is maximally effective when the aid and assistance is congruent with the help seeker's appraisal of his or her problem or need" (p. 162). The professional's perspective of the adolescent's needs should, however, also be considered.

Sometimes, adolescent parents do not perceive themselves in need whereas social service professionals do. For example, although our research has identified a multitude of potential problems related to the teen parents' attitudes, expectations and knowledge, the teen mothers were often not aware of these problems. Weed (1997) found that almost all of a sample of 84 adolescent mothers of 6-month-old infants felt "capable and on top of things" when taking care of their infants More than 75% believed that they were better than average parents, and all of the others believed they were at least average parents. The majority did not perceive a need for intervention. This type of perception may account in part for the high rates of absenteeism in intervention programs for adolescent mothers. Wolfe, Edwards, Manion, and Koverola (1988) surmised that a certain level of discontentment is needed to motivate clients to participate in parenting programs. From this perspective, an early goal of any intervention program for adolescent parents should involve insuring that the parent fully recognizes the need for the services to be provided and that these services be delivered in a culturally sensitive fashion.

Summary of Recommendations

In developing intervention programs for adolescent mothers, a comprehensive array of services to address mothers' cognitive, socioemotional, self-sufficiency, social support, educational, and vocational needs should be available. Interventions should be both parent- and child-focused and developmentally appropriate. Assessment at the time of the mother's pregnancy is important for determining as early as possible which teens are most at risk and the extent of their needs. Provision of services also should begin early, and be individualized, based on both the professionals' and the teens' perception of their needs. Every effort should be made to ensure that the teen mothers understand the rationale for the services actually provided. Programs should be designed so as to be culturally appropriate, social supports need to be structured to encourage the teens active and continuing program participation. Interventions should be empowering, helping the teens to assume responsibility for themselves and their children. In order for service provision to be cost effective, local community services need to be utilized to the extent possible (e.g., using paraprofessionals from the teen mother's neighborhood).

Implementing the Recommendations: An Example

An example of a program that includes many of our intervention recommendations is the Mothers as Mentors program, initiated in South Carolina in the early 1990s (Weed, 1997). In this program, educational and other services were provided to pregnant adolescents, beginning early in the prenatal period, and continuing through the child's early years. One-on-one support by the mentor was given to the teen mother (mentee) until her child reached 1 year of age. Subsequently, the mentee was either enrolled in mentor training or continued her participation in group educational and social activities. Mentees were matched with mentors from their own neighborhoods and backgrounds to ensure services would be culturally relevant. Parental needs were met in homes and in neighborhoods, not in agency offices. Both one-on-one and group services focused on socioemotional, parenting, and educational issues. Referrals were made as appropriate to mental health, vocational, and/or educational agencies. Both mentors and mentees were supported by concentrating on their respective strengths rather than dwelling on areas of weakness.

More specifically, intervention services occurred on two levels. Initially, mentors, older (18- to 22-year-old) adolescent mothers, were given training to enhance their parenting attitudes, knowledge and skills, self-esteem and self-efficacy. The training format for mentors included group instructional classes and individualized case management training. Training services were provided by a professional social worker and a developmental psychologist. Younger pregnant adolescents (mentees) were subsequently matched one-on-one with a mentor who had successfully completed the training program. The initial goals of the mentoring process were to help the mentees obtain adequate prenatal care and delay subsequent pregnancies. All services provided to both mentors and mentees were tailored to their individual needs and background characteristics.

Instructions for the mentors consisted of two dozen 2-hour sessions. Critical components of the training program included instruction regarding delivery of the curriculum, incentives for attendance and participation, proficiency testing and ongoing monitoring of program effectiveness, and provision of transportation and child care. All information presented was accompanied by written handouts that were reviewed and discussed during class. In-class exercises and out-of-class homework assignments reinforced the application of important concepts.

For example, a module on child development involved handouts describing norms for physical and cognitive growth. The in-class exercise involved mentors watching a video on infant development during the first year, then "introducing" their own child to the group using information from the video. Homework assignments included mentors observing their toddlers and interpreting the possible meanings of nonverbal behaviors, such as crying, fussing, smiling, and throwing toys. Class discussions also focused on methods of presenting information to the mentees. These discussions were designed to ensure that the mentors responded to the material in an in-depth and personalized fashion. The intervention stressed proficiency in learning the materials so that the mentors would be able to teach their mentees. In addition to the group instructional sessions, the program coordinator worked with each prospective mentor to model the steps the mentor would subsequently go through with her mentee as well as to develop an individualized service plan for the mentor's own life.

The empowerment philosophy was integrated into the fabric of the program. Instead of focusing on young mothers' difficulties and deficiencies, the training motivated the young mentors to help pregnant teenagers by utilizing the wisdom they gained through their experience with pregnancy, childbirth, and parenting. The challenges and successes they encountered as pregnant adolescents were reviewed as lessons they had learned and could share with the mentees. Mentors were also instructed on how to intervene on behalf of their mentees with personnel from various community agencies (e.g., Social Services, Health Department, Mental Health). Mentors were encouraged to be role models for their mentees, helping them to make good decisions, to solve their own problems, and to follow through with good prenatal care, while reinforcing the attitude, "If I could do it, you can to."

The training of the mentors also considered the broader social and developmental context of their lives. Discussion centered on how they dealt with identity and social relationship issues as they struggled to make the transition from adolescence to adulthood (e.g., how having a child forced them to make choices about whether to focus on motherhood or on the formation of intimate peer relationships). In addition, attention was given during training concerning how to resolve issues from their own childhoods, particularly those involving conflicts with their parents, and how such conflicts affected their childrearing approach.

These discussions were designed to provide young mothers with the feeling that they were adults and could control their lives.

Five mentor training classes were conducted over a 3-year period. Each class contained between 4 and 10 participants. The promise of a supplemental income from being a mentor functioned as an incentive for successful program completion. Of the 53 mentors enrolled, 34 graduated (64%), and all but 3 were subsequently paired with a mentee. Evaluation focused on mentor changes in such areas of cognitive readiness, self-esteem, and optimism from the beginning to the end of the intervention program. Mentor adolescent mothers who participated in the training were compared with a nonrandom sample of same-aged peers. Results suggested that the young women who participated in the Mothers as Mentors program showed positive changes in their parenting attitudes and knowledge from 6 to 36 months postpartum and a generally healthy adaptation to their maternal role. In contrast, adolescent mothers who did not receive intervention, continued to hold unrealistic expectations concerning their maternal role and the psychological benefits associated with being a mother. The majority of these young mothers also had inappropriate parenting attitudes and expectations for their children; and were deficient in their knowledge of infant development.

In summary, the Mothers as Mentors program is an example of an effective intervention program that incorporated most of the recommendations discussed previously. One-on-one support was provided by young mentors to pregnant adolescents beginning early in the prenatal period, and continued through the child's first birthday. Subsequently, the mentee herself had the opportunity to enroll in mentor training, or if she wasn't yet old enough, continued her participation in group educational and social activities. Both one-on-one and group services focused on socioemotional, educational, and parenting issues. Referrals were made as appropriate to mental health, vocational, and/or educational agencies. Matching mentees with mentors from their own neighborhoods and backgrounds helped ensure that services would be culturally appropriate. Needs were met in homes and in neighborhoods when they arose, not in an agency office. Finally, both mentors and mentees were empowered by supporting their respective strengths rather than dwelling on areas of weaknesses.

FINAL RECOMMENDATIONS

Once a decision is made to intervene with adolescent mothers, a critical question remains: Who should be the target of the prevention/intervention program? One approach is to select all adolescent mothers and their children because these mothers are at risk as a group by virtue of their young age. A second approach is to target only those who appear at special risk. If the second approach is adopted, our study suggests that a systematic assessment strategy be adopted that considers the relationship of the mothers' prenatal characteristics—including IQ, cognitive readiness, socioemotional adjustment, and social supports—to parenting and child development.

We suggest that a combination of both universal and more focused intervention strategies be adopted. Certain universal or communitywide strategies should be applied to all teen mothers. Based on our results, and past research, we recommend that all mothers be cognitively prepared for their parenting role and all mothers be provided sufficient child care to allow them to finish their education and receive job training. In addition to such universal programs—which are to varying degrees already in place in many communities—more focused intervention strategies need to be implemented for those at special risk, that is at risk for reasons other than being an adolescent mother or being a child of an adolescent mother. For example, based on our data, mothers who score low on IQ tests (especially those with an IQ below 75), are more likely to be deficient in their knowledge and attitudes about parenting and child development, be depressed, have minimal or inadequate social supports from their partner or family, manifest punitive parenting practices, and/or be evaluated as at risk for child abuse, need to be targeted for additional specialized interventions in order to improve their own and their children's developmental trajectories. Moreover, child-centered educational programs should be made available early to children of these at-risk parents.

A second important issue regarding intervention/prevention programs concerns the role of the public school system. Schools are ideally situated to provide physical facilities and support programs for both adolescent parents and their children. Many schools serving adolescents have already incorporated parenting classes into their curriculum. However, the scope of educational services is usually narrow, and many teens do not seem to take advantage of or benefit from them. Special efforts should be made to reach those adolescents who are failing academically, who drop out of school, and who have socioemotional problems. Information on how adolescent parents can access community services should also be provided by the schools. Ideally, the many community services offered to teen mothers through hospitals, family practice clinics, mental health centers, and parent support groups, should be integrated into the school setting as outreach programs. Finally, adolescents need to be educated concerning the value of services offered to them (Zaslow et al., 1998).

A third issue centers on welfare reform and its long-term impact on mothers and children. Yoshikawa (1999) analyzed data from 614 mother–child dyads, examining the impact of welfare reform on children's development through the first 8 years of life. The project evaluated both types of child care (relative, babysitter, and center-based) and "human capital" (child support, education, and job training) supports. A number of important results emerged:

1. Controlling for background factors and patterns of welfare change, positive, but small, relationships were found between child support, education, job training, and mothers' income.
2. Moderate positive correlations were found between center-based child care and both mothers' earnings and children's receptive language.
3. The positive effects of support services on earnings were strongest for mothers with more "human capital."
4. Type and quality of early child support influenced both child math and reading scores.

Both mothers and children seemed to benefit most from a comprehensive approach to welfare reform. The results underscored the importance of broad-based, high intensity welfare reform that integrates four components: high quality child care, child supports (e.g., receipt of support payments across the first 5 years), education, and job training. We believe that effective welfare reform needs to routinely incorporate these types of supports and services in order to improve the life course of teen mothers and their children.

Several comments are in order regarding the policy implications of recent welfare reform legislation, in particular the Personal Responsibility and Work Reconstruction Act of 1996. Although the intent of this type of legislation was to reduce the number of mothers on welfare and to help adolescent mothers, their families and fathers financially support themselves rather than relying on the government, the Act seems to be based on a number of assumptions that may well be untrue—these include the following three assumptions:

1. Mothers with minimal education, low IQ, and personal problems can obtain and maintain steady employment.
2. Jobs the mothers obtain will provide sufficient income for their family.
3. The family of adolescent mothers have sufficient income to support their daughters and their grandchildren, and that fathers, if located, can and will pay support.

If any of these three assumptions are false—and that seems likely for many families—then both mothers and children will probably suffer. In order to make welfare reform work, programs must ensure that a mother's employment does not result in her living below the poverty line and that children whose mothers are in the workforce are provided quality day care. These are fundamental components of successful welfare reform and necessary for long-term success (cf. Yoshikawa, 1999).

In summary, short-term, narrowly focused interventions make little to no impact on the lives of most adolescent parents and their children. Although community or school-based interventions are expensive, the costs to the mothers and children involved, and to society in the long term, if interventions are not provided, are even more staggering. As federal, state, and local agencies institute welfare reform policies, the impact of these policies need to be evaluated, along with related intervention programs. Although clear-cut outcomes of comprehensive interventions may not emerge for several years, it is unlikely that programs will have positive long-term effects without observable short-term gains. These gains need to be closely monitored and enhanced as necessary through ongoing program modification.

AND IN CONCLUSION

Our data highlight the interwoven nature of the lives of adolescent mothers and their children. The findings emphasize the critical importance of meeting the developmental needs of both mothers and children early in life. Infant development and early maternal parenting skills are highly malleable and can be enhanced through appropriate interventions. We simply need the "societal will" to help adolescent mothers create more adaptive environments for themselves and their children. Society suffers, not only financially, but also psychologically, when its children are abused, neglected, put into foster care, or incarcerated. Although Maynard (1997) and her colleagues have tried to evaluate the costs of inaction, an economic measuring stick does not begin to capture the benefits derived by helping adolescent mothers and their children reach their full potential.

References

Abidin, R. R. (1983). *Parenting Stress Index–Manual.* Charlottesville, VA: Pediatric Psychology Press.

Achenbach, T. M. (1991a). *Manual for the Child Behavior Checklist 4-18 and the 1991 Profile.* Burlington: University of Vermont, Department of Psychiatry.

Achenbach, T. M. (1991b). *Manual for the Teacher Report Form and 1991 profile.* Burlington: University of Vermont, Department of Psychiatry.

Achenbach, T. (1991c). *Manual for the Youth Self-report and 1991 profile.* Burlington: University of Vermont, Department of Psychiatry.

Ainsworth, M., Blehar, M. C., Waters, E., & Walls, S. (1978). *Attachment: A psychological study of the Strange Situation.* Hillsdale, NJ: Lawrence Erlbaum Associates.

Ainsworth, M. D., & Wittig, B. A. (1969). Attachment and exploratory behavior of one-year-olds in a strange situation. In B. M. Foss (Ed.), *Determinants of infant behavior* (Vol. 4, pp. 129–173). London: Netheum.

Alan Guttmacher Institute. (1994). *National teenage pregnancy rate.* New York: Author.

Alan Guttmacher Institute (1999, April). *Teenage pregnancy: Overall trends and state-by-state information.* Washington, DC: Author.

Allen, J. P., Philliber, S., Herrling, S., & Kuperminc, G. P. (1997). Preventing teen pregnancy and adademic failure: Experimental evaluation of a developmentally-based approach. *Child Development, 64,* 729–742.

Angelou, M. (1983). *I know why the caged bird sings.* New York: Bantam Books.

Angelou, M. (1984). *The heart of a woman.* New York: Bantam Books.

Angelou, M. (1985a). *Gather together in my name.* New York: Bantam Books.

Angelou, M. (1985b). *Singin' and swingin' and getting' merry like christmas.* New York: Bantam Books.

Apfel, N., & Seitz, V. (1999, April). *Support predicts teen mother's subsequent childbearing and parenting success.* Paper presented at the biennial meeting of the Society for Research in Child Development, Albuquerque, NM.

Arend, R., Grove, F., & Sroufe, L. A. (1979). Continuity of individual adaptation from infancy to kindergarten: A predictive study of ego resiliency and curiosity in preschoolers. *Child Development, 50,* 950–959.

Armsden, G., & Greenberg, M. (1987). The inventory of parent and peer attachment: Individual differences and their relationship to psychological well-being in adolescence. *Journal of Youth and Adolescence, 16,* 427–454.

Arnett, J. (1992). Reckless behavior in adolescence: A developmental perspective. *Developmental Review, 12,* 339–373

Azar, S. T. (1991). Models of child abuse: A metatheoretical analysis. *Criminal Justice and Behavior, 18,* 30–46.

Barkley, R. A. (1997). Behavioral inhibition, sustained attention, and executive functions: Constructing a unifying theory of ADHD. *Psychological Bulletin, 121,* 65–94.

Barth, R. (1983). Social support among mothers. *Journal of Community Psychology, 16,* 132–143.

Battle, L. S. (1995). Teenage mothers' narratives of self: An examination of risking the future. *Advanced Nursing Science, 17,* 22–36.

Baumeister, A. A. (1988). The new morbidity and the prevention of mental retardation. *Research Progress, 7* (1).

Baumrind, D. (1971). Current patterns of parental authority. *Developmental Psychology Monograph, 4* (1, Pt.2).

Baumrind, D. (1980). New directions in socialization research. *Psychological Bulletin, 35,* 639–652.

Bavolek, S. J. (1984*). Handbook for the Adult-Adolescent Parenting Inventory.* Schaumberg: Family Development Associates.

Bayley, N. (1969). *Bayley Scales of Infant Development.* New York: The Psychological Corporation.

Beardslee, W., Zukerman, B., Amaro, H., & McAllister, M. (1988). Depression among adolescent mothers: A pilot study. *Developmental and Behavioral Pediatrics, 9,* 62–65.

Beck, A. T., (1967). *Depression: Causes and Treatment.* Philadelphia: University of Pennsylvania Press.

Beck, A. T. (1987). *Beck Depression Inventory.* San Antonio, TX: The Psychological Corporation.

Beery, K. (1989). *The Administration, Scoring, and Teaching Manual for the Development Test of Visual-Motor Integration Third Revision.* Cleveland: Modern Curriculum Press.

Bell, R. Q. (1976). Reduction of stress in childrearing. In L. Levi (Ed.), *Social stress and disease* (Vol. 2, pp. 183–207). London: Oxford University Press.

Belmont, L., Cohen, P., Dryfoos, J., Stein, Z., & Zayac, (1981). Maternal age and children's intelligence. In K. G. Scott, T. Field, & E. G. Robertson (Eds.), *Teenage parents and their offspring* (pp. 177–194). New York: Grune & Stratton.

Belsky, J. (1980). Child maltreatment: An ecological integration. *American Psychologist, 35,* 320–335.

Belsky, J. (1984). The determinants of parenting: A process model. *Child Development, 55,* 83–96.

Bennett, V. C., & Bardon, J. I. (1977). The effects of a school program on teenage mothers and their children. *American Journal of Orthopsychiatry, 47,* 671–678.

Black, C., & DeBlassie, R. R. (1985). Adolescent pregnancy: Contributing factors, consequences, treatment, and plausible solutions. *Adolescence, 20,* 281–290.

Bolton, F. G. (1990). The risk of child maltreatment in adolescent parenting. *Advances in Adolescent Mental Health, 4,* 223–237.

Borkowski, J., & Dukewich, T. (1996). Environmental covariations and intelligence: How attachment influences self-regulation. In D. K. Delterman (Ed.), *Current topics in human intelligence* (Vol. 5, pp. 3–15). Norwood, NJ: Ablex.

Bouchard, T. J., & McGue, M. (1981). Familial studies of intelligence: A review. *Science, 212,* 1055–1059.

Bourne, L. E., & Ekstrand, B. R. (1973). *Psychology: Its principles and meanings.* Hinsdale, IL: Dryden Press.

Broman, S. (1981). Long-term development of children born to teenagers. In K. G. Scott, T. Field, & E. G. Robertson (Eds.), *Teenage parents and their offspring* (pp. 195–225). New York: Grune & Stratton.

Broman, S., Nichols, P. L., Shaughnessy, P., & Kennedy, W. (1987). *Retardation in young children.* Hillsdale, NJ: Lawrence Erlbaum Associates.

Brooks-Gunn, J. (1995). Strategies for altering the outcomes of poor children and their families. In P. L. Chase-Lansdale & J. Brooks-Gunn (Eds.), *Escape from poverty: What makes a difference for children?* (pp. 87–117). New York: Cambridge University Press.

Brooks-Gunn, J., & Furstenberg, F. F. (1986). The children of adolescent mothers; Physical academic, and psychological outcomes. *Developmental Review, 6,* 224–251.

Broughton, J. M. (1983). The cognitive-developmental theory of adolescent self and identity. In B. Lee & G. Noam (Eds.), *Developmental approaches to the self* (pp. 215–266). New York: Plenum.

Brown, H., Adams, H., & Kellam, S. (1981). *The longitudinal study of teenage motherhood and symptoms of distress: Research and community mental health* (pp. 82–213). Greenwich, CT: JAI.

Bugental, D. B., Blue, J., & Cruzcosa, M. (1989). Perceived control over caregiving outcomes: Implications for child abuse. *Developmental Psychology, 25,* 532–539.

Burke, R. J., & Weir, T. (1979). Helping responses of parents and peers and adolescent well-being. *Journal of Psychology, 102,* 49–62.

Camp, B. W., Holman, S., & Ridgway, E. (1993). The relationship between social support and stress in adolescent mothers. *Developmental and Behavioral Pediatrics, 14,* 369–374.

Card, J., & Wise, L. (1978). Teeneage mothers and teenaege fathers: The impact of early childbearing on the parents' personal and professional lives. *Family Planning Perspectives, 10,* 199–205.

Carey, W., & McDevitt, S. (1978). Revision of the Infant Temperament Questionnaire. *Pediatrics, 6,* 735–769.

Cassidy, J. A., & Marvin, R. S., with the MacArthur Working Group on Attachment. (1992). *Attachment organization in Preschool Children: Procedures and coding manual.* Unpublished Coding Manual, University of Virginia, Charlottesville.

Cobb, N. J. (1988). *Adolescence: Continuity, change, and diversity.* Mountain View, CA: Mayfield.

Coley, R. L., & Chase–Lansdale, P. L. (1998). Adolescent pregnancy and parenthood: Recent evidence and future directions. *American Psychologist, 53,* 152–166.

Colin, V. L. (1996). *Human attachment.* New York: McGraw Hill.

Coll, G. G., Hoffman, J., & Oh, W. (1987). The social ecology and early parenting of Caucasian adolescent mothers. *Child Development, 58,* 955–963.

Colletta, N. D. (1981). Social support and the risk of maternal rejection by adolescent mothers. *Psychology, 109,* 191–197.

Connelly, C. D., & Strauss, M. A. (1992). Mother's age and risk for physical abuse. *Child Abuse and Neglect, 16,* 709–718.

Contreras, J. M., Mangelsdorf, S. C., Diener, M. L., & Rhodes, J. E. (1995, May). *Correlates of parent–child interaction among adolescent Latina mothers.* Paper presented at the meeting of the Midwestern Psychological Association, Chicago, IL.

Coopersmith, S. (1981). *Self-esteem inventories.* Palo Alto, CA: Consulting Psychologists Press.

Crnic, K. A., Greenberg, M. T., Ragozin, A. S., Robinson, N. M., & Basham, R. B. (1983). Effects of stress and social support on mothers of premature and full-term infants. *Child Development, 54,* 209–217.

Crnic, K. A., Greenberg, M. T., & Slough, N. M. (1986). Early stress and social support influences on mothers' and high-risk infants' functioning in late infancy. *Infant Mental Health Journal, 7,* 19–33.

Crockenberg, S. B. (1981). Infant irritability, mother responsiveness, and social support influences on the security of infant–mother attachment. *Child Development, 52,* 857–865.

Crockenberg, S. B., & Smith, P. (1982). Antecedents of mother–infant interaction and infant irritability in the first three months of life. *Infant Behavior and Development, 5,* 105–119.

Culp, A. M., Osofsky, J. D., & O'Brien, M. (1996). Language patterns of adolescent and older mothers. *First Language, 16,* 61–75.

de Anda, D., Darroch, P., Davidson, M., Gilly, J., & Morejon, A. (1990). Stress management for pregnant adolescents and adolescent mothers: A pilot study. *Child and Adolescent Social Work, 7,* 53–67.

DeLissovoy, V. (1973). Child care by adolescents. *Children Today, 2,* 22–25.

Demographic and Behavioral Sciences Branch. (1999, June). *Report to the NACHHD Council.* Bethesda, MD: NICHD, NIH.

Dix, T. (1991). The affective organization of parenting: Adaptive and maladaptive processes. *Psychological Bulletin, 110,* 3–25.

Dodge, K., Bates, J., & Pettit, G. (1990). Mechanisms in the cycle of violence. *Science, 250,* 1678–1683.

Dubow, E. F., & Luster, T. (1990). Adjustment of children born to teenage mothers: The contribution of risk and protective factors. *Journal of Marriage and the Family, 52,* 393–404.

Dukewich, T. L., Borkowski, J. G., & Whitman, T. L. (1996). Adolescent mothers and child abuse potential: An evaluation of risk factors. *Child Abuse and Neglect, 20,* 1031–1047.

Dukewich, T. L., Borkowski, J. G., & Whitman, T. L. (1999). A longitudinal analysis of maternal abuse potential and developmental delays in children of adolescent mothers. *Child Abuse and Neglect, 23,* 405–420.

Duncan, G. J., & Brooks-Gunn, J. (1997). *Consequences of growing up poor.* New York: Russell Sage.

Duncan, G. J., Brooks-Gunn, J., & Klebanov, P. (1994). Economic deprivation and early-childhood development. *Child Development, 62,* 296–318.

Dunn, L. M., & Dunn, L. M. (1981). *Peabody Picture Vocabulary Test–Revised.* Circle Pines, MN: American Guidance Service.

Dunn, L. M., & Markwardt, F. C., Jr. (1970). *Peabody Individual Achievement Test.* Circle Pines, MN: American Guidance Service.

Dunst, C. J., & Trivette, C. M. (1988). A family systems model of early intervention with handicapped and developmentally at-risk children. In D. R. Powell (Ed.), *Parent education as early childhood intervention: Emerging directions in theory, research and practice* (pp. 131–180). Norwood, NJ: Ablex.

East, P. L., & Felice, M. E. (1996). *Adolescent pregnancy and parenting: Findings from a racially diverse sample.* Mahwah, NJ: Lawrence Erlbaum Associates.

Egeland, B., & Farber, E. A. (1984). Infant–mother attachment: Factors related to its development and changes over time. *Child Development, 55,* 753–771.

Egeland, B., & Sroufe, L. A. (1981). Developmental sequelae of maltreatment in infancy. In R. Rizley & D. Cicchetti (Eds.), *Developmental perspectives in child maltreatment.* San Francisco: Jossey-Bass.

Elder, G. H., & Rockwell, R. (1976). Marital timing in women's life patterns. *Journal of Family History, 1,* 34–53.

Elkind, D. (1961). Quantity conception in junior and senior high school students. *Child Development, 32,* 551–560.

Elkind, D. (1967). Egocentrism in adolescence. *Child Development, 38,* 1025–1034.

Elman, J. L., Bates, E. A., Johnson, M. H., Karmiloff-Smith, A., Parisi, D., & Plunkett, K. (1996). *Rethinking Innateness.* Cambridge, MA: The MIT Press.

Elo, I. T., King, R. B., & Furstenberg, F. F. (1999). Adolescent females: Their sexual partners and the fathers of their children. *Journal of Marriage and the Family, 61,* 4–84.

Epstein, A. (1980). *Assessing the child development information needed by adolescent parents with very young children* (a report to the Department of Health, Education, and Welfare). Ypsilanti, MI: High/Scope Educational Research Foundation.

Erikson, E. H. (1960). Youth and the life cycle. *Children, 7,* 43–49.

Erikson, E. H. (1963). *Childhood and society.* New York: Norton.

Erikson, E. H. (1968). *Identity: Youth and crisis.* New York: Norton.

Field, T. M. (1980). Interactions of preterm and term infants with their lower- and middle-class teenage and adult mothers. In T. Field, S. Goldberg, D. Stern, & A. Sostek (Eds.), *High-risk infants and children.* New York: Academic Press.

Field, T. M., Widmayer, S. M., Stringer, S., & Ignatoff, E. (1980). Teenage, lower-class, black mothers and their pre-term infants: An intervention and follow-up. *Child Development, 51,* 426–436.

Frodi, A., Keller, B., Foye, H., Liptak, G., Bridges, L., Grolnick, W., Berko, J., McAnarney, E., & Lawrence, R. (1984). Determinants of attachment and mastery motivation in infants born to adolescent mothers. *Infant Mental Health Journal, 5,* 15–23.

Furstenberg, F. (1976). The social consequences of teenage parenthood. *Family Planning Perspective, 8,* 148–164.

Furstenberg, F. F. (1998, January). *Teenage parenthood.* Paper presented at the 35th anniversary of NICHD, Bethesda, MD.

Furstenberg, F. F., Brooks-Gunn, J., & Morgan, S. P. (1987). *Adolescent mothers in later life*. New York: Cambridge University Press.

Furstenberg, F. F., & Crawford, A. G. (1978). Family support: Helping teenage mothers to cope. *Family Planning Perspectives, 10*, 322–333.

Garber, H. (1988). *The Milwaukee project: Preventing mental retardation in children at risk*. Washington, DC: American Association of Mental Retardation.

Garmezy, N., Masten, A. S., & Tellegen, A. (1984). The study of stress and competence in children: Building blocks for developmental psychopathology. *Child Development, 55*, 97–111.

George, C., & Main, M. (1979). Social interactions of young abused children: Approach, avoidance, and aggression. *Child Development, 50*, 306–318.

Goldberg, W. A., & Easterbrooks, M. A. (1984). The role of marital quality in toddler development. *Developmental Psychology, 20*, 504–514.

Gottman, J. M. (1997). *The heart of parenting*. New York: Simon & Schuster.

Gottman, J. M., Katz, L. F., & Hooven, C. (1997). *Meta-emotions: How families communicate emotionally*. Mahwah, NJ: Lawrence Erlbaum Associates.

Greenberg, M. T., Siegel, J. M., & Leitch, C. J. (1983). The nature and importance of attachment relationships to parents and peers during adolescence. *Journal of Youth and Adolescence, 12*, 373–386.

Greene, R. W. (1998). *The explosive child*. New York: HarperCollins.

Greenough, W. T., Black, J. E., & Wallace, C. S. (1987). Experience and brain development. *Child Development, 58*, 539–559.

Grow, L. J. (1979). Today's unmarried mothers: The choices have changed. *Child Welfare, 58*, 363–371.

Halpern, R., & Larner, M. (1988). The design of family support programs in high-risk communities: Lessons from the Child Survival/Fair Start Initiative. In D. R. Powell (Ed.), *Parent education as early childhood intervention: Emerging directions in theory, research and practice* (pp. 181–208). Norwood, NJ: Ablex

Hamburg, B. A. (1986). Developmental issues in school-age pregnancy. In E. Purcell (Ed.), *Aspects of psychiatric problems of childhood and adolescence* (pp. 299–325). New York: Josiah Macy, Jr. Foundation.

Hardy, J. B., Welcher, D. W., Stanley, J., & Dallas, J. R. (1978). Long-range outcome of adolescent pregnancy. *Clinical Obstetrics and Gynecology, 21*, 1215–1232.

Harris, K. M. (1997). *Teen mothers and the revolving welfare door*. Philadelphia: Temple University Press.

Hart, B., & Risley, T. (1995). *Meaningful differences in the everyday experience of young American children*. Baltimore, MD: Paul H. Brooks.

Haveman, R. H., Wolfe, B., & Peterson, E. (1997). Children of early child-bearers as young adults. In R. A. Maynard (Ed.), *Kids having kids: Economic costs and social consequences of teen pregnancy* (pp. 257–284). Washington DC: The Urban Institute Press.

Hayes, C. E. (Ed.). (1987). *Risking the future: Adolescent sexuality, pregnancy and childrearing* (Vol. 1). Washington, DC: National Academy Press.

Hechtman, L. (1989). Teenage mothers and their children: Risks and problems: A review. *Canadian Journal of Psychiatry, 34,* 569–575.

Hill, R. (1958). Social stressors on the family. *Social Casework, 37,* 139–150.

Hoffman-Plotkin, D., & Twentyman, C. T. (1984). A multimodal assessment of behavioral and cognitive deficits in abused and neglected preschoolers. *Child Development, 55,* 794–802.

Hollingshead, A. (1965). *Two factor index of social position.* New Haven, CT: Yale Station.

Horowitz, S. M., Klerman, L. V., Kuo, H. S., & Jekel, J. F. (1991). Intergenerational transmission of school-age parenthood. *Family Planning Perspectives, 23,* 166–172.

Horwitz, F. D. (1999, April). *Child development and the PITS — Simple questions, complex answers, and developmental theory.* Presented at the biennial meeting of the Society for Research in Child Development, Albuquerque, NM.

Hotz, V. J., McElroy, S. W., & Sanders, S. G., (1997). The impacts of teen-age childbearing on the mothers and the consequences of those impacts for government. In R. A. Maynard (Ed.), *Kids having kids: economic costs and social consequences of teen pregnancy* (pp. 55–94). Washington DC: The Urban Institute Press.

Jarrett, G. E. (1982). Childrearing patterns of young mothers: Expectations, knowledge and practices. *Maternal-Child Nursing, 7,* 119–124.

Jorgensen, S., King, S., & Torry, B. (1980). Dyadic and social network influences on adolescent exposure to pregnancy risk. *Journal of Marriage and the Family, 42,* 141–155.

Josselson, R. (1989). Identity formation in adolescence: Implications for young adulthood. In S. C. Feinstein (Ed.), *Adolescent psychiatry* (Vol. 16, pp. 142–154). Chicago: University of Chicago Press.

Kaufman, J., Cook, A., Arny, L., Jones, B., & Pittinsky, T. (1994). Problems defining resiliency: Illustrations from the study of maltreated children. *Development and Psychopathology, 6,* 215–229.

Klaczynski, P. A. (1997). Bias in adolescents' everyday reasoning and its relationship with intellectual ability, personal theories, and self-serving motivation. *Developmental Psychology, 33,* 273–283.

Klerman, L. V. (1981). Programs for pregnant adolescents and young parents: Their development and assessment. In K. G. Scott, T. Field, & E. G. Robertson (Eds.), *Teenage parents and their offspring* (pp. 227–248). New York: Grune & Stratton.

Lamb, M. E. (1988). The ecology of adolescent pregnancy and parenthood. In A. R. Pence (Ed.), *Ecological research with children and families: From concepts to methodology* (pp. 99–121). New York: Teachers College Press.

Lamb, M. E., Hopps, K., & Elster, A. B. (1987). Strange Situation behavior of infants with adolescent mothers. *Infant Behavior and Development, 10,* 39–48.

Lapsley, D. K. (1990). Continuity and discontinuity in adolescent social cognitive development. In R. Monterrayo, G. R. Adams, & T. P. Gullota (Eds.), *From childhood to adolescence: A transitional period?* (pp. 183–204). Newbury Park, CA: Sage.

Leadbeater, B. J., & Bishop, S. J. (1994). Predictors of behavior problems in preschool children of inner-city Afro-American and Puerto Rican adolescent mothers. *Child Development, 65,* 638–648.

Leadbeater, B. J., & Bishop, S. J., & Raver, C. C. (1996). Quality of mother–toddler interactions, maternal depressive symptoms, and behavior problems in preschoolers of adolescent mothers. *Developmental Psychology, 32,* 280–288.

Leadbeater, B. J., & Linares, O. (1992). Depressive symptoms in black and Puerto Rican adolescent mothers in the first three years postpartum. *Development and Psychopathology, 4,* 451–468.

Levinson, R. A. (1995). Reproductive and contraceptive knowledge, contraceptive self-efficacy, and contraceptive behavior among teenage women. *Adolescence, 30,* 65–86.

Linares, L. O., Leadbeater, B. J., Jaffe, L., Kato, P. K. & Diaz, A. (1992). Predictors of repeat pregnancy outcome among Black and Puerto Rican adolescent mothers. *Developmental and Behavioral Pediatrics, 13,* 89–94.

Lindberg, L. D., Sonenstein, F. L., Ku, L., & Martinez, G. (1997). Age differences between minors who give birth and their adult partners. *Family Planning Perspectives, 29,* 61–66.

Lutes, C. J. (1981). Early marriage and identity foreclosure. *Adolescence, 16,* 809–815.

Luthar, S. S., & Zigler, E. (1991). Vulnerability and Competence: A review of research on resilience in childhood. *American Journal of Orthopsychiatry, 61,* 6–22.

Lynch, M. A., & Roberts, J. (1982). *Consequences of child abuse.* New York: Academic Press.

Lyons-Ruth, K., Alpern, L., & Repacholi, B. (1991). Disorganized infant attachment classification and maternal psychiatric problems as predictors of hostile-aggressive behavior in the preschool classroom. *Child Development, 64,* 572–585.

Main, M., & Solomon, J. (1986). Discovery of an insecure-disorganized/disoriented attachment pattern: Procedures, findings and implications for the classification of behavior. In T. B. Brazelton & M. Hogman (Eds.), *Affective development in infancy* (pp. 95–124). Norwood, NJ: Ablex.

Main, M., & Solomon, J. (1990). Procedures for identifying disorganized/disoriented infants in the Ainsworth Strange Situation. In M. Greenberg, D. Cicchetti, & M. Cummings (Eds.), *Attachment in the preschool years: Theory, research, and intervention* (pp. 121–160). Chicago: University of Chicago Press.

Maracek, J. (1979). *Economic, social, and psychological consequences of adolescent child bearing: An analysis of data from the Philadelphia collaborative perinatal project* (Final report to NICHD). Bethesda, MD: NICHD.

Marcia, J. E. (1966). Development and validation of ego-identity status. *Journal of Personality and Social Psychology, 3,* 551–558.

Markwardt, F. L. (1989). *Peabody Individual Achievement Test–Revised.* Circle Pines, MN: American Guidance Service.

Matas, L., Arend, R. A., & Sroufe, L. A. (1978). Continuity of adaptation in the second year: The relationship between quality of attachment and later competence. *Child Development, 49,* 547–566.

Maynard, R. A. (1997). The costs of adolescent childbearing. In R. A. Maynard (Ed.), *Kids having kids: economic costs and social consequences of teen pregnancy* (pp. 285–338). Washington DC: The Urban Institute Press.

McCourt, F. (1998). *Angela's Ashes.* New York: Simon & Schuster.

McDevitt, S., & Carey, W. (1978). The measurement of temperament in 3–7 year old children. *Journal of Child Psychology and Psychiatry, 19,* 245–253.

McKenry, P., Browne, D., Kotch, J., & Symons, M. (1990). Mediators of depression among low-income, adolescent mothers of infants: A longitudinal perspective. *Journal of Youth and Adolescence, 19,* 327–347.

McLanahan, S. (1999). Father absence and the welfare of children. In E. M. Hetherington (Ed.), *Coping with divorce, single parenting, and remarriage: A risk and resiliency perspective* (pp. 117–145). Mahwah, NJ: Lawrence Erlbaum Association.

McLanahan, S., & Sandefur, G. (1994). *Growing up with a single parent: What hurts, what helps.* Cambridge, MA: Harvard University Press.

McLaughlin, F. J., Sandler, H. M., Sherrod, K. S., Vietze, P. M., & O'Conner, S. (1979). Social-psychological characteristics of adolescent mothers and behavioral characteristics of their first-born infant. *Journal of Population, 2*, 69–73.

Medora, N. P., Goldstein, A., & von der Hellen, C. (1994). Romanticism and self-esteem among pregnant adolescents, adolescent mothers, and nonpregnant, nonparenting teens. *Journal of Social Psychology, 134*, 581–591.

Miller, B., & Moore, K. (1990). Adolescent sexual behavior, pregnancy, and parenting: Research through the 1980s. *Journal of Marriage and the Family, 52*, 1025–1044.

Miller, C. L., Heysek, P. J., Whitman, T. L., & Borkowski, J. G. (1996). Cognitive readiness to parent and intellectual emotional development in children of adolescent mothers. *Developmental Psychology, 32*, 533–541.

Miller, S. A., Manhal, M., & Mee L. L. (1991). Parental beliefs, parental accuracy, and children's cognitive performance: A search for causal relations. *Developmental Psychology, 27*, 267–276.

Milner, J. S. (1986). *The child abuse potential inventory: Manual* (2nd ed.). Webster, NC: Psytec.

Moore, K., Hofferth, S., Wetheimer, R., Waite, L., & Caldwell, S. (1981). Teenage childrearing: Consequences for women, families, and government welfare expenditures. In K. G. Scott, T. Field, & E. G. Robertson (Eds.), *Teenage parents and their offspring* (pp. 35–54). New York: Grune & Stratton.

Moore, K. A., Morrison, D. R., & Greene, A. D. (1997). Effects on the children born to adolescent mothers. In R. A. Maynard (Ed.), *Kids having kids: Economic costs and social consequences of teen pregnancy* (pp. 145–180). Washington DC: The Urban Institute Press.

Moore, K. A., Sugland, B. W., Blumenthal, C., Glei, D., & Snyder, N. (1995). *Adolescent pregnancy prevention programs: Interventions and evaluations.* Washington, DC: Child Trends, Inc.

Mott, F., & Marsigliano, W. (1985). Early childbearing and completion of high school. *Family Planning Perspectives, 17*, 234–237.

Musick, J. S., & Barbera-Stein L. (1988). The role of research in an innovative preventive initiative. In D. R. Powell (Ed.), *Parent education as early childhood intervention: Emerging directions in theory, research and practice* (pp. 209–228). Norwood, NJ: Ablex.

Musick, J. S., & Stott, F. (1990). Paraprofessionals, parenting, and child development: Understanding the problems and seeking solutions. In S. J. Meisels & J. P. Shonkoff (Eds.), *Handbook of early childhood intervention.* Cambridge, MA: Cambridge University Press,.

Mylod, D. E., Whitman, T. L., & Borkowski, J. G. (1997). Predicting adolescent mothers' transition to adulthood. *Journal of Research in Adolescence, 7,* 457–478.

Nath, P., Borkowski, J., Whitman, T., & Schellenbach, C. (1991). Understanding adolescent parenting: The dimensions and functions of social support. *Family Relations, 40,* 411–420.

National Research Council. (1993). *Understanding child abuse and neglect.* Washington, DC: National Academy Press.

National Survey of Family Growth. (1997). *Vital and health statistics: Fertility, family planning, and women's health* (Series 23: No. 19). Hyattsville, MD: Department of Health and Human Services.

National Survey of Family Growth, Cycle III. (1982). *National Center for Health Statistics.* Washington, DC: Department of Health and Human Services.

Navarro, S. (1996, May 6). Teenage mothers viewed as abused prey of older men. *The New York Times,* pp. B1 – B10.

Nover, A., Shore, M., Timberlake, E., & Greenspan, S. (1984). The relationship of maternal perceptions and maternal behavior: A study of normal mothers and their infants. *American Journal of Orthopsychiatry, 54,* 211–223.

Oates, R. K., Peacock, A., & Forrest, D. (1984). Development in children following abuse and nonorganic failure to thrive. *American Journal of Diseases of Children, 138,* 764–767.

O'Callaghan, M. F. (1996). *Temperamental instability in children of adolescent mothers: Correlates of change and implications for development.* Unpublished doctoral dissertation.

O'Callaghan, M., Borkowski, J. G., Whitman, T. L., Maxwell, S. E., & Keogh, D. A. (1999). A model of adolescent parenting. *Journal of Research on Adolescence, 9,* 203–225.

Orlofsky, J. L., Marcia, J. E., & Lesser, I. M. (1973). Ego identity status and the intimacy versus isolation of young adulthood. *Journal of Personality and Social Psychology, 27,* 211–219.

Osofsky, H. J., & Osofsky, J. D. (1970). Adolescents as mothers: Results of a program for low-income pregnant teenagers with some emphasis upon infant's development. *American Journal of Orthopsychiatry, 40,* 825–834.

Passino, A., Whitman, T. L., Borkowski, J. G., Schellenbach, C. J., Maxwell, S. E., Keogh, D. A., & Rellinger, E. (1993). Personal adjustment during pregnancy and adolescent parenting. *Adolescence, 28,* 97–122.

Patten, M. A. (1981). Self-concept and self-esteem: Factors in adolescent pregnancy. *Adolescence, 26,* 765–778.

Piaget, J. (1926). *The language and thought of the child.* New York: Harcourt, Brace, & World.

Piaget, J. (1950). *The psychology of intelligence.* New York: International Universities Press.

Piaget, J. (1952). Jean Piaget. In C. A. Murchison (Ed.), *A history of psychology in autobiography* (Vol. 4). Worcester, MA: Clark University Press.

Piaget, J. (1972). Intellectual evolution from adolescence to adulthood. *Human Development, 15,* 1–12.

Plomin, R., Loehlin, J. C., & DeFries, J. C. (1985). Genetic and environmental components of "environmental" influences. *Developmental Psychology, 21,* 391–402.

Ramey, C. T., & Campbell, F. A. (1987). The Carolina Abecedarian Project: An educational experiment concerning human malleability. In J. J. Gallagher & C. T. Ramey (Eds.), *The malleability of children* (pp. 127–139). Baltimore, MD: Paul H. Brookes.

Ramey, C. T., & Ramey, S. L. (1990, April). *Prevention of intergenerational mental retardation.* Paper presented at the Gatlinburg Conference on Research and Theory in Mental Retardation and Developmental Disabilities, Gatlinburg, TN.

Ramey, C. T., & Suarez, T. (1984). Early intervention and the early experience paradigm: Toward a better framework for social policy. *Journal of Children in Contemporary Society, 17,* 3–13.

Rauch-Elnekave, H. (1994). Teenage motherhood: Its relationship to undetected learning problems. *Adolescence, 29,* 91–103.

Record, R., McKeown, T., & Edwards, J. (1969). The relation of measured intelligence to birth order and natural age. *Annual of Human Genetics, 33,* 61–69.

Resnick, M. D., Blum, R. W., Bose, J., Smith, M., & Toogood, R. (1990). Characteristics of unmarried adolescent mothers: Determinants of child rearing versus adoption. *American Journal of Orthopsychiatry, 60,* 577–584.

Ricks, M. H. (1985). The social transmission of parental behavior: Attachment across generations. In I. Bretherton & E. Waters (Eds.), *Growing points in attachment theory and research* (pp. 211–227). *Monographs of the Society for Research in Child Development, 50.*

Roosa, M. W. (1983). A comparative study of pregnant teenagers' parenting attitudes and knowledge of sexuality and child development. *Journal of Youth and Adolescence, 12,* 213–223.

Roosa, M. W. (1984). Short-term effects of teenage parenting programs on knowledge and attitudes. *Adolescence, 19,* 659–666.

Roosa, M. W., Fitzgerald, H., & Carson, N. (1982). Teenage and older mothers and their infants: A descriptive comparison. *Adolescence, 65,* 1–17.

Roosa, M. W., & Vaughn, L. (1983). Teen mothers enrolled in an alternative parenting program: A comparison with their peers. *Urban Education, 18*, 348–360.

Roosa, M. W., & Vaughn, L. (1984). A comparison of teenage and older mothers with preschool age children. *Family Relations, 33*, 259–265.

Rosenberg, M. (1965). *Society and adolescent self-image*. Princeton, NJ: Princeton University Press.

Roth, R. M. (1980). *The Mother–Child Relationship Evaluation Manual*. Los Angeles: Western Psychological Services.

Russell, (1980). Unscheduled parenthood: Transition to "parent" for the teenager. *Journal of Social Issues, 36*, 45–63.

Rutter, M. (1985). Resilience in the face of adversity: Protective factors and resistance to psychiatric disorder. *British Journal of Psychiatry, 147*, 598–611.

Rutter, M. (1989). Pathways from childhood to adult life. *Journal of Child Psychology and Psychiatry, 30*, 23–51.

Sandler, J. (1979). *Effects of adolescent pregnancy on mother–infant relations: A transactional model of reports to the Center for Population Research*. Bethesda, MD: National Institutes of Health.

Sattler, J. M. (1990). *Assessment of children* (3rd ed.). San Diego: Author.

Sattler, J. M. (1992). *Assessment of children: WISC–III and WPPSI–R Supplement*. San Diego: Author.

Sattler, J. M. (1994). *Assessment of children* (4th ed.). San Diego: Author.

Scarr, S., & McCartney, K. (1983). How people make their own environments: A theory of genotype–environment effects. *Child Development, 54*, 424–435.

Schellenbach, C. J., Whitman, T. L., & Borkowski, J. G. (1992). Toward an integrative model of adolescent parenting. *Human Development, 35*, 81–99.

Schinke, S., Gilchrist, L., & Small, R. (1979). Preventing unwanted adolescent pregnancy: A cognitive behavioral approach. *American Journal of Orthopsychiatry, 49*, 81–88.

Seitz, V., & Apfel, N. H. (1993). Adolescent mothers and repeated childbearing: Effects of a school-based intervention program. *American Journal of Orthopsychiatry, 63*, 572–581.

Shearer, D. (1999, March). *Adolescent childbearing in young women with low cognitive ability*. Paper presented at the Gatlinburg Conference on Research and Theory in MR/DD, Charleston, SC.

Sigel, I. E., McGillicuddy-DeLisi, A. V., & Goodnow, J. J. (1992). *Parental belief systems: The psychological consequences for children*. Hillsdale, NJ: Lawrence Erlbaum Associates.

Smetana, J. (1994). *Beliefs about parenting: Origins and developmental implications*. San Francisco: Jossey-Bass.

Smith, J. R., Brooks-Gunn, J., & Klebanov, P. K. (1997). Consequences of living in poverty for young children's cognitive and verbal ability and early school achievment. In G. J. Duncan & J. Brooks-Gunn (Eds.), *Consequences of growing up poor* (pp. 132–189). New York: Russell Sage Foundation.

Sommer, K. S., Whitman, T. L., Borkowski, J. G., Gondoli, D. M., Burke, J., Maxwell, S. E., & Weed, K. (2000). Prenatal maternal predictors of cognitive and emotional delays in children of adolescent mothers. *Adolescence, 35*, 87–112.

Sommer, K., Whitman, T. L., Borkowski, J. G., Schellenbach, C. J., Maxwell, S. E., & Keogh, D. (1993). Cognitive readiness and adolescent parenting. *Developmental Psychology, 29*, 389–398.

Sparrow, S. S., Balla, D. A., & Cichetti, D. V. (1984). *Vineland Adaptive Behavior Scales.* Circle Pines, MN: American Guidance Service.

Spieker, S. J., & Bensley, L. (1994). Role of living arrangement and grandmother social support in adolescent mothering and infant attachment. *Developmental Psychology, 30*, 102–111.

Spieker, S. J., Larson, N. C., Lewis, S. M., Keller, T. E., & Gilchrist, L. (1999). Developmental trajectories of disruptive behavior problems in preschool children of adolescent mothers. *Child Development, 70*, 443–454.

Spielberger, C. D. (1983). *Manual for the State-Trait Anxiety Inventory* (Form 4). Palo Alto, CA: Consulting Psychological Press.

Sroufe, L. A. (1983). Infant–caregiver attachment and patterns of adaptation in preschool: The roots of maladaption and competence. In M. Perlmutter (Ed.), *Minnesota Symposia in child psychology* (Vol. 16, pp. 41–83). Hillsdale, N J: Lawrence Erlbaum Associates.

St. Pierre, R. G., & Layzen, J. I. (1998). Improving the life chances of children in poverty: Assumptions and what we have learned. *Social Policy Report, 12.*

Stevens, J. H. (1984). Child development knowledge and parenting skills. *Family Relations, 33*, 237–244.

Stoiber, K. C., & Houghton, T. G. (1993). The relationship of adolescent mothers' expectations, knowledge, and beliefs to their young children's coping behavior. *Infant Mental Health Journal, 14*, 61–79.

Streitmatter, J. L. (1989). Identity development and academic achievement in early adolescence. *Journal of Early Adolescence, 9*, 99–111.

Terman, L., & Merrill, M. (1972). *Stanford–Binet Intelligence Scale Manual for the Third Revision, Form L–M.* Boston: Houghton-Mifflin.

Thomas, A., & Chess, S. (1977). *Temperament and development.* New York: Brunner-Mazel.

Tomlinson-Keasey, C. (1972). Formal operations in females from 11 to 54 years of age. *Developmental Psychology, 6*, 364.

Troy, N., & Sroufe, L. A. (1987). Victimization among preschoolers: Role of attachment relationship history. *Journal of American Academy of Child and Adolescent Psychiatry, 26,* 166–172.

Unger, D. G., & Wandersman, L. P. (1985). Social support and adolescent mothers: Action research contributions to theory and practice. *Journal of Social Issues, 41,* 29–45.

Unger, D. G., & Wandersman, L. P. (1988). A support program for adolescent mothers: Predictors of participation. In D. R. Powell (Ed.), *Parent education as early childhood intervention: Emerging directions in theory, research and practice* (pp. 105–130). Norwood, NJ: Ablex.

Vaughn, B., Egeland, B., Sroufe, L. A., & Waters, E. (1979). Individual differences in infant–mother attachment at twelve and eighteen months: Stability and change in families under stress. *Child Development, 50,* 971–975.

Ventura, S. J. (1980). Trends and differentials in births to unmarried women: U.S., 1970–1976. *Vital Health Statistics,* Series 21, No. 36.

Vondra, J., & Belsky, J. (1993). Developmental origins of parenting: Personality and relationship factors. In T. Luster & L. Okagaki (Eds.), *Parenting: An ecological perspective* (pp. 1–33). Hillsdale, NJ: Lawrence Erlbaum Associates.

Vukelich, C., & Kliman, D. S. (1985). Mature and teenage mothers' infant growth expectation and use of child development information sources. *Family Relations, 34,* 189–196.

Ward, M. J., & Carlson, E. A. (1995). Associations among adult attachment, representations, maternal sensitivity, and infant–mother attachment in a sample of adolescent mothers. *Child Development, 66,* 69–79.

Waterman, A. S. (1985). Identity in the context of adolescent psychology. In A. S. Waterman (Ed.), *Identity in adolescence: Process and contents* (pp. 5–24). San Francisco, CA: Jossey-Bass.

Wechsler, D. (1974). *Manual for the Wechsler Intelligence Scale for Children–Revised.* San Antonio, TX: The Psychological Corporation.

Wechsler, D. (1981). *Manual for Wechsler Adult Intelligence Scale–Revised.* San Antonio, TX: The Psychological Corporation.

Wechsler, D. (1991). *Manual for the Wechsler Intelligence Scale for Children–Third Edition.* San Antonio, TX: The Psychological Corporation.

Week, K. (1997, April). *The USCA Mother's as Mentors program.* Presented at the Society for Research in Child Development Biennial Conference, Washington DC.

Weed, K., Keogh, D., & Borkowski, J. G. (2000). Predictors of resiliency in adolescent mothers, *Journal of Applied Developmental Psychology, 21,* 207–231.

Werner, E. E. & Smith, R. S. (1992). *Overcoming the odds: High risk children from birth to adulthood*. Ithaca, NY: Cornell University Press.

Whitman, T. L., Borkowski, J. G., Schellenbach, C. J., & Nath, P. S. (1987). Predicting and understanding developmental delay of children of adolescent mothers: A multi-dimensional approach. *American Journal of Mental Deficiency, 92*, 40–56.

Wolfe, D. A. (1985). Child abusive parents: An empirical review and analysis. *Psychological Bulletin, 97*, 462–482.

Wolfe, D. A. (1987). *Child abuse: Implications for child development and psychopathology* (Vol. 10). Newbury Park, CA: Sage.

Wolfe, D. A., Edwards, B., Manion, L., & Koverola, C. (1988). Early intervention for parents at risk of child abuse and neglect: A preliminary investigation. *Journal of Consulting and Clinical Psychology, 56*, 40–47.

Yeates, K. O., MacPhee, D., Campbell, F. A., & Ramey, C. T. (1983). Maternal IQ and home environment as determinants of early childhood intellectual competence: A developmental analysis. *Developmental Psychology, 19*, 731–739.

Yoshikawa, H. (1999). Welfare dynamics, support services, mothers' earnings, and child cognitive development: Implications for contemporary welfare reform. *Child Development, 70*, 779–801.

Yussen, S. R., & Santrock, J. W. (1984). *Children and adolescents: A developmental perspective*. Dubuque, IA: W. C. Brown.

Zaslow, M., Tout, K., Smith, S., & Moore, K. (1998). Implications of the 1996 welfare legislation for children: A research perspective. *Social Policy Report, 12*, 1–27.

Zimmerman, M. A., & Arunkumar, R. (1994). Resiliency research: Implications for schools and policy. *Social Policy Report, 8*.

Author Index

A

Abidin, R. R., 57, 58
Achenbach, T. M., 56, 62, 72, 101, 110
Adams, H., 92
Ainsworth, M. D., 61, 121
Allen, J. P., 6
Alpern, L., 165
Amaro, H., 93, 111
Angelou, M., 171
Apfel, N. H., 8, 16, 39, 104
Arend, R. A., 165, 166, 168
Armsden, G., 57
Arnett, J., 29
Arny, L., 176
Arunkumar, R., 20, 172
Azar, S. T., 105, 106, 110

B

Balla, D.A., 62
Barbera-Stein L., 223
Bardon, J. I., 225
Barkley, R. A., 40
Barth, R., 67
Basham, R. B., 35
Bates, E. A., 229
Bates, J., 164
Battle, L. S., 29, 30
Baumeister, A. A., 15
Baumrind, D., 23, 41, 42
Bavolek, S. J., 55
Bayley, N., 59
Beardslee, W., 93, 111

Beck, A. T., 56
Beery, K., 61
Bell, R. Q., 35
Belmont, L., 36, 119, 120
Belsky, J., 23, 24, 25, 26, 34, 37, 42, 93, 95, 96, 105, 110, 115, 156
Bennett, V. C., 225
Bensley, L., 31, 32, 104, 121, 144, 155, 166, 224
Berko, J., 121
Bishop, S. J., 155
Black, C., 29
Black, J. E., 229, 230
Blehar, M. C., 61, 121
Blue, J., 35
Blum, R. W., 30
Blumenthal, C., 65
Bolton, F. G., 104, 162
Borkowski, J. G., 12, 26, 30, 33, 34, 35, 36, 37, 40, 41, 42, 43, 45, 65, 67, 90, 91, 95, 100, 101, 103, 104, 108, 109, 110, 114, 116, 146, 150, 154, 155, 162, 163, 164, 165, 168, 173, 175, 176, 221, 222, 227
Bose, J., 30
Bouchard, T. J., 150
Bourne, L. E., 54
Bridges, L., 121
Broman, S., 16, 119, 121, 147, 149
Brooks-Gunn, J., 1, 8, 9, 10, 11, 15, 16, 18, 19, 65, 66, 68, 92, 93, 119, 120, 122, 147, 149, 165, 173, 174, 175, 219, 225

Subject Index